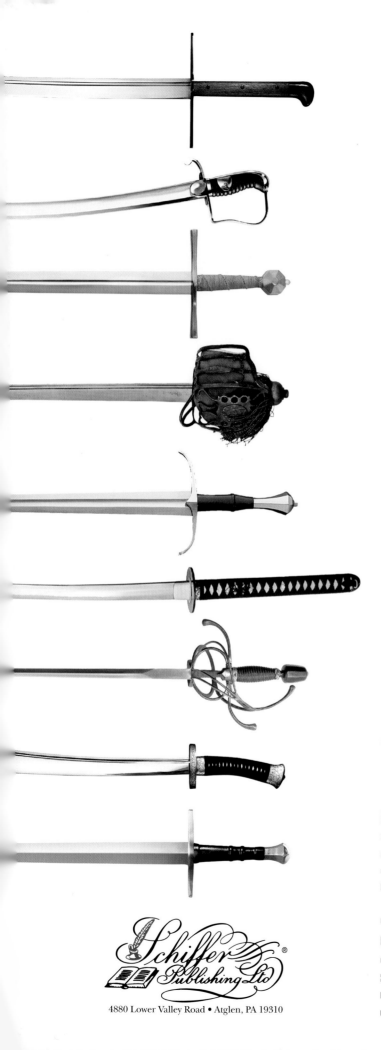

Thomas Laible

THE SWORD

TECHNOLOGY ◆ HISTORY ◆ FIGHTING ◆ FORGING ◆ MOVIE SWORDS

MYTH & REALITY

Schiffer Publishing Ltd

4880 Lower Valley Road • Atglen, PA 19310

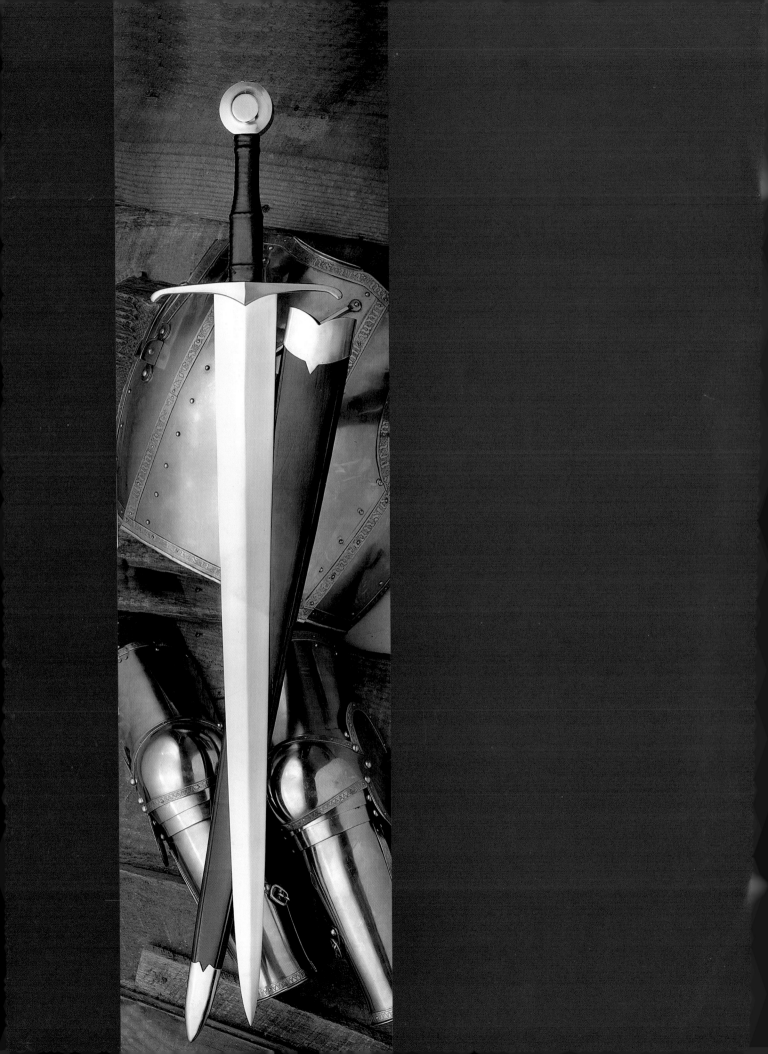

Trusty friend, well-tried sword;
worth gold in time of need.

– Medieval Proverb

Fortunately, I have never been in need of a "well-tried sword," and – much more important – have never lacked trusty friends.

This book is dedicated to Georg and the others.

Type set in Farrier ICG/Minion Pro/Gill Sans Std

ISBN: 978-0-7643-4877-8
Printed in China

Published by Schiffer Publishing, Ltd.
4880 Lower Valley Road
Atglen, PA 19310
Phone: (610) 593-1777; Fax: (610) 593-2002
E-mail: Info@schifferbooks.com

For our complete selection of fine books on this and related subjects,
please visit our website at www.schifferbooks.com. You may also write for a free catalog.

This book may be purchased from the publisher. Please try your bookstore first.

We are always looking for people to write books on new and related subjects.
If you have an idea for a book, please contact us at proposals@schifferbooks.com.

Schiffer Publishing's titles are available at special discounts for bulk purchases for sales promotions or premiums. Special editions, including personalized covers, corporate imprints, and excerpts can be created in large quantities for special needs. For more information, contact the publisher.

Contents

Foreword

The sword is an archetype that fascinates us. There is no boy in existence, I believe, who has never had a sword fight with his playmates (and this is also certainly true for many girls). We encounter the sword in all periods of history, whether in the Bible, the medieval sagas, or modern fantasy films such as *Star Wars*. The sword is a phenomenon.

We can approach this phenomenon from different aspects. One point of view is that of an art or cultural historian. You can write entire monographs about ornamentation, inscriptions, or the role of the sword in medieval symbolism. All of this is important and the relevant research is absolutely justified. But this is not the issue here. "Form follows function," and a sword primarily has a function: A sword is a close-combat weapon. And we are approaching swords from the perspective of this functional viewpoint. In this respect, this book has a different focus from previous ones on the subject.

This book is no comprehensive encyclopedia – it is a comprehensible representation of medieval combat swords and their functional properties. Our emphasis on a sword's suitability for use in fighting, is particularly evident in our description of how swords are manufactured – here, the focus is on the quality of the blade and not on techniques used for decoration. The successors to the sword, the various types of broadsword or *Degen* [a German sword, military form of the rapier], are discussed only briefly here. In contrast, Japanese swords are discussed in detail in a separate chapter – because they are consistently used as comparisons for European medieval weapons. The conclusion discusses modern swords and training weapons for re-enactors – all those swordsmen who want to experience history up close and as authentically as possible. Overall, this work makes no claims to completeness.

This book also has no aspirations about presenting new and groundbreaking scientific discoveries. It is rather a summary and a popular scientific presentation of already known, but often widely dispersed facts. The text is written so that even a complete novice will be able to gain a useful introduction to the topic of "swords." This, of course, means that at some times, we will be presenting facts that other readers would consider "commonplace" and self-evident. I ask the more experienced reader's understanding for this.

Globalization doesn't spare the sword either – as all the international discussion forums on the Internet demonstrate. For this reason, I have, when possible, used the general, international, and mostly English, technical terms: For example, bastard sword and falchion instead of *Anderthalbhänder* (hand-and-a-half) and *Malchus*.

Astute readers will notice that there are hardly any photos of original weapons in this book, but rather, that most of the weapons pictured are replicas. There are several reasons for this circumstance: First, we are discussing "living history" and "experimental archeology" – that is, the re-creation of functional swords. This book documents for future or already dedicated collectors, just how many historically accurate replicas there are, who is making them, and where from they are available (more on this in the chapter "Sword Replicas"). Secondly, it is an "old hat" of media pedagogy that you can very often demonstrate the facts of the case better with a model than a photo. It is the same with swords: You can see more from a good reproduction than with a poorly preserved original. Or, as a friend of mine put it after visiting a museum: "Oh well, just some rusty swords."

The prefatory words in the individual chapters are usually taken from the writings of historical master swordsmen. These include the mnemonic of Meister Johannes Liechtenauer, the forefather of the German sword-fighting school, as they were handed down from Meister Sigmund Ringeck. Others are from the declarations of an anonymous 14th-century German sword master, which are written in the so-called Manuscript HS 3227a. At the end, comes a quote from the *Book of the Five Rings* – the work on strategy by Japan's greatest swordsman, Myamoto Musashi.

Finally, I would like to thank all those who have contributed to this book. In addition to the sword-smith Peter Johnsson, who explained the mysteries of sword physics to me with infinite patience, are Herbert Schmidt of Ars Gladii, who contributed several suggestions for improvement, as well as all the members of swordforum.com and myarmoury.com, who were happy to make contributions, listed here by name:

20th Century Fox, Agilitas.tv, Albion Armorers, Armart-Antiquanova, Arms & Armor, ASA Swordworks, Patrick Barta, Jirka Bükow, Cas Iberia, Cold Steel, Harvey Dean, Del Tin Armi Antiche, Dublin City Council, Arno Eckhardt (Traumschmiede), Vince Evans, Wally Hayes, John Howe, Kai Corporation, Lutel, Jens Nettlich, New Line Cinema, Paul Mortimer, Museum Replicas, Karlheinz Peuker, Phoenix Metal Creations, Pieces of History, Stephan Roth (Seelenschmiede), Torsten Schneyer, Hebsacker Sthalenwarenhaus [steel warehouse], United Cutlery, VS-Books, Wilkinson Sword.

Thomas Laible
December 2007

A sword for a king – pictures like
this shape our ideas about
medieval swords.

An Introduction to the History of the Sword

Practice knighthood and learn the art that becomes you, and pays court to honor in war.
— Meister Liechtenauer's Verses, after Sigmund Ringeck

I will never forget the feeling, when I touched a real sword for the first time. Until then, I only had contact with more or less well-made decorative swords or relatively inexpensive stage-combat swords from the Czech Republic. Now, however, I was holding a handcrafted weapon by the Swedish sword-smith Peter Johnsson in my hands. The difference between a decorative sword and a sharp combat sword is only really apparent at such a time: A feeling as if a blind person has just started to see. A genuine sword is light, flexible, and balanced; an extension of my arm. Such a sword comes alive in your hand! To look at it philosophically, this sense of being alive, is the quality that constitutes the essence of a sword.

When we deal seriously with the sword, we have to come to terms with prejudices. Medieval swords are the targets of many prejudices that come from different directions. On the one hand, there are "positive prejudices," the totally excessive beliefs about a sword's power that many people get from books, movies, and television. On the other hand, there are the "negative stereotypes," generated by the rusty remnants in museums and the dismissive judgments of so-called experts. A medieval sword is neither a super-weapon, nor a crude, hammered together blunt steel bat. Swords are designed and made, "to dispatch" opponents—and they fulfill this purpose perfectly.

The Sword as a Weapon
Independent of all its other functions, the sword is first and foremost a weapon. It is not a tool like the machete, but a weapon.

A sword is a balanced, flexible, and sharp piece of steel, which is intended to send an opponent to eternity, as quickly and efficiently as possible. And precisely for this purpose, to be able to fight the opponent effectively—regardless of his armor –various forms of swords were developed over the centuries.

The medieval sword is a weapon that was in use for about 1,000 years. In the fifth century, an ancestor of the knightly sword emerged as the Germanic spatha, and in the course of the 16th century, a slow replacement of the sword by the Renaissance weapon, the *Degen* or broadsword, begins. During these 1,000 years, the sword was perhaps the most famous weapon, but by no means the most important. In terms of a military and war technology viewpoint, the sword actually plays a minor role. The most important close combat weapons of the Early and High Middle Ages were the lance (or the spear) and the ax. However, in terms of society, the sword is the most important weapon of the Middle Ages.

The actual military importance of the various edged weapons finally emerges in the Late Middle Ages: Armies of foot soldiers equipped with pole-arms repeatedly win victory over armies of knights previously held to be unconquerable. Of special historical importance were the victories of Morgarten (1315) and Sempach (1386). In these battles, Swiss infantry mostly armed with *Helmbarte* (an early forerunner of the halberd) defeated heavily armored and well-armed armies of knights from Austria and Burgundy, who had seemed to be their complete superiors. In contrast to the knights'

Many people only know swords as rusted remains in museums.

9

Despite all their beauty, swords are primarily weapons, which were often enough bloodstained (scene from *Kingdom of Heaven*).

Photo: 20th Century Fox/Museum Replicas

Swordsmanship flourished in the late Middle Ages. The longsword was the "queen of weapons."

Photo: Agilitas.tv

From a military standpoint, the spear was much more important than the sword (drawing after the Bayeux Tapestry, around 1077).

Until the Late Middle Ages, knights in armor were also an important factor in war (drawing after a 15th-century woodcut).

Over the centuries, various types of swords were developed to combat the enemy.

Photo: Del Tin

swords, the foot soldiers' pole-weapons were a decisive factor in war. However, the outstanding victories at Morgarten and Sempach also had a great deal to do with the noble commander's tactical mistakes. For this reason, infantry should not be overrated nor cavalry be underestimated because of these battles: "Dramatic defeats of knightly armies are pitted against brilliant victories over infantry. Therefore, until the 16th century, heavily armored horsemen formed the army's reserve force, but there were ever fewer knights and ever more mercenaries in the military formations," (Schlunk and Giersch, p.11).

Although the sword's primary function lies more in its symbolic character, it should by no means be dismissed as any secondary weapon. Of course, the sword was used in all the battles during the Middle Ages, and used successfully. It was especially important for personal self-defense (such as against robbers and highwaymen) and as a weapon for a judicial duel. Beyond this, "the sword had an advantage over all other [weapons]: It is the most versatile weapon that can be carried easily," (Windsor, p.12).

Since, during the Late Middle Ages, the sword represented an important weapon not only in war but also in everyday life—on the road, in court proceedings, and on other occasions—the martial art of swordsmanship was continuously developing, and sword masters were able to make a full-time living from their skills, and publish numerous textbooks. The most important weapon here was the long-sword. The need for sword masters became so great, that the masters later organized themselves into guilds, to protect this art from charlatans and incompetents. Some of these guilds existed until the Thirty Years' War.

Taking into account both these circumstances and the social significance of medieval swords, it is not surprising that they were the object of a veritable arms race during this thousand-year history. This affected both the sword's shape and the material used—in this case concretely, the quality of the steel. The sword-smith had to design a sword in such a way that you could use it as effectively as possible against a soldier with helmet and shield, as well as additional body armor. As a result, already in the Early Middle Ages methods were in use to—according to our present

conceptions—further refine inferior bloomery hearth iron, such as Damascus steel. As we will see later, the work of a sword-smith is a real art, which the master held as a well-kept secret. High quality swords were a hot commodity, which were traded from northern Europe to the Near East (for this reason, the place where an historical sword is found is not necessarily the country it was made).

For us, what is especially interesting—next to forging methods—are all the various forms of swords that were developed during the Middle Ages. Amazingly, the sword remains largely unaltered during the early centuries: Early medieval swords did not differ much, apart from shape and the decoration of the hilt. It was not until the 10th century that swords began to change more and more. Different blade shapes emerged, and their development was specifically related to the prevailing type of armor worn.

Two main changes in the shape of swords are particularly important. The first alteration is size. At the end of the 12th and beginning of the 13th centuries, the first two-handed battle swords made their appearance. The fighting technique for wielding a two-handed sword is totally different than that for a one-handed weapon. With a two-handed sword, you are either unable to use a shield at all, or only rarely. As a result, you have to pay much greater attention to cover by means of the sword blade. Fighting with a two-handed sword eventually led to the heyday of swordsmanship—the techniques for wielding a late medieval long-sword.

The second change concerns the shape of the sword blade, especially the cross-section. In the 13th century, full plate armor begins to develop—the warrior's body is always better protected. As a result, you need a weapon that is able to penetrate gaps in the armor. The flat cutting blade [*Hiebklinge*] of the Early and High Middle Ages, became the thrust-oriented blade typical of the Late Middle Ages.

The Sword as Symbol

The sword is much more than just a weapon; it is a symbol. The strong symbolic character of the sword is apparent up to the present time. Swords are constantly used as emblems, and still play a role in the military ceremonials of countless armies around the world.

It appears we will still be employing these emblems, even into the distant future. This is how *Star Wars* creator George Lucas explains the development of the lightsaber: "To create a group of peacekeepers who were noble and honorable above all, who made decisions and brought peace to the galaxy, I needed a weapon worthy of a Jedi Knight. It was much more a symbol of a simpler time—before the Empire was in power—and still meant something in terms of honor. So it was thus more a symbol than a weapon in the film. […] Initially, the Jedi are supposed to be armed with swords, but I wanted a futuristic sword—a lightsaber […]." The sword unquestionably possesses a symbolic value which can almost be called archetypal. But what does the sword really symbolize?

First, the sword—at least in the Middle Ages— represents an ideological symbol. It is no coincidence that the knightly sword resembles the Christian cross in profile. Downward curved cross-guards only become more common first in the 15th century; until then, we find almost exclusively straight cross-guards—though there is no functional basis for this. For four centuries, a sword almost always has the form of the cross—actually, in the Middle Ages, the cross-guard was also known as the *Creutz* (conversely, the Islamic saber corresponds to the curvature of the crescent). The weapon was thus deliberately adapted as the symbol of the Christian ideals of chivalry. An aspiring knight was also often given a consecrated sword by a priest during the ceremony in which he was dubbed a knight. Further ideological symbolism was described in the 13th-century poem *L'ordène de la Chevalerie*: Not only the profile, but also the two cutting edges have a special meaning. One edge is to protect the weak against the strong, the other the poor against the rich.

Many Christians of the 21st century might not be entirely at ease with any comparison equating the sword with the Cross and Christendom, but two Bible passages, "swords into plowshares" (Isaiah 2:4 and Micah 4:3), which are so often preached in churches today, are also in complete contrast to other passages: "Prepare yourselves for the holy war! Offers to the strong! Wake up the mighty men, let all the men of war draw near! Beat your plowshares into swords, and your pruning hooks into spears, (Joel 4, 9-10).

Development of full plate armor in the 13th century changed the sword blade.

Photo: Agilitas.tv

The first two-handed swords appeared towards the end of the 12th century.

Development of the sword from the 10th to 15th centuries.

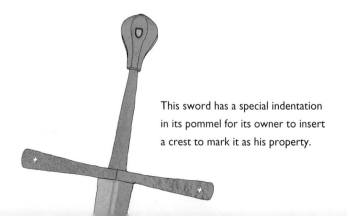

This sword has a special indentation in its pommel for its owner to insert a crest to mark it as his property.

The sword was in use as a weapon for some 1,000 years. Here is a typical, narrow 15th-century thrusting sword.

Photo: Museum Replicas

The sword became the symbol of Chivalry (scene from *Kingdom of Heaven.*)

Photo: 20th Century Fox/Museum Replicas

Different types of body armor, such as helmet and chain mail, impacted the shape of the sword.

Photo: Museum Replicas

The "new" blade cross-section: A late medieval sword is designed for a powerful thrust into gaps in the armor.

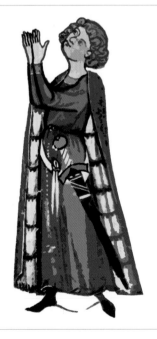

Only a knight was allowed to carry a sword on his belt (graphic after the Manesse manuscript).

And this propensity to violence and war is not only found in the Old, but also in the New Testament. Thus, Jesus, commonly held to be absolutely peaceful, says: "Think not that I am come to bring peace on the earth. I came not to bring peace, but a sword," (Matthew 10:34).

The most important aspect of the medieval sword is perhaps its function as a status symbol. Already in the Early Middle Ages, you could distinguish a leader from a common soldier by his possession of a sword. By the High and Late Middle Ages, ordinary warriors also had swords, and the sword becomes the symbol *par excellence* of chivalry. A knight began to learn how to handle weapons already in childhood. At about seven years old, he left home and joined the household of a friendly knight, to be educated there as a page. In addition to countless other skills, the page also learned to use a wooden sword. At about thirteen, the page became a squire, who was now also deployed in combat. After about six to seven years, his training was completed. Now the squire could either himself become a knight, or continue to offer his services as a squire. The difference between a squire and a knight was not particularly great: "In battle, he wore the same armor as the knights, he only could not wear his sword on his belt; and he fastened it upon the pommel of his saddle," (Schlunk and Giersch, p.21). If the squire then was knighted, he was dubbed a knight with a sword—for the nobility, a knighting ceremony was also celebrated—and he was solemnly girded with his sword.

Possession of a sword marked a free man of noble origin; wearing his sword on his belt, the knight himself. Accordingly, it was generally forbidden for the commoners, the serfs, to own and, even more, to carry swords. This situation altered in the Late Middle Ages, when the citizens of the free cities were granted such privileges, and a sword also became the mark of a free citizen. This situation also led, as we shall see later, to a blossoming of swordsmanship.

The sword was thus from the beginning a status symbol for the upper classes. This is also reflected in the sword itself. In many historical documents there is evidence that even an average sword had about the equivalent value of four cows—in an agrarian society, that means a real asset. Really excellent swords could easily cost many times more. Compared to other weapons—such as an ax, war hammer, and halberd—swords were incredibly costly objects. In addition to the skill required to forge a good weapon, swords were often also sumptuously decorated. As a result, we learn from the *Vita Karoli Magni*, that Charlemagne, "constantly [wore] a sword at his side, which had a hilt and sword belt hanger made of gold or silver. At times he also wore a sword studded with precious stones, but only for particularly festive occasions or when the embassies of foreign nations appeared before him." The higher the wearer's rank, the more impressive the sword was. Nevertheless, medieval swords are not to be compared with Renaissance weapons, which were absolutely overloaded with adornments. It is striking that even royal swords—despite their gilded hilts and engravings—are often relatively plain and practical, well-balanced weapons which represent the highest quality (consider the swords of St. Maurice and Edward III, to be discussed later.).

Not only kings, but knights also often had—according to their wealth—more than one sword. As Charlemagne did, it was customary to distinguish special swords for representative purposes and those for "everyday" use. In the Late Middle Ages, warriors often also had a one-handed sword and a two-handed long-sword or battle sword. In the 9th century, it was reported of the Margrave Eberhard of Friuli that he possessed nine swords, and an 11th-century Anglo-Saxon prince even possessed twelve swords of his own, which were distributed among his sons after his death.

Besides its function as a status symbol, the sword was also a sign of official authority. This started already at the very highest rank. There is a well-known representation in the *Sachsenspiegel* [Mirror of the Saxons], in which Jesus is giving over the sword of secular power to the king, and the sword of spiritual power to the Pope. Just as in dubbing a knight, a sword always plays a role in the coronation of an emperor or king, and since the beginning of feudalism, swords belonged among the imperial insignia, along with crown and scepter. Thus, the St. Maurice sword—the Imperial Sword of the Holy Roman Empire: "Kings of the Middle Ages were girded at their coronation by the Pope in Rome. The ruler thus received this

weapon, as it were, from the hands of the Apostles (Peter and Paul) with the order, to lead with this weapon [ad vindictam quidem malorum, ad laudem vero bonorum] (to fight evil and for the good of the righteous) (1 Pet. 2:14). At the recessional from the church it was borne ahead by the Schwertführer [bearer of the Imperial Sword]—with the point upwards—as a sign of worldly power and authority. It was to remind the ruler of the fact that he was the defender of the Empire as well as of the Church," (Schulze-Dörrlamm, p.9). Accordingly, the office of royal sword bearer was one of the highest honors throughout the Middle Ages.

In the 14th century, it was also customary to represent official civic power by a sword. Mayors and judges, for example, were given special ceremonial swords to be carried before them as a sign of their power. These swords were usually a more or less pompous bastard sword or two-handed sword. A fine example of such an "official sword" is the Sword of the city of Dublin. This is a classic Type XVa weapon (more on this typology in the following chapter). The gilded hilt of this bastard sword has a facetted "scent-stopper" (pear-shaped) pommel, very long cross-guard, and a metal rain-guard (the scabbard is not original). Unlike many other swords, we know the exact historical background of this specimen: it was forged in 1396 for the future King of England, Henry IV. He apparently also used this sword in battle, because the blade shows typical signs of wear and nicks. When municipal rights and privileges were awarded to Dublin in 1403, Henry IV gave the city its sword—as the mayor's official symbol. It is still used for special ceremonies.

The Sword in Legend and Myth

Given its special social significance, soon countless legends and tales were spun around the sword. Swords were magical, indestructible, and much more: if you disregard the magical properties, we still find a kernel of truth in many legends.

Perhaps the best-known sword of all is Excalibur, the sword of King Arthur. The figure of Arthur became known throughout Europe through the literature of the High Middle Ages; historically, he lived in the 5th or 6th century. The sword Caliburn—old English for "Excalibur"—is inextricably linked to the Arthurian

A newly made knight girded with sword and spurs (drawing after a miniature from the biography of King Offa, around 1300).

Sigurd (Siegfried), the dragon slayer, with the help of master smith Regin, repaired his father's broken sword (drawing from Sigurd carvings in the Hyllestad stave church, around 1200).

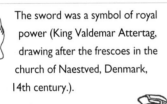

The sword was a symbol of royal power (King Valdemar Attertag, drawing after the frescoes in the church of Naestved, Denmark, 14th century.).

The sword in the hand of a judge was a symbol of judicial authority (drawing after a woodcut, around 1500).

The Lady of the Lake receives the magical sword Excalibur (drawing after a French 14th-century miniature).

Today, swords are made everywhere in the world. Here, a modern interpretation by hobby knife maker Herbert Schmidt.

Photo: Herbert Schmidt

The sword of the city of Dublin symbolizes the Mayor's authority.

Photo: Dublin City Council

story. Caliburn was forged on the island of Avalon; King Arthur pulled it out of the stone, and after his death, it was returned to the "Lady of the Lake." Again, there is a core of truth here—the legend reflects the religious practices of the pagan Celts. The two historians Graham Phillips and Martin Keatman describe this as follows: "Archaeological excavations have uncovered many valuable artifacts, including swords, which were thrown by the Celts of northern Europe as a sacrifice to the water gods in sacred lakes and ponds." They present the following cogent theory: "Could the theme of Excalibur being thrown into the water to the Lady of the Lake, therefore, be an ancient Celtic practice of making a sacrifice to a water goddess, perhaps in hope of curing the king?" (Phillips and Keatman, pp. 68, 69).

In contrast to the popular Arthurian author Geoffrey Ashe, Phillips and Keatman remained largely unnoticed. However, I believe that they provide the best clarification of the historical King Arthur, and I am not aware that it has been scientifically refuted to date. They also convincingly explain another detail of the Caliburn legend: the oldest description of Caliburn is found in the Welsh poem "Dream of Rhonabwy" (around 1150). This poem states that the golden hilt was decorated with two coiled snakes. The Roman garrison in the Kingdom of Gwynedd—home of the historical Arthur—actually had two crossed snakes as its emblem. "If Arthur had inherited the sword of his office from his predecessors, the pro-Roman rulers of Gwynedd […], it is historically conceivable that such a sword bore the motif of a double snake, the insignia of the former Roman authorities in this area," (Phillips and Keatman, p.298).

The great majority of legends about swords occur in the Germanic heroic legends of the Early Middle Ages. Such stories include that about the cursed sword Tyrfing, which constantly had to taste blood. Or about Sigurd's sword Gram: broken by Odin himself and re-forged with the help of the dwarf Regin, so that it could cleave through the anvil. There are a surprisingly number of realistic core elements in the magical or alchemical processes of sword forging described here. Entire books have been written just about Völund (Wieland), the blacksmith, and his sword Mimung (more on this in the chapter on sword forging). While

this book is not about sword legends, it should be clearly emphasized at this point that many legends contain important historical information, and we should be open-minded when we consider it.

Swords Today

Although the craft of both the sword-smith as well as the swordsman had died out for five hundred years, today, the sword is in a brilliant situation. Swords are being forged all over the world—whether by professionals in well-equipped forges or by amateurs in backyard workshops. Internet forums are making every effort to extend knowledge about swords all over the world.

Until the 1980s, interest in swords was no more than moderate. Only the cheapest decorative swords—so-called wall hangers—were commercially available, usually made of stamped sheet metal. At the other end of the scale were some hand-forged stainless Damascus steel swords, but these also only served decorative purposes. Hardly anyone was interested in the art of manufacturing a fully functional sword that could be used in combat. This changed when, in the late 1970s and early 1980s, literature and movies began to make fantasy and historical themes very popular. *The Lord of the Rings, Conan the Barbarian*, & Co., made for renewed interest in the medieval sword. The fantasy film *Highlander* (1985) can be considered a groundbreaker in this development, followed in the nineties by its own TV series. Inspired by *Highlander*, people all over the world became increasingly interested in the function of historical swords.

The Internet is another influential factor in the history of modern swords. It was cyberspace which first gave sword fans the opportunity to network and exchange information worldwide. Today, the Internet offers literally tens of thousands of pages about swords. They range from an outrageous article "How little Hans Miller imagines himself a sword" on fantasy and role-playing sites, to Internet forums that function on a scientific level (more on this in the section "Addresses").

In the 1990s, groups increasingly began to concern themselves with medieval sword fighting, in addition to the historical, theoretical components of the field. Centuries-old fencing books were unearthed in archives, translated, and studied. The demand for genuine, sharp swords kept growing. As a result, today, for the first time in 500 years, there are companies, small manufacturers and individual swordsmiths who earn their living making swords designed for fighting.

There is a very wide range of swords being made today. There are purely decorative pieces (wall hangers), replicas of middle and high quality that can be used in practice, up to modern interpretations of historic swords. They are made at individual sword forges, in factories in the Czech Republic, India, or Mongolia, or by advanced companies in the USA. The techniques used range from traditional forging methods to computer controlled milling machines. The selection of models has become too enormous. From a Viking sword to the classic long-sword of the late Middle Ages, to fantasy designs fit for dueling, everything is available. The only thing that matters here is the buyer's taste and the size of his wallet.

Modern replica of a Viking sword.

Photo: Armart Antiquanova

More and more people are interested in historical swordplay.

Photo: Agilitas.tv

The swords featured in Peter Jackson's
The Lord of the Rings have influenced many
modern manufacturers and swordsmiths.
Photo: New Line Cinema/United Cutlery

Nomenclature and Classification of Swords

Swords belong to the edged weapons or cut and thrust weapons. Within this category of weaponry, swords are defined by their size. For antique weapons, anything with a total length of more than 15.75 inches (40 centimeters) is no longer considered a dagger, but rather a short sword. For the Middle Ages and modern times, this measurement shifts upward, to about 19.7 inches (50 centimeters). These boundaries are relatively arbitrary and represent only a guideline, since, in reality, there are fluid transitions and exceptions. We find a similar problem in the groups of sword types, which occur in both dagger and sword length—such as for the Germanic *Sax* or seax, which is considered both a sword and a combat knife. For samurai swords, there are in any case different rules that apply.

A sword can be roughly divided into two sections:

- the blade
- the hilt or mounting.

If the hilt is removed, the blade itself consists in turn of two parts:

- the actual blade
- the tang: the shank that is connected to the hilt and is usually hidden in it.

The parts of the blade which project at the base of the tang are called shoulders.

Apart from this rough classification, we distinguish many smaller parts and pieces:

- pommel-nut or pommel-rivet
- pommel
- grip, or the sword's handle
- cross-guard; if disc-shaped: hand guard
- ricasso, the unsharpened base of the blade
- cutting edge
- fuller
- point.

The pommel of a sword fulfills several functions:

- It acts as a counterweight to the blade, thus improving balance.
- It prevents the hand from slipping backwards from the grip.
- You make backhand strokes with the pommel.
- A hand on the pommel gives more pressure to a thrust, effectively making it bore into the target, as can be seen in historical illustrations.

Over the centuries, various forms of pommels were developed. However, it is clear that the various versions of the disc pommel have been the most popular and common form for almost 500 years.

The cross-guard performs several functions:

- They are used to parry, entrap, and block the opponent's blade.
- It protects the hand against the opponent's blade and also prevents the sword hand from slipping forward onto the blade.
- It is used for parrying, catching, and leveraging techniques.
- If necessary, they protect the sword hand upon impact with the opponent's shield.

The term cross-guard or quillons first emerged in the 16th century; in the Middle Ages the guard was often referred to simply as the "cross" because of its shape. The name quillons is now common only in English, in addition to the terms derived from its function of protecting the hand: "hand-guard" or simply "guard." In German, the term *Parierstange* (parrying bar or rod) is generally used.

In the Middle Ages, the pommel was called a "lump" or "knob." In the English re-enactment scene, participants try to consistently use the medieval names. I am using instead the now-general names, to make interdisciplinary communication on these matters possible.

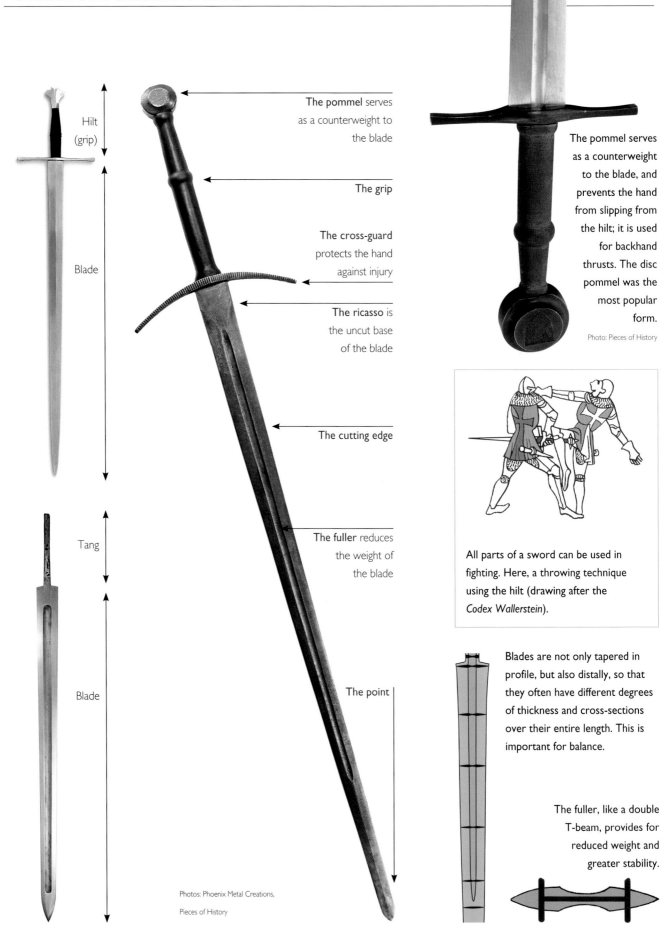

Hilt
(grip)

Blade

Tang

Blade

The **pommel** serves as a counterweight to the blade

The **grip**

The **cross-guard** protects the hand against injury

The **ricasso** is the uncut base of the blade

The **cutting edge**

The **fuller** reduces the weight of the blade

The **point**

Photos: Phoenix Metal Creations, Pieces of History

The pommel serves as a counterweight to the blade, and prevents the hand from slipping from the hilt; it is used for backhand thrusts. The disc pommel was the most popular form.

Photo: Pieces of History

All parts of a sword can be used in fighting. Here, a throwing technique using the hilt (drawing after the *Codex Wallerstein*).

Blades are not only tapered in profile, but also distally, so that they often have different degrees of thickness and cross-sections over their entire length. This is important for balance.

The fuller, like a double T-beam, provides for reduced weight and greater stability.

The geometry of the blade is complicated. This primarily means the different blade cross sections. In addition to the shape of the blade's side, the cross section—that is, the wedge or sharpening angle—also gives an indication of its purpose and proper functioning. For example, the wedge angle of a seax (*Hiebschwert*) must, understandably, be much greater than that of a small knife for fine cutting (i.e., a utility knife and not the "long knife" type of sword). On a seax, a razor sharp, thin blade would be badly nicked by the first powerful blow.

Throughout history, most blade cross sections were given their own names. The differences between the swords of the High and Late Middle Ages are characteristic (more on individual blade cross sections under the respective sword types). At this point I should note that the blade has very different thickness and cross sections over its entire length (which is extremely important for overall weight and balance). The blades of medieval swords taper towards the point not only in profile, but also distally, and thus in thickness. The distal taper must especially be kept in mind when considering such features as balance and the sword's harmony. This is one of the main points of criticism of modern replicas.

The fuller is also part of the blade geometry. This is a forged or ground-in polished groove along the blade. The fuller has two effects on a sword:

- first, it makes it lighter
- second, it gives more stability, on the physical principle of the double T-beam.

Usually, the fullers are symmetrical on both sides of the blade. On early medieval swords, fullers are usually broad and flat; later, they were made much narrower, and often there can be two or three fullers on one side of a blade.

The fuller is sometimes referred to by the popular name a "blood groove." Unfortunately, even in the recent literature, fairy tales are often spread about the blood groove: That the blade would often block up a stab wound and would prevent major bleeding. Therefore, the blood groove was invented to let the blood drain from a stab wound, making the opponent bleed to death. All this, of course, is total nonsense.

First, stab wounds are very dangerous because of internal bleeding, and secondly, were the fuller to make blood flow, it would mean that a swordsman, in the midst of battle, would have to leave his blade stuck in his defeated enemy so that he would bleed to death. And finally, this does not explain just why seaxes—which are only intended for a stroke or cut—have pronounced fullers. To finally put all the fairy tales about the blood grooves to rest, we should consistently use the technically correct term fuller, and avoid "blood groove."

The only terms that are now still missing do not concern the sword itself, but its accessory, the scabbard. The scabbard opening is called the throat, and the metal reinforcement on leather or wood scabbards are also called the locket, and the chape on the scabbard tip. If there is a third reinforcement, it is logically called the middle band.

The terms we have not yet mentioned are not universal, but type-specific and are explained along with the individual weapons.

Classification of Medieval Swords

Swords can be divided into several different categories. One of the most important categories is the size—that is, is it a one-handed sword or a long-sword? The term long-sword is used here as a generic term for all swords that have a long grip for two hands, although bastard swords (= hand-and-a-half) and battle swords essentially represent categories of their own (more on this in the relevant chapters). Besides the size, swords can be also distinguished by their form. The largest and best-known groups in terms of form, are the straight and double-edged swords.

In addition to the two-edged sword, we also find swords that are sharpened only on one side. This type is referred to in German as *Rückenklinge* ("back blade"); the English equivalent is "backsword." Straight backswords are rare. The sword pictured far right on the opposite page is of German origin and dates from around 1500 to 1520. The forward third of the blade has a sharp back cutting edge.

Contrary to popular belief, there were also a relatively large number of single-edged swords in the European Middle Ages, with blades that are more or less sharply curved or asymmetrically shaped, and are thus counted among the curved swords and sabers. Types such as the falchion and the "long knives" were particularly popular among common soldiers and also the rural population. The perfectly straight backsword is seen more often beginning in the Renaissance, especially in basket-hilted swords; it has developed into a very popular style since the 18th century.

In addition to the straight swords of the Middle Ages, we find swords with curved or asymmetric blades: sabers and scimitars. Compared to backswords, they are numerous, but in comparison to the straight, double-edged types, they are still rarely represented in museums.

The typical medieval sword is thus straight and double-edged. As we will see in more detail later, this design goes back to the swords of the Population Migration and Viking periods, which are classified by the shape of their grip. This system is useful, because the blades do not vary much, and, by and large—up to the single-edged swords—can be all designated as a particular basic type. In the High and Late Middle Ages, however, we come across such a large variety of blade forms, that you can no longer in good conscience classify them according to the grip shape.

With swords, as in many other areas, the saying "form follows function" applies. In the High Middle Ages, completely new sword types are invented which are designed for different functions and types of fighting. Despite these differences, for a long time it was customary among historians to distinguish high medieval swords by their hilts. This only changed when the sword expert Ewart Oakeshott presented a new system for the classification of two-edged swords in 1958 (see page 26). By the beginning of the 1990s, Oakeshott's typology had developed into the undisputed international standard—classifications designed later on, that were competing and sometimes more in-depth, could not become established.

The "Broadsword" Mischief

We are constantly encountering the term "broadsword" in books, movies, and television – and usually it is applied completely incorrectly to medieval swords. Actually, "broadsword" means a heavy *Degen* – at this time, there was no specific English term for the *Degen*; only "rapier" and the generic term "sword" were known. The term "broadsword" emerged in the 18th century and was used to distinguish a sword with a wide blade from the slender rapiers. The types of weapons which come under the term "broadsword," are usually referred to in German as a *Reitschwert* [riding sword], *Korbschwert* [basket(-hilt) sword, a *Pallasch*, or simply as *Degen*. They have absolutely nothing to do with medieval swords!

Swords may have one or more fullers of different diameters. Often, the fullers also show inscriptions.

Photo: Armart Antiquanova

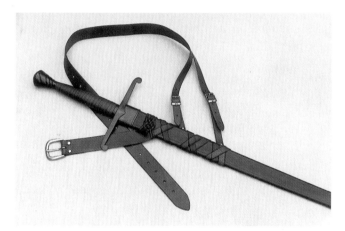

The scabbard is usually made of leather or leather-covered wood and often decorated with metal fittings.

Photo: Lutel

The sword was worn on a special belt.

Photo: Museum Replicas

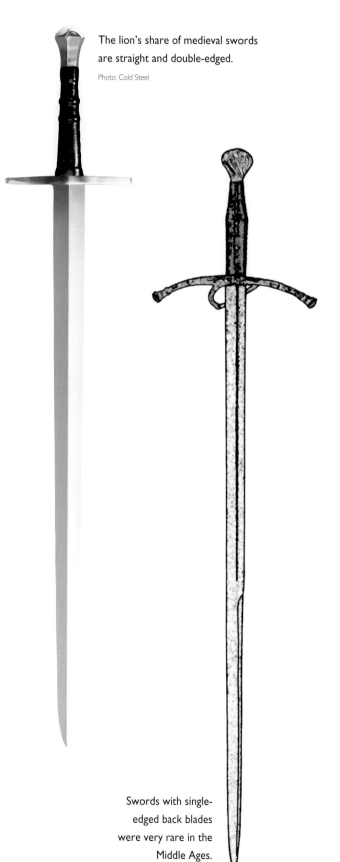

The lion's share of medieval swords are straight and double-edged.

Photo: Cold Steel

Swords with single-edged back blades were very rare in the Middle Ages.

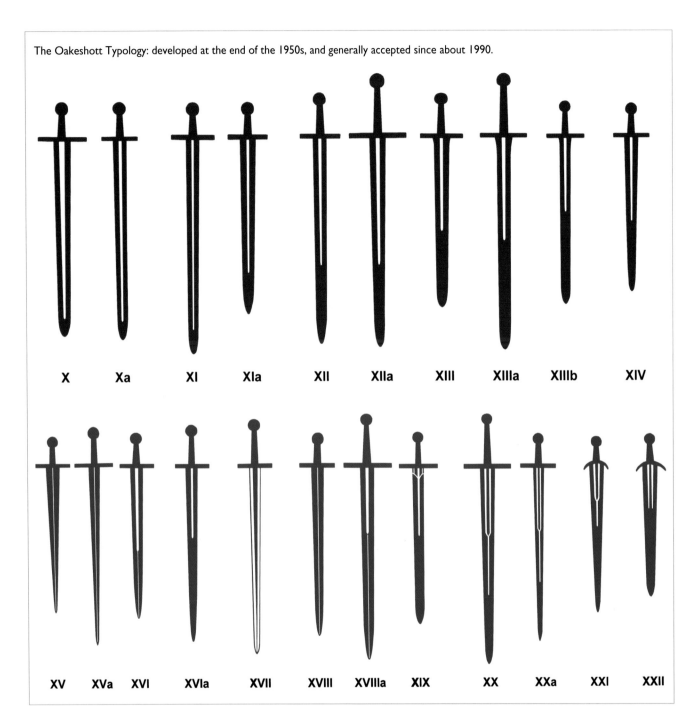

The Oakeshott Typology: developed at the end of the 1950s, and generally accepted since about 1990.

X   Xa   XI   XIa   XII   XIIa   XIII   XIIIa   XIIIb   XIV

XV   XVa   XVI   XVIa   XVII   XVIII   XVIIIa   XIX   XX   XXa   XXI   XXII

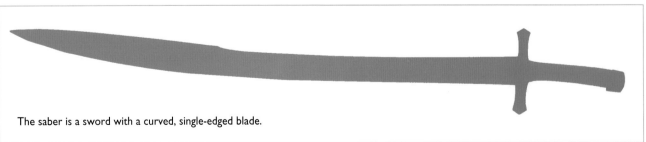

The saber is a sword with a curved, single-edged blade.

The Oakeshott Typology

Swords are primarily weapons—sometimes, they are also works of art, but that's really just a pleasing side effect. For this reason, artistic design cannot play a role in sword classification. Beyond this, the artistic design—since it does not affect the weapon's purpose—is often determined by fashion trends and the personal taste of the sword owner. In this respect, the basic Oakeshott typology totally disregards the form of the hilt and its decoration. The blade is especially important: It primarily constitutes the sword.

The Oakeshott typology is based on two factors:

- the shape of the blade (width, length, shape of the point, tapering of the blade, the blade cross section and the form of the fullers)
- the proportions of the sword (consisting of the relative proportions of hilt and blade to each other).

Using this approach, we can identify thirteen major types (X to XXII) and various sub-types. The Oakeshott numbering starts where the Viking swords end (I to IX), and the different types run through the entire world of medieval swords.

Moreover, Oakeshott also developed a "sword formula." He categorized thirty-five different forms of sword pommels and twelve different forms of cross-guards. The basic sword type is combined with the shape of the pommel and the cross-guard, and the resulting formula describes the sword exactly. The sword pictured on page 29, for example, has a relatively slender blade with diamond-shaped cross section and short fuller, as well as a two-handed grip (type XVIIIa). The disc pommel has a slight ridge on its flat surface, which is defined as concave (J), and the cross-guard is straight and slightly tapered (2). The formula is: XVIIIa-J-2.

The various pommel and cross-guard types, as defined by Oakeshott, are presented in an outline for reference in the table on page 226.

Regardless of these types, you can still distinguish thirteen different "families" of swords. This deals with the characteristic form of the hilt design, combinations of pommel and cross-guard which cut across the sword types. These various designs have no functional background, but are largely determined by the influence of fashion or trends—hence, only the most important families are presented in the appropriate places in this book. Oakeshotts' typology, however, is of

The "Dean of Swords"

As so often happens in life, it was not any graduate historian who accomplished perhaps the greatest scientific achievements in the field of swords, but rather an amateur and layman. Ewart Oakeshott (1916-2002), respectfully known by sword fans as the "Dean of Swords," studied art at the London Central School of Art, and later worked as a freelance illustrator. His uncle – a successful author of chivalric and cloak-and-dagger stories – brought him into touch with the field of old swords: a fascination that would accompany Ewart Oakeshott his entire life. In the 1930s and 1940s, he started collecting and studying medieval swords. Right from the beginning, his work was interdisciplinary: he did not consider the swords as art objects, but looked at them "through a knight's eyes" – as functional weapons. He made replicas himself, carried out cutting tests with valuable original historical weapons, and attempted sword-fighting in armor – in short: he was the pioneer of the modern sword customer.

In the 1950s and 1960s, Oakeshott increasingly made his name as an expert in historical weapons and was increasingly consulted by private individuals, as well as by famous museums and institutions. In addition to numerous articles and several children's books, he wrote three standard works on swords, which remain in print today: *The Archaeology of Weapons* (1960), *The Sword in the Age of Chivalry* (1964) and *Records of the Medieval Sword* (1981). Oakeshott's greatest achievement was probably the creation of a typology which has now became the international standard.

paramount importance—it is essential for international communication among sword enthusiasts.

Oakeshott bases his fundamental differentiation of swords on their intended target, the enemy's armor. He differentiated between swords which:

a) are primarily used against chain mail
b) primarily against plate armor.

Swords of the first group (red) can be approximately dated to the period 1050-1350. The blades are generally broad and flat, and usually have one or more fullers. The cutting edges are ground slightly convex, intended for a stroke or cut. The swords of the second group (blue) are from the period 1350-1550. The blades taper more distinctly and have a rhombic cross section—diamond-shaped, as they say in international usage. These blades are no longer primarily designed for a cut, but rather for a thrust into unprotected areas in plate armor.

Classification of Swords

In the classification of swords – by whatever typology and classification – it is essential to remember that historical swords are handmade single pieces. Each sword is unique, and none really is exactly like another. Therefore, they sometimes cannot be clearly assigned to a particular type, and there are hybrid forms and exceptions.

Pommels were made in a variety of shapes. An outline based on Oakeshott's work appears on page 226.

Flattened mushroom shape (Type B).

Flattened triangle (Type T1).

Octagonal pommel (Type I1).

Blades of group I (red) are designed for fighting opponents in chain mail; group 2 (blue) for fighting opponents wearing plate armor.

Swords of Group I (left, center) and Group 2 (right) have significantly different blade shapes.

Photo: Museum Replicas

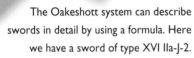

The Oakeshott system can describe swords in detail by using a formula. Here we have a sword of type XVI IIa-J-2.

Photo: Pieces of History

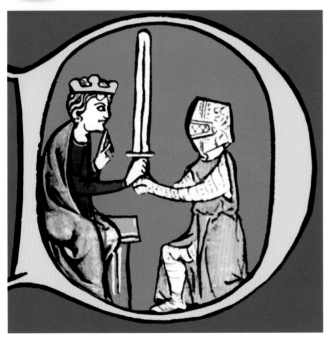

Swords of the 1050-1350 period are characterized by broad cutting blades (sketch from an English illumination, around 1300).

CIRCA 1250

CIRCA 1100-1200

CIRCA 1400

Medieval Swordsmanship

I would now like to ask the reader to say goodbye to a cherished prejudice. It is frequently stated that the Japanese art of swordsmanship—*Kenjutsu*—is the most perfect in the world, while swordsmen of the European Middle Ages battled each other using brute force, raw strength, and without skill, as if true to the motto: "The loser was he whose arm was first paralyzed." A superstition! Medieval swordsmanship was much more elaborate than is commonly believed—in fact, there was no need for it to yield to Japanese *Kenjutsu*.

I would like to begin this chapter with a comment by the famous sword expert Heribert Seitz. In his standard work *Blankwaffen* [*Edged Weapons*], he writes on medieval swordsmanship: "They ruthlessly deployed everything which promised success. [...] Based on this conception, the art of fencing was without rules—raw and primitive," (Seitz, vol.1, p.166).

As fundamental as Seitz' work on weaponry is, this comment is also much influenced by the morality and prejudices of the 20th century—it confuses ethics with skill. There is no question that the medieval art of sword fighting focused on victory, on survival by all means: the fencer Hans Sachs (1494-1576) described "breaking the leg, thrusting at the testicles and breaking the arm, the death stroke, breaking fingers, stabbing in the face." But these techniques are not a sign of general brutality, but of the simple need for effective self-defense. The modern sword-fighting expert Guy Windsor comments here: "If the punishment for losing is death or being seriously mutilated, of course you must win at all costs," (Windsor, p.9).

Swordsmanship really did mean that "no rules apply"—but it definitely was not "raw and primitive." To begin with, presumptions assert that the strongest always wins, but as an anonymous master swordsman stated already in 1389, technique could defeat pure force: "If it should be strength against strength, the stronger is always victorious, for that reason, Lichtenauer's swordsmanship goes to a right and true skill, so that a weaker, with his art and cunning, can win as surely as the powerful one with his strength—

why otherwise would it be an art?" The old masters' fencing manuals show us a sophisticated, clever, and strategy-oriented art of sword fighting that goes far beyond mere force.

What do we know about medieval swordsmanship, comes mostly from the so-called *Fechtbücher* [sword fighting or fencing manuals]. This was a widespread literature that constituted, together with manuals on some other subjects (such as herbalism) the most widely read literature in the Middle Ages. Translated into modern bibliographic terms, we would describe them as "manuals." The oldest recorded *Fechtbuch* dates from the late 13th or the early 14th century. This is the "Manuscript I.33," which is erroneously known as the "Tower Fencing Book." The manuscript portrays dueling with sword and shield, described in a mixture of Latin and German. It is interesting that a sword master in the I.33 is clearly identified as a priest (*sacerdos*); in many pictures we see both his cowl and tonsure.

One fencing book very interesting in art historical terms is the one commissioned by Emperor Maximilian around 1512. The illustrations were provided by none other than Albrecht Dürer; the texts are by Dürer himself, his friend Willibald Pirckheimer (who had gained combat experience in various military campaigns) and a third author, to date still unidentified. Most of the historical illustrations used here come from the so-called *Codex Wallerstein*, a fencing book from the 15th century (very interesting background information on the *Codex* is available free on the Arma websites: www. thearma.org).

Medieval swordsmanship is traditionally also described with the vocabulary of fencing. However, "fencing" is a somewhat misleading term here. Medieval fencing used all kinds of edged weapons—from the dagger up to the halberd and lance. Unarmed melee or close combat played a major role, in addition to the sword. During the Early Middle Ages, fighting was essentially done with the one-handed sword and shield. During this time, the term *schirmen* (to shield or protect) developed (from *"mit dem Schild abschirmen"* ["to shield with a signboard or screen"]). Later, *Schirmen* was used synonymously for *Schwertkampf* (sword fight), and the sword master called himself the *Schirm-Meister* ("*schirmaister*") [sign or shield master]. The terms shielding and fencing were used in parallel for a long time, until fencing prevailed in the early modern period.

During the Middle Ages, there were two major schools of swordsmanship—the Italian and the German style. Of these two styles, the German apparently became much more significant. While the Italian style is actually represented by only two manuscripts and masters—Fiori de Liberis *"Flos Duellatorum"* (1409) and Filippo Vadis *"De Arte Gladiatora Dimicandi"* (about 1482-1487)—all other existing medieval fencing manuals come from the pens of the German masters: Johannes Liechtenauer, Hans Talhoffer, Hanko Döbringer, Sigmund Ringeck, Peter von Danzig, der Jude [the Jew] Ott, and Paulus Kal are only the best known among many.

In the early Middle Ages, fencing [*Schirmen*] was passed down within the family, with the son learning from his father. At larger princely courts, the most talented fighters usually undertook the training of the other warriors, although in some few places, the presence of specialized *Schirm-Meister*, or fencing masters, were also already being reported. In contrast, in the High and Late Middle Ages, fencing or sword fighting was a genuine profession, and it was at this time that the fencing books were written.

In the Late Middle Ages, there was also a change in weapons technology and warfare. Plate armor replaced chain mail, and the shield was usually no longer needed. The fighter thus had a free hand and could hold his sword with both hands. Accordingly, hilts and blades became longer. Over time the wielding the long-sword developed into the crowning discipline of all swordsmanship.

At the time, a *Schirm-Meister* earned his keep as an intermittently engaged teacher. One must remember that at that time, there was great demand for melee or close combat skills. The rural and urban communities lived in constant insecurity, since there was perpetually some kind of "small" or turf war being fought. Therefore, sword masters were hired to train the troops of noblemen or militias in the use of weapons.

But civilians were also interested in the art of fencing. First, people had to defend themselves against bandits and highwaymen, and secondly, it was a widespread custom to "fight out" legal disputes in court—in the most literal sense of the word. Before such a day in court, the adversaries usually took additional lessons from a sword master. In certain cases, the adversaries could have their judicial duel fought by a hired fighter. Those who did this included the old and infirm, women, children, clergy, and at times, those who were Jewish. "With this, a separate occupation developed, which, because duels were not that common, was practiced as an itinerant trade. These travelers could even create their family names: Kempe, Kemper, etc. [likely from Kampf or battle, combat]," (Schubert, p.234). In contrast to the reputable fencing masters, these itinerate warriors were regarded as outside the law in the High Middle Ages; they could by no means make any claims for damage suffered. "Everyone who let himself be nominated as a deputized fighter in a trial by ordeal, had to [...] commit themselves by oath, that he was convinced of the justness of the matters represented. In case he was defeated, he had to expect the same penalty in the criminal trial as the person he represented would, in the worst case, death," (Hils, p.225).

This situation changed during the 14th century—the trial by ordeal was increasingly out of fashion. This meant that the *Kempen*'s lives changed for the better. They moved about the country and showcased their art as *Klopffechten* [knockabout fighting]—show fighting. *Klopffechter* became a recognized means of livelihood, and in the 15th century there is even occasional mixing with the "serious" fencing masters, who normally set themselves strictly apart from the *Klopffechtern*.

As we can see, the fencing master was therefore a real professional. Accordingly, the masters also tried to protect their trade secrets. They would pass on their knowledge in the form of rhyming slogans—the *Merkeversen* [memorized or noted verses]—a tradition that dates back to Meister [Master] Liechtenauer. This secrecy is also reflected in the later books on fencing. The *Merkeverse* were not intended as textbooks in the modern sense, but as secret memory aids, containing tricks and tactics. The only people who could correctly interpret or decipher the verses, had

Legal judgments were "fought" in the Middle Ages in the most literal sense of the word.

Photo: Agilitas.tv

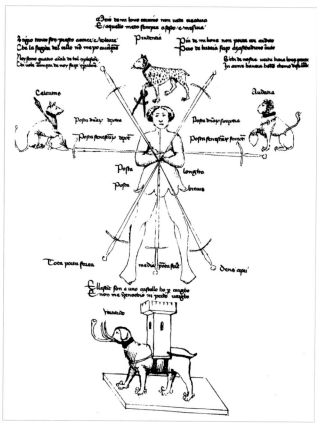

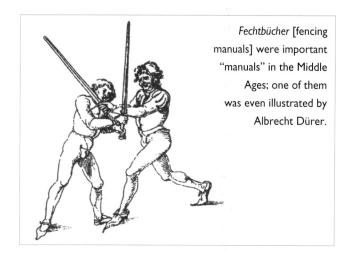

Fechtbücher [fencing manuals] were important "manuals" in the Middle Ages; one of them was even illustrated by Albrecht Dürer.

In 1409, Master de Liberi wrote the lines of attack and the principles of swordsmanship: A swordsman must be as quick as a tiger, have the eye of a lynx, be as brave as a lion, and as steadfast as an elephant.

Medieval "fencing" included using all types of edged weapons, such as the dagger.

Photo: Agilitas.tv

In the Early and High Middle Ages, fighting was basically done with sword and shield (scene from *Kingdom of Heaven*).

Photo: 20th Century Fox/Museum Replicas

Fechtschulen [fencing schools] were schools as well as popular amusement and a type of "fitness center." (Late medieval woodcut).

Swordplay in the Middle Ages (drawing from the *Codex Wallerstein*).

More and more people are attempting to reconstruct and resurrect medieval swordsmanship, by using the writings of the masters.

Photo: Agilitas.tv

Hans Talhoffer was one of the greatest fencing masters of the 15th century.

Image: VS-Books

previously been trained by a fencing-master, as Master Ringeck explains: "... written with hidden and covert words, so that the art shall not become public."

During the 15th century, the free bourgeoisie developed in Germany. The cities and their citizens increasingly competed with the nobility and often had to defend themselves against robber barons. The free citizens were granted a number of privileges by the Emperor, which included wearing swords. "The long-sword was [...] an obvious medium not only to demonstrate their own orientation to what was socially and culturally classified as superior lifestyle of the nobility [...], but at the same time to register their right to personal respect, which, if needed, could be sufficiently claimed/enforced," (Hils, p.310).

This new consciousness as free citizens, and the need to defend their rights, gave rise to a previously unprecedented demand for sword fighting lessons and fencing masters. Medieval swordsmanship experienced a revival, especially in Germany. Accordingly, in contrast to the case for Renaissance and modern fencing, a large number of the medieval fencing books appeared in the German language.

To protect themselves from charlatans and abuse, the fencing masters began to organize themselves in guilds know as *Fechter Gesellschaften* (Fencing Societies). These societies were structured like the craftsmen's guilds. The oldest and most powerful of the *Fechter-Gesellschaften* was founded in Nuremberg as the *Bruderschaft von St. Markus vom Löwenberg* (Brotherhood of St. Mark of Löwenberg). In 1487, the "Marx [Mark] Brothers" were given a letter of protection by Emperor Frederick III and were allowed to call themselves "masters of the long-sword": "So that now, everywhere in the Holy Empire, no one shall call himself a master of the sword, keep a school, nor teach for money, unless he previously has been tested approved in his art by the masters of the sword."

If a swordsman wanted to be a member of the Brotherhood, he had to be schooled by a master and later, as a journeyman, embark on a journey to develop his art in strange places. Finally, he was subjected to extensive testing by the masters in the Frankfurt headquarters of the Marx Brothers (Mark Brothers). Most of these tests were held in public at a great show and prize fencing event during the Autumn Fair.

Those who had passed the test, received the "Secrecy"—these were the *Merkeverse*—and was henceforth allowed to bear the title of "master of the long-sword" and himself accept and teach students.

It was customary to carry out fencing as "moonlighting." Thus, there are teachers known who taught their students both writing and reading as well as sword fighting. In the preface of a fencing book from the year 1600, we read: "Hanns Görg Deckinger I'm called, Ulm is my homeland. My praiseworthy craft is a glazier also a master and free swordsman of the manly and chivalrous free art of fencing, citizen and inhabitant of the princely capital city of Munich."

The Marx Brothers were the dominant society for about eighty years; in a sense the *Hanse* or "guild of swordsmanship." Then gradually competition grew from independent *Freifechter* (free fencers) who also produced a number of outstanding masters. The important fencing master Joachim Meyer published his textbook *Gründtliche Beschreibung der freyen ritterlichen und adelichen Kunst des Fechtens* (*Basic Description of the Free Chivalric and Noble Art of Fencing*) in 1570, describing himself as a proud

The Secret Merkeverse

An excerpt from Meister Liechtenauer's verses (in Middle High German original)

The Crooked Stroke

Crooked on him with nimbleness,
throw the point on the hands.
Who performs the crooked well,
with stepping he hinders many a stroke.
Strike crooked to the flats
of the Masters if you want to weaken them.
When it clashes above,
Then move away, that I will praise.
Don't do the Crooked, strike short,
Changing through show with this.
Strike crooked to who irritates you,
the Noble War will confuse him,
that he will not know truthfully
where he can be without danger.

"Freyfechter und Burger zu Strassburg (free fencer and citizen of Strasbourg.)" Later, Emperor Rudolf II granted the free fencers, who were then known as *Federfechter* [literally, feather fencers] the same privileges as the Marx Brothers. After the *Federfechter*, the *Lukas Fechter* (*Luxfechter*) [Luke's fencers] also arose, but did not reach the level of the other two fencing societies. "The rivalry between two fraternities was great. Each claimed to represent the true art of fencing. For the spectators then, it must have created a real pleasure when the Marx and Federfechter competed against each other; these were no longer any expositions, but fights in which rivalry and competition could lead to a bloody result," (Schubert, p.141).

Abraham a Sancta Clara (1644-1709) reports: "Nevertheless, it happens very often that a Marks brother could become a *Merksbruder* ('marked' brother) when he had lost an eye, and a *Federfechter* would be called a *Lederfechter* (leather fencer) when he dances his one last dance with his lacerated skin."

The fencing societies created a 16th-century boom in swordsmanship. The so-called fencing schools were a special attraction. In addition to the permanent fencing schools, the travelling category was especially important. Although the traveling swordsmen naturally also taught the citizenry, their main function was to stage large-scale demonstration fencing events, a kind of shooting match with swords. Like an annual fair, the fencers moved from place to place to showcase their skills with all kinds of weapons, for the price of an entrance fee. Of course, all fencers could participate in the competition. The Brotherhood, which won most of the victor's wreaths, shared the prize money. They fought without body armor, often with naked torso—their weapon was their only protection. A duel during a fencing school usually ended with the flourish of the "red flower," the first drawn blood. This ancient symbol of victory seems to have survived until today in the *Schmiss*, the fencer's dueling scar of the student *Burschenschaften* [university fraternal societies]. The rules during the fencing school were clearly defined: "However, everyone should know what is banned at this fencing school, as position, pommel, point, running-in breaking arms, a thrust at the private parts, strike at the eyes, throwing stones, and all dishonest items that some well know how to use, which I can not all recount, and have not learned, also no one strikes me still under the bars. Everyone will protect himself and hold a shield like the others, likewise I will have asked that where envy and hatred enter here together, he does not fight it out in this school [...]." Despite all these rules, the fencing schools often degenerated into a ruckus and were thus not

Training Swords

While training was usually with wooden swords, during the 16th century, steel training swords also emerged. These typical weapons have been passed down to us in representations of fencing schools and in Joachim Meyer's fencing book. They included bastard swords and two-handed swords with a slender, blunt blade. One particular characteristic was a significantly widened base, which apparently serves as a cross-guard. According to some historians, such training swords were called "feathers."

Photo: Pieces of History

Why Feathers?

The origin of the name *Federfechter* is unclear. Many historians have different interpretations. Some explain the name by a feather on the crest or emblem. Others attribute it to an alleged colloquial term for a *Degen* [German term for broadsword]. This "new" weapon allegedly initially was much more widely used by the *Federfechter* than the Marx Brothers, but later also spread rapidly among them. The third explanation is that it is a blunt training sword that, according to some historians, was also known as a "feather." The most likely explanation is its derivation from a patron saint, as for the Marx Brothers: The *St.-Viti-Fechter* or *Viterfechter* derived their name from Saint Vitus, and *Viterfechter* was later bowdlerized to *Federfechter*.

welcomed by the authorities. Already by 1286, fencing schools were prohibited within the city limits of London, and, "in the files of the first Rector of the University of Heidelberg, founded in 1386, there is a ban on students attending the fencing schools." (Hils, p.308).

The atmosphere at a fencing school seems to be like that a football or soccer game today: The teams entered the competition in a large show, accompanied by their fans. The opposing teams and fans greeted each other with *Trutzreimen* [defense rhymes], the historical ancestors of today's football theme songs. I will render one of these combative dialogues here:

"Only just now bold and stiffly trembling,
you feather-fencers are embittered;
but are specially ready with sword,
Dussack [war knife], with poles,
to get the best blows!
The fight is crowned with your blood!"

"While your daring Marx Brothers,
set aside the first attempts,
more with their mouths than any deed:
But let it be! The end will show,
which of us will yield to the other,
and likely gets the most hits."

It often happened that the referee had to separate the opponents with a long pole, and sometimes the fans joined the fight from the spectators' stands, so that the *Platzwärtel* [guard or referee] had to keep order with a leather *Dussack*. A football game is certainly the best modern comparison for the atmosphere at a fencing school.

Because of the show character of fencing schools, the fencing masters accordingly maintained a strict distinction between "serious fencing" and "school fencing," with some fencing masters magnanimously conceding to the school fencers that, with diligent practice, they might amount to something. In any case, the majority of the guild members were themselves not above taking part in fencing schools many a time. Altogether, the sword masters ensured that they set themselves apart, as fencing masters, from the ordinary duelers and school fencers, also known as *Leicht-Meister*, or lightweight masters.

In addition to the entertainment value of the show fighting, a fencing school offered the citizenry one of the few occasions when they could just engage in sports. An historic etching by Balthasar Schön carries the inscription: "I also have a craving for fighting and knightly games; I like to exercise my body, and then with good companions do springing, wrestling, running, fencing, and the like. [...] But I don't like it when things get abusive and too serious." Next to gymnastics, it is clear that for fun, they wrestled and dueled with swords. A fencing school is thus a kind of late medieval fitness center. All the sweating caused by this physical exertion led to the phrase, "It stinks here like a fencing school."

If a traveling fencing master wanted to open up a fencing school in a city, he usually needed the permission of the Council. He also had to face any challenger. Often, two competitors had to compete against each other in battle, and the loser would have to leave the city.

The decline of civilian sword fighting and fencing begins with the Thirty Years' War (1618-1648), which brought the German-speaking countries to utter ruin. Even after the war, the cities and free citizens increasingly lost their influence. Correspondingly, demand for fencing masters also fell. The fencing societies lost their privileges: The letter of protection was extended for the last time in 1688, and the fencers were no longer able to finance their livelihood with their skills. The only way that remained to many of them, was to degrade their once deadly art purely into a show and to eke out a living as a traveling *Klopffechter* or pugilists.

By this time, *Degen* or broadsword fencing had long found its way into swordsmanship. Innovations in this style of swordsmanship no longer came from Germany, but from Italy and Spain. With this development, fencing itself began to alter—from a hallmark of the free citizen to an expression of the aristocratic lifestyle. "Horseback riding and fencing are status symbols in an upper class that was no longer just distinguished by the nobility. This is the background for the ban on urban fencing schools as places of enjoyment for the normal citizens, while the academic fencing instructor obtains a permanent job to educate the sons of the nobility and the upper class gentry" (Schubert, p.407). This development also marks the

Classic German school swordfighting positions: right *Ochs* [ox], *vom Tag* [from the roof] from the shoulder, left *Alber* [fool], and left *Pflug* [plow].

Photos: H. Schmidt/Ars Gladi

Winden [winding]: Without resolving the "bind" with the opposing blade, you change the angle of your sword, so that the sword is wound against the other blade in your opponent's weak points.

Photos: H. Schmidt/Ars Gladi

demise of the long-sword—the broadsword makes its entrance, for its ultimate triumph.

The Art of the Master

Johannes Liechtenauer can certainly be seen as the greatest swordsman of the Middle Ages. Very little is known about Liechtenauer's life. Apparently, during the 14th century, he travelled to many European countries, to learn the art of the long-sword from different masters everywhere: "which could have been founded and conceived some hundred years ago, and Meister Lichtenauer has completely and correctly had and practiced [this skill]. Not that he himself had founded or conceived [this art], since it was previously written about, but he has traveled and searched through some lands and sought through the same just and true art the will, that he wanted to experience and know." (Anonymous sword master).

Master Liechtenauer combined his hard-earned knowledge into a systematic field of learning and formulated it in encoded rhymes. The earliest surviving record of Liechtenauer's *Merkeversen* (the manuscript *HS 3227a*) from the year 1389, comes from the pen of an anonymous master (who is often considered to be his direct disciple Hanko Döbringer). Liechtenauer's teachings became the origin of the German school of the art of the long-sword.

Master Liechtenauer's influence can be seen in all subsequent sword masters; it became the convention to repeat his verses completely once, at the beginning of a fencing book. The Liechtenauer tradition lasted for more than 250 years and is reflected in the work of the second outstanding German sword master: Hans Talhoffer. Although the *HS 3227a* already provides some clarification of Master Liechtenauer's cryptic verses, our primary knowledge about the details of the Liechtenauer combat system comes mainly from *Ringecks Kommentare*. *Ringeck's Commentary* is a manuscript written around 1440. The section on the long-sword was composed by Sigmund Ringeck—*Schirm-Meister von Albrecht, Pfalzgraf vom Rhein und Herzog von Bayern* (fencing master of Albrecht, Count Palatine of the Rhine and Duke of Bavaria) (he is likely Albert III of Bavaria). We do not know whether Ringeck himself or someone else wrote the other chapters, but the whole manuscript is known today as *Ringeck's Commentary*. It contains detailed explanations of Liechtenauer's verses, making it possible for today's enthusiasts to reconstruct the Liechtenauer system—as well as that is at all possible without a teaching master and only with the help of a book.

If Liechtenauer is the most important of the fencing masters of the 14th century, in the 15th century, this honor goes to the Marx Brother Hans Talhoffer. Master Talhoffer had paid "ghost writers" to produce a fencing book in each of the years 1443, 1459, and 1467. Thus, his "career" encompassed a period of at least twenty-four years. We can scarcely even imagine today just what this meant. From Master Talhoffer's works, we know that he was primarily concerned with judicial duels and probably even fought many—if not most—of them. In effect, this means that Talhoffer was engaged in a deadly occupation in both Germany and Switzerland for a quarter century—and not only survived, but rose to the top level. According to existing research, Master Talhoffer was still living in 1482. Assuming that he wrote his first fencing book at about twenty-years-old, one can conclude that he lived to be about sixty to seventy: "for a man of the 15th century, a remarkable life span. When we look at Talhoffer's occupation, there is every reason to consider his life and his ability to survive as amazing. Not only for that reason, it can be said of him that he must have been not only the best but also the most successful and most experienced fencing master of his time," (Hils, p.175). Talhoffer was so influential and powerful that he even had his own coat of arms.

Although Talhoffer's system is based on that of Master Liechtenauer, he not only continued the tradition, but also developed his own approach. One of the differences from Liechtenauer is shown in the choice of weapons: based on the requirements for judicial duels, Talhoffer had to deal a lot with dagger fencing and unarmed wrestling, as well as with fighting with mace and shield and other methods of dueling. In addition to different priorities, Talhoffer also discussed such matters as movement dynamics, physical training, and the science of nutrition: Master Talhoffer raised sword fighting and his teaching to a quasi-"scientific" level.

Liechtenauer's combat system can be divided into several categories:

- *Bloßfechten* or bare-handed fighting: a duel without armor
- *Harnischfechten*: dueling in armor
- *Rossfechten*: combat on horseback

In addition to the long-sword, we also find other techniques: fighting with a spear, wrestling (unarmed close combat), *Kampfringen* (combat wrestling) (wrestling in armor), and techniques using a (one-handed) using sword and shield.

Figuratively, you can consider medieval fencing as a diverse, but self-contained blend of sword cuts, sword parries, kicking, using strangleholds, and throwing techniques. This is certainly not the right place to go into detail on this system of combat and the individual techniques, but I want—as much as my theoretical knowledge permits—to introduce some basic aspects.

Master Liechtenauer presented seventeen "main matters" (basic techniques), which include, in addition to the five master strokes *Zornhau* (stroke of wrath), *Krumphau* (crooked stroke), *Zwerchhau* (crosswise stroke), *Schielhau* (squinting stroke), and *Scheitelhau*) (crown stroke) also the four "casual" (the four basic defensive positions: *Ochs, Pflug, Alber, vom Tag* [ox, plow, fool, from the roof).

Liechtenauer's basic tactic is the *Vor und Nach* [before and after]. "Before" means that one should attack the enemy before he strikes (even with the first blow, the *Vorschlag* (offer or proposal), thus forcing him on the *Versetzen* (defensive). If you get into the *Nach* yourself and must react to an opponent's attack defensively with a following stroke, you do this best, *indes* (simultaneously) using a defense that includes a counter-attack in the same motion. Thus, you retake the offensive, forcing the opponent on the defensive. *"So you win the* Vor, *and he remains* Nach," as Sigmund Ringeck wrote. Master Liechtenauer never tired of stressing this tactic:

> *"vor und nach, die zwei Ding*
> *[before and after, these two things]*
> *sind aller Kunst ein Ursprung*
> *[are the source of all skill"]*

A hotly discussed aspect of medieval swordsmanship is the technique of parrying. Almost certainly, the art of swordsmanship was not to "drive" the blade edges of the swords at each other using brute force, as is shown in movies and show fights (and is unfortunately often considered to be medieval swordsmanship). The issue is much more, not to use your own strength against the opponent's stroke—if you can't avoid it at the outset—but to divert his energy with his own sword. This is also behind the principle of the *"Stärke" und "Schwäche"* ["strong" and "weak"] areas of the blade.

The technique of *Winden* [winding] is also of fundamental importance. When winding, without resolving the "bind" with the opposing blade, you change the angle of your sword, so that the sword is wound against or around the other blade. In this way, you attack your opponent's weak points from out of a bind. *Winden* is one of the most important techniques of German swordsmanship school.

The art of parrying is an important aspect of medieval swordsmanship. The view is often expressed that knights only struck at each other with brute force—and in such a way that the sword edges hit each other. This view is reinforced by movies and stage matches, as this is how they show sword fights. But even the best sword blade could not long survive such treatment: It gets nicked and there is risk it will break. In reality, everything was quite different: the swordsman parried using the flat side of the lower part—the *Stärke* or strong part—of the blade! This is emphasized repeatedly in the medieval fencing books, and the swords themselves are further evidence: On many historical swords we find the traces of such parrying on the flat side.

The technique of *Winden* (winding) is also of fundamental importance. Sword fighting expert Christian Tobler explains: "Winding is swinging or pivoting the sword around the axis of the blade. The result is superior leverage in a bind and/or bending the sword point to find another vulnerable area." Winding is one of the most important techniques of the German swordsmanship school.

One aspect, described fully by both Masters Liechtenauer and Talhoffer, are unorthodox (from today's perspective) methods for using a sword. These are primarily techniques of striking with the sword pommel and the half-sword technique (the latter is explained in the chapter on long-swords). Techniques using the pommel are very important in medieval sword fighting. This involved not only backhand thrusts with the pommel; at times you would turn the sword around by the blade and use the pommel like a club—called the death blow.

Thus, as you can see, medieval sword fighting is far more than just "hitting hard." A variety of intricate and imaginative techniques utilizing all the available parts of the sword, were used in devising a strategy and tactics. This summation of the subject of sword fighting should be sufficient here, since I do not have any significant personal experience and this book is not about sword fighting, but about swords themselves. Suggestions for further reading can be found in the bibliography at the end of the book.

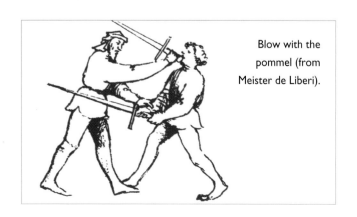

Blow with the pommel (from Meister de Liberi).

In half-sword technique, you aim with your left hand, while the right gives momentum.

Photo: Agilias.tv

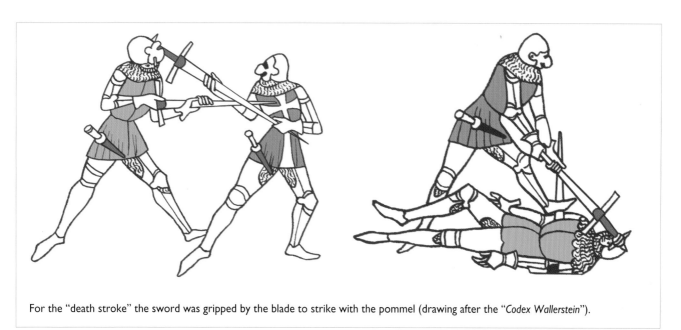

For the "death stroke" the sword was gripped by the blade to strike with the pommel (drawing after the "*Codex Wallerstein*").

The Secret of Sword Physics

While the sagas and early fantasy stories mostly concentrated only on their decorations, magical properties, or "unbreakable super steel" when describing swords, it has meanwhile now got around among recent authors that the real secret of a good sword lies elsewhere—in the balance. Ever more frequently, we find the adjective "well balanced" applied to swords. However, you rarely find any information about what now constitutes a well-balanced sword. The aspect we are now discussing could be described as "sword physics," but in international parlance, the term "sword harmony" has been adopted (this is due to the harmonic vibrations in the sword; more on that later).

In the historical literature, sword harmony is almost never discussed. This is due to the fact that it is only in recent years, that research and experiments have been done on this. Previously, the sword was regarded as an object of research in terms of art and military history, and statements about its suitability for fighting and "performance" were almost always speculation. Thanks to the efforts of many re-enactors, swordsmiths and sword fans, in the meantime many swords have been tried out and tested. As a result, completely new insights into swords have come to light.

A good sword has a blade that is hard and able to hold an edge, but is also springy and flexible at the same time. Beyond this, it must be properly balanced, or it will be cumbersome, awkward, and difficult to wield properly. A poorly balanced sword makes it simply impossible to use some techniques, while a balanced weapon supports the strokes. "If the blade of a sword is well proportioned and has a corresponding flexibility, the sword will have a balance that generates to a smooth forward thrust without making it unwieldy and cumbersome. The blade is easier to direct when wielding it," according to the Swedish swordsmith Peter Johnsson. Of course, not all medieval swords were perfectly balanced; there were significant differences in quality.

Three factors are crucial for the balance of a sword:

- the total weight of the sword
- the center or point of balance
- distribution of its mass

The total weight of the sword is of course a very important factor. Unfortunately, completely wrong ideas prevail on this point. These are not only created by scenes in novels or movies in which ordinary people (as opposed to muscle-bound heroes) can either only lift a sword with both hands or not at all, but also by statements by modern sport fencers—compared to a modern sports foil or sword, which is guided by the fingertips and is not intended to cause any injury, medieval swords are of course much heavier. Unfortunately, however, historians often make false statements regarding weight and balance. This was done, for example, in an otherwise very well made TV documentary, which discussed sword weights of 33-44 pounds (15-20 kilograms). This is utter nonsense! In reality, swords were much lighter. This is actually logical: after all, your life often depended on whether you could maneuver a sword easily and quickly.

Studies on historical swords have revealed the following average weights:

- one-handed swords (10th to 15th centuries) => about 2.2 pounds (1.0 kilograms)
- long-swords => about 3.3 pounds (1.5 kilograms)
- two-handed swords => 4.4-5.5 pounds (2.0 to 2.5 kilograms)

Stage or re-enactment swords weigh about forty percent more than a corresponding sharp sword ("cheap" stage combat swords even more). This is because they have no sharp edges, but a blunt edge about three to four millimeters thick. Thus, the blade does not have the original cross section, but is much thicker. To the regret of many re-enactors, this affects not only the total weight, but also the balance of a stage combat sword. Visitors to medieval markets usually only come in contact with stage combat swords, and understandably confuse them with "real" swords, getting a completely false impression of the weight of a genuine sword.

A Modern Swordsmith

The Swede Peter Johnsson is a pioneer in research on "sword physics." He has been fascinated by swords since his earliest childhood. On his eighth birthday, Peter Johnsson was given a small anvil, on which, with his father's help, he forged knives and miniature swords. After he completed his schooling, he trained as a graphic designer and began a career as an illustrator of children's and schoolbooks. In addition, he studied metal-smithing for four years. As his master's piece, he reconstructed the sword of the Swedish regent Svante Nilsson Sture.

In recent years, Peter Johnsson has been completely dedicated to the study and reconstruction of medieval swords. He has precisely measured and documented about a hundred historical originals. He places particular emphasis on the study of "sword harmony." According to Johnsson, you can recognize basic rules for proportions, and sometimes even the "golden section," in the various types of swords. As a result, he is able to create not only reconstructions, but also completely new models: "Sometimes I combine features of different swords and make a new one, which always has the handling characteristics of an original." An entire series of these "new models" is available at Albion Armorers under the name "Albion Mark Next Generation."

Although sharp swords are much lighter than is generally assumed, I want to emphasize that sword fighting is still an athletic performance. Just try once to wield a weight of 3.3 pounds (1.5 kilograms) (longsword) over a longer time at a fast pace and in a controlled way. You must not forget that being a knight was not only a privilege, but also was a "profession." Most knights had trained with their weapons every day from their childhood; they were professional fighters! Furthermore it is clear that weight is just a secondary factor. As sword fighting expert Guy Windsor explains: "The importance of balance cannot be overemphasized: A heavy, well-balanced blade can be wielded more easily than a light, poorly balanced one," (Windsor, p.38).

The definition of the center of balance is clear: At this part of the sword, the weapon is in equilibrium. Depending on the size and shape of the sword, the center of balance is about 5.9 inches (15 centimeters) below the cross-guard. If the center of balance is too far down in the blade, the sword stroke indeed will achieve great force, but the blade is, in overall comparison, too clumsy, and the sword is difficult to handle. If the center of balance is too close to the grip, the sword will at first be easier to handle, but the sword stroke loses force and the blade (especially the point) will be difficult to control. In addition, the heavy grip will constantly "tug" on the sword hand. It is therefore of utmost importance that the center of balance be in the right place.

It must be easy to direct a sword when wielding it. "The total weight and mass at a specific distance from the center of movement—the sword hand—affect both the speed and the power of the sword stroke," states Peter Johnsson. Therefore, the mass must be properly distributed along the entire sword. Here one can find, however, sharp differences—depending on the method of use. In a pure seax, the mass must be distributed relatively evenly over the entire length. In a sword also intended for thrusting, the mass is more concentrated around the grip area—the sword must be easy to control by the movements of one hand. Even if a sword, because its mass is concentrated at the grip, has a greater total weight than another type, it still appears to the user to be lighter and easier to guide. To compensate for the overall balance, the mass of the pommel must be adjusted to the rest of the sword, as an anonymous sword master explains: "If a sword is large and heavy, so the pommel must be heavy." In the end, the mass must not be too great, or the sword cannot be controlled precisely.

Now we have addressed the three factors of total weight, center of balance, and weight distribution. Beyond this, the so-called nodes are important for the harmony of the sword. A heavy blade is flexible—it must be in order to cushion the blows from the opponent's sword. When you wield the sword, it vibrates almost imperceptibly. Greatly simplified, one could say that it is a gigantic tuning fork.

When a sword strikes another sword or a shield, the vibrations are naturally stronger. A bad sword begins to tremble in the hand, and the vibrations are transmitted from the blade to the grip. A good sword, however, lies firmly in the hands, as the vibration-free zones—the nodes—are exactly in the right places. "The handling of vibration-free nodes is one of the secrets of a skilled swordsmith," Peter Johnsson states in this regard.

The primary node is also called the "center of percussion" (CoP) (sometimes called a salopp or "sweet spot" by sword fans). The CoP is the point on the blade where the impact on some resistance will transmit the least amount of shock effect to your own sword hand. As can be seen in the amplitude in the graph on page 46, the vibration-free node in the blade harmonizes with another, secondary node in the grip, also known as a "resonance point." That is, if the sword strikes another sword at the CoP, the vibrations are not transmitted—or almost not—to the resonance point.

Ideally, the CoP should lie on a sword—depending on the center of balance—at about one-third of the blade length (measured from the point). The resonance point in the grip should lie behind the cross-guard—near the sword hand. No matter how hard a sword stroke may be: the shock effect is relatively low on the sword hand.

Sword fighting expert Guy Windsor explains the effects of nodes as follows: "To chop off limbs, use the CoP, but for a swift stroke to the head, the last few centimeters of the blade. The best compromise for general use of a long-sword is to strike with the area three-quarters down the blade—just behind the

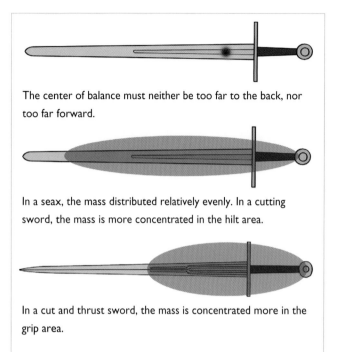

The center of balance must neither be too far to the back, nor too far forward.

In a seax, the mass distributed relatively evenly. In a cutting sword, the mass is more concentrated in the hilt area.

In a cut and thrust sword, the mass is concentrated more in the grip area.

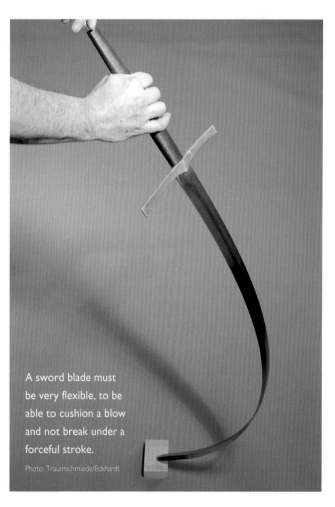

A sword blade must be very flexible, to be able to cushion a blow and not break under a forceful stroke.

Photo: Traumschmiede/Eckhardt

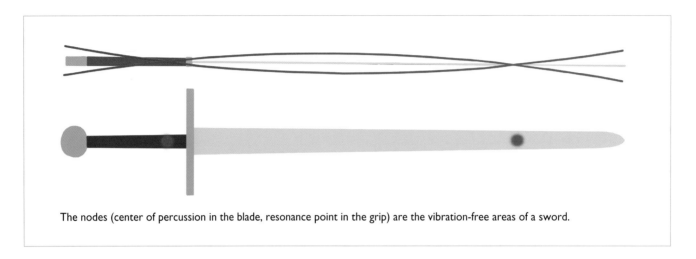

The nodes (center of percussion in the blade, resonance point in the grip) are the vibration-free areas of a sword.

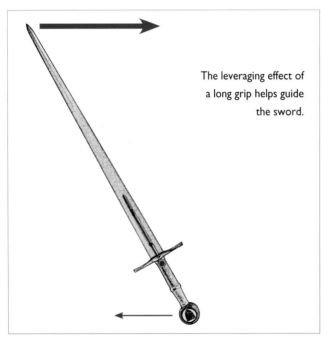

The leveraging effect of a long grip helps guide the sword.

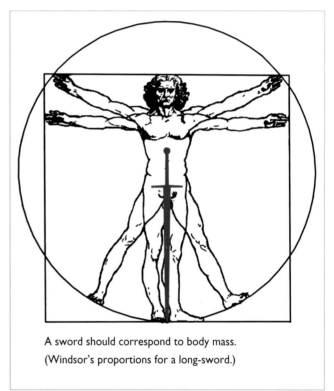

A sword should correspond to body mass. (Windsor's proportions for a long-sword.)

The pommel is a counterweight to the blade. The tang runs through the pommel and is riveted around the end. Riveting finally holds the sword parts together.

Photo: Poenix Metal Creations

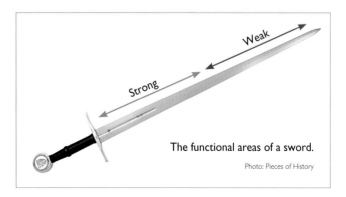

Weak

Strong

The functional areas of a sword.

Photo: Pieces of History

CoP. This delivers a lot of clout, a calculable and controllable shock [to the sword hand, TL] and the option to continue to thrust further or draw the blade," (Windsor, p.84).

You can determine a sword's nodal points by using two simple tricks. It is childishly easy to find the CoP (even for a known butterfingers like myself). Hold the sword so that the blade is aligned vertically and the point pointing upwards. Then hit the pommel with your free hand so that the sword begins to vibrate. In doing this, observe the front of the blade very carefully. A particular area of the blade will not, or at least almost did not, vibrate: The primary node.

The resonance point is much more difficult to find, since here you must rely on your sense of touch rather than your eyes. To determine it, hold the sword so that the point is downward. The weight is borne by the thumb and index finger, and the other fingers are only loosely on the grip. Strike the pommel lightly with your palm, so that the sword begins to vibrate, and try to feel the vibrations with your fingers. The secondary node is at the point on the grip where you feel no or virtually no vibration. With a seax, it is usually in the area of the index, middle, or ring finger. However, on a cut and thrust sword, is close to the cross-guard. The CoP can usually be found on the first try, but it usually takes several attempts to find the resonance point, since you have to develop a sort of feeling for it. If it does not work right away, let your hand slide up and down the grip, and then try again.

According to the swordsmith Jim Hrisoulas, the pommel is another critical point for the vibrations: "If the blade strikes an object, vibrations run along it. Generally these have no (and if any, only a little) influence on the sword as a whole. But sometimes they can be so severe that the blade breaks at its weakest point. This point is normally the connection of tang and pommel." The riveted-on tang holds the pommel fast, and thus also secures the individual parts, the blade, cross-guard, and grip. If this riveting fastening the pommel and tang breaks, in the worst

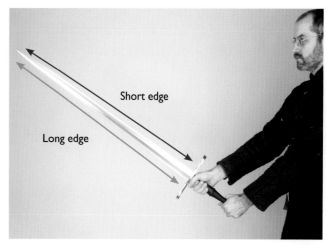

The "long" and "short" cutting edges.

Photo: Herbert Schmidt

Sword Anatomy

Sword master Joachim Meyer described the four areas of the sword:

"The first is called the Bind or Haft, including Pommel and Cross, for charging, wrenching, grappling, throwing, and of service in other work. The other is the Strong, used in cutting, winding, impacting, and otherwise where the Strong is useful in fencing. The third part is the Middle, which lies between Strong and Weak on the halfway part and is used when needing to close in, in the changeful work, where it will be resorted to at every opportunity when needed. The fourth is the Weak, through which changing, rushing, slinging, and similar such, which, beyond length, are used in fencing."

case, the sword can break apart into its separate parts. Therefore, the swordsmith, starting from the blade, has to so calculate the size and mass of the pommel, that it both has the necessary counterweight to the blade, and at the same time is as light as possible, to compensate for the effect of the vibrations.

M, L or XL?—The "Right" Sword Size

At this point, I would like to deal with an aspect that, although it only marginally is part of "sword physics," in my opinion is best brought up here. For you to be able to wield a sword in the most effective way, it must correspond to your own body measurements. In Japan, for example, we have been handed down a rule of thumb for the size of a *katana*: If you let the sword hang down from your arm, the blade should nearly touch the ground, and the grip should be about three times as long as your hand width. The information in the fencing books on this topic is pretty sparse. The sword master of *HS 3227a* only notes the length of the grip. In his opinion, the grip must be long enough for both hands:

> "Know also that a good fencer should above all, guide his sword certainly and securely, and grasp it with both hands between grip and pommel, this way he holds the sword much more securely, than if he grasps it with one hand by the pommel. And he also strikes much harder and more surely, if the pommel throws over and swings with the stroke, so that he can land the stroke much more powerfully than if he grasped the sword by the pommel. Thus, when he leads the stroke with the pommel, it will not come home so fully and strongly."

Bastard swords with a shorter grip, allowing the left hand only to cover the pommel, are—according to this opinion—to be avoided. A longer grip primarily supports leverage in swordplay: While the pivot point lies by the right hand, shifting the left hand causes a change in the blade position, without exertion (this example demonstrates once again the fundamental differences between one-handed swords and long-swords).

One of the few medieval swordsmen who holds forth a little more on sword's measurements is Master Vadi. In his opinion, a two-handed sword should reach from the floor almost to the armpit. The pommel should be round so it does not affect the closed hand. The grip should be a "span" long (a span is a measure from the elbow to the wrist). The cross-guard should be square and thick in cross section and as long as grip and pommel together, so that the hands are well protected. The ends of the cross-guards should be pointed and sharp so that you can "wound and cut." Such pointed cross-guards are illustrated in some panels in Talhoffer's Fencing Book, but almost no specimens have survived—we can conclude that they were relatively rare in reality.

Descriptions such as those by Master Vadi are very rare, as already noted. The other fencing masters seem to have taken it for granted that their readers have mastered the basics of sword fighting and are

Sword Anatomy

The "Golden Section" is a design principle for achieving harmonious proportions that are not only functional but also aesthetically pleasing. The golden section was widely used by artists and architects of antiquity, the Middle Ages, and the Renaissance, including such geniuses as Pythagoras or da Vinci. In nature, one finds many instances of golden section proportions, which are particularly attractive to the human eye. Therefore, this quasi-natural law was also known as the "Divine Proportion" in the Renaissance. Mathematically, the golden section can be expressed with the number $Pi – 3.14$. Pi is closely related to the Fibonacci number series. In the 12th century, the mathematician Leonardo Fibonacci discovered that in nature, such as in plant growth, specific numerical values occur repeatedly (1, 1, 2, 3, 5, 8, 13, 21, …). These numbers can also be calculated. A number is given by the sum of the previous two. And if you divide a number by the one that follows (for example, 3/5, 5/8, 8/13, …) then the result is again almost *pi*.

According to the findings of the sword researcher Peter Johnsson, quite a few medieval swords have proportions based on the Fibonacci numbers. The sword of Svante Nilsson Sture has a blade eight units long, the grip three units and the cross-guard two units. Blade and pommel are each half a unit wide. Other similarities can be determined by the distal taper (the decreasing cross section to the point) of the blade. The Sture sword deviate from the Fibonacci proportions by less than one millimeter. Giving

knowledgeable enough to choose a sword suitable to them (Master Ringeck suggests, for example, that only a reader who already has such basic knowledge can correctly interpret the *Merkeverse*). The modern sword fighting expert Guy Windsor recommends the following dimensions for a long-sword:

- Total length should be approximately from the floor to the sternum.
- The grip should be about two and a half to three handbreadths long.
- The cross-guard should be between about one and two hand lengths.
- The center of balance should lie about three to five finger widths below the cross-guard.

Functional Areas of the Sword

A swordsman divided his weapon into three functional areas:

- The "hilt" naturally serves as the means for grasping the sword. In addition, it is also used for hitting, choking, and ripping.
- While nowadays we use the diameter of the blade cross section to denote the blade *Stärke* or thickness, in the Middle Ages, the *Stärke* ["strong"—the forte] of a sword meant the area from the wide base of the blade to its center. You used the forte to parry—here the leverage which your opponent can deploy, is lesser than at the *Schwäche* ["weak" or foible].
- The foible of the sword blade extends from the center to the blade point. This area was used for the more refined techniques. ... *"here you want to use you skill and put up a defense,"* is how Master Ringeck commented on the foible in the 15th century.

Not only the forte and foible of your own sword, but also of your opponent's weapon, are of tactical importance. Thus, you must observe the following: "If you strike the foible, the impact will push his blade away slightly downward and to the side. If you hit on the forte, it will tend to stop the blade in position." (Lindholm and Svärd, p.34). Several weapon historians have determined that this division of the sword into foible and forte, just like the division of the body into four target areas, was first made in the 16th century; although both concepts were already known at least two centuries earlier by Master Liechtenauer (see Tobler, p.34).

We also frequently find the terms "long and short edge" in the medieval fencing books. This is a method to distinguish the cutting edges while fighting: "The long edge is the full edge from your fingers facing against your opponent, the short or half edge is nearest the thumb, or between thumb and index finger turned towards the fencer himself, as if it wants to be an allegory for the other's weapon, so to speak, the sword's back, [...]," explains Joachim Meyer; he summarizes: "the short and long cutting edges: that is front and back."

For a saber or a scimitar with a back edge, this designation would be clearly evident, but for a straight sword—whose edges are the same length—it is, and remains, paradoxical. We cannot determine just where these terms came from.

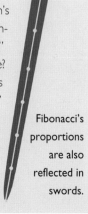

a sword these harmonious proportions not only appeals to the eye, but, according to Johnsson's findings, it also has an effect on nodes and balance, and thus affects the sword's "performance."

So, where do we stand today on this issue? Johnsson's findings indicate that some swords were made based on "Fibonacci proportions." We do not know if swordsmiths deliberately applied these proportions, or whether they were "only" using rules of thumb. Johnsson himself does not want to make any further statements here, since a lot more research is required.

Fibonacci's proportions are also reflected in swords.

Handcrafted replicas.

Sword: Katachi Art [Katachi Style]

Photos and graphic design: Clemens Richardson

Sword Replicas – An Introduction

As I mentioned in the introduction, as a side aspect of this book, I would like to give an overview of the sword replicas commercially available today. Therefore, most of the illustrations in the book are categorized so you can classify the replicas. I have divided the commercial (industrially produced) replicas—admittedly simplistically—into four categories, A to D.

Category D

These replicas are decorative swords, which generally correspond to the historical originals in appearance. The reader can recognize the characteristic features of a sword type, and recognize these characteristics in other replicas or historical pieces. The grips are usually made of die-cast metal; sometimes, at least in part, of plastic. The tang mostly just goes partly into the grip: The mounting is therefore not stable enough for practical use. The blades are made of stainless steel (usually 420 steel, are blunt, and they usually have "cutting edge" of 0.11-.019 inches (three to five millimeters) thick.

The tang usually does not pass through the pommel, but is only bolted to it. The profile of the blade half way corresponds to the original, but the blade cross section, not at all. Therefore, the replicas are much heavier than the historical swords. On average, they weigh about twice what the historical originals or good replicas do. For this reason, these replicas do not have a true balance. Anyone who has had the opportunity to compare a category D replica with one of categories A and B, knows what I'm talking about. While good swords come "alive" in the hand, a category D model is only a "dead" piece of steel—a wrist-breaking weight, which is only shaped like a sword. Category D replicas are purely decorative, and are classified as non-battle-ready, based on material and workmanship. Swords of category D are widely available commercially.

Category D swords are "wall hangers," purely decorative pieces. You cannot compare them to a real sword. A real sword is characterized by the following properties:

- The blade is hard enough to be polished sharp and hold a cutting edge.
- The blade is flexible enough to give on impact and not break.
- The sword is balanced and easy to wield.

While category D swords have nothing near these qualities, swords in categories C and B, at least try to approximate them.

Category C

In contrast to category D, replicas in this group correspond to historical swords not only in approximate design, but also in dimensions and weight. The blades are forged from non-stainless, flexible steel and are hardened; the cutting edges have a thickness of 0.039-0.059 inches (1 to 1.5 millimeters). The tang runs the full length of the grip and is usually bolted, and in many cases even riveted at the grip

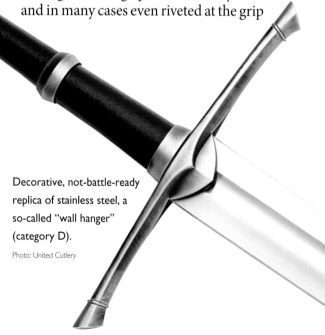

Decorative, not-battle-ready replica of stainless steel, a so-called "wall hanger" (category D).

Photo: United Cutlery

Swords of Stainless Steel

So-called "stainless steel" (or rather tool (D2) steel) is rated positively for making knives (although there are those who prefer non-stainless steels because of their cutting properties), but for swords, everything looks different. Due to the high chromium content of stainless steels – steel is considered rust-free only if it is at least 10.5 percent chromium – they have a different crystal structure and are therefore less resilient and flexible than non-stainless steels. Of course, even swords made of stainless steel can be bent, but not nearly to the extent as swords made of carbon steel. I've seen how a knife maker could bend a sword made of stainless ATS-34 steel about 5.9 inches (15 centimeters), using his foot. At this time, I was impressed – until I saw how a sword made of carbon steel could be effortlessly bent almost 19.6 inches (50 centimeters).

This lack of resilience in longer swords is, of course, something quite different than it would for a knife. However, to achieve a certain level of resilience in sword blades of stainless steel, they are often only minimally hardened. As a result, the blade acquires some amount of flexibility, but at the same time its ability to hold an edge is lessened (see chapter on sword forging). Another method is to harden a stainless steel blade to the required level and make it stronger and thicker in cross section, to compensate for the lack of resilience. But the changed thickness makes the blade heavier, and alters the balance and cutting qualities. Overall, for these reasons, stainless steel is unfit for use in sword blades intended for real use – it can only be used for purely decorative swords and, within certain limits, for exhibition-fight swords.

end. Natural materials like wood and leather are used for the grips. The balance is at least about that of the original weapons. The profile of the blade is usually quite accurate, however, the distal taper is sometimes not adhered to. The blades are usually subjected to an appropriate tempering process. Category C replicas are commercially available.

Expert Judgment

"You don't have to be a car mechanic to buy a good car, and you don't have to be a metallurgist or swordsmith to buy a good sword."

John Clements, Director of the Association of Renaissance Martial Arts, the "absolute authority" on sword forging and other manufacturing.

Category B

These swords are modeled on specific original historical pieces, and have the same design and same mass. Therefore, in such replicas you can recognize not just a sword type, but also a very specific historical sword. Category B sword mountings are made of metal and organic materials. The blades have similar cross sections and thickness as the originals; the cutting edges are 0.039-0.059 inches (1 to 1.5 millimeters). The balance is roughly equivalent to that of the original weapons. The tang goes completely through the grip and is bolted or riveted to the pommel. The blades are subjected to a suitable tempering, are flexible, and in general battle-ready.

There has been significant progress in recent years in industrial mass production of categories B and C sword replicas. At many companies, flexible carbon steel and full-length, bolted tangs are now standard. Also, the balance and center of balance now approach those of historical swords. However, the emphasis here is on "approach." Even good replicas generally cannot be compared to the originals. An examination of an original and a category B replica revealed, for example, that the center of balance of the replica was

Fulvio Del Tin has, like some other entrepreneurs, specialized in the manufacture of high-quality replicas.

Photo: Del Tin

A functional
replica of
the sword of
King Edward III
(category B).

Photo: Pieces of History

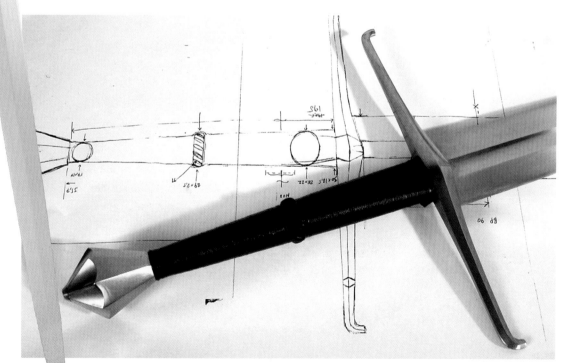

The first step in making a good replica/reconstruction, is an accurate drawing of the historical original in a 1:1 scale, which also reflects its three-dimensional appearance.

Photo: Albion Armorers

twice as far away from the cross-guard as on the original. The results of another comparison between replica and original is summarized by the sword fighting expert John Clements: "Although they both had the same dimensions, the small and subtle differences in the blade geometry (the weight distribution in the tang, the shoulders, the cutting angle …) were large enough to significantly affect the balance—and thus the feeling when handling [the sword]."

Category A

These are the best industrially made replicas currently available. The blades are made of flexible and hardened carbon steel, with grips made of wood and leather. The tang is riveted or screwed to the pommel. Most important, however, is that both the original tapering in profile and the distal taper are respected: as a result, the balance is, as much as possible, closer to the originals. Category A replicas are battle-ready, which is covered by the appropriate guarantees.

All the categories listed comprise just mass-produced replicas, because these—roughly—dominate ninety-five percent of the market. In addition, there are special pieces custom-made by knife makers and modern swordsmiths. These have a much higher quality because they are 100 percent handcrafted. A skilled smith is able to create a totally different performance from the steel and works in very different tolerances than is possible in mass production.

Battle Readiness of Replicas

The question whether a replica sword is battle ready or not is very difficult to answer. Many manufacturers attribute "battle-ready" quality to their products. With few exceptions, however, the sword manufacturers provide only a limited or no guarantee. Since there is no such thing as the *Stiftung Warentest* [German equivalent of *Consumer Reports* magazine] for swords, usually only the statements and reports of private users are available. And these can differ considerably, even for the same sword. First, there is the user's attitude: some will only accept a "perfect" sword as battle-ready, while others are not so demanding. For example, there are re-enactors who basically reject bolted tangs and only accept swords with riveted tangs. Secondly, in cutting tests, you have to take the tester's skills into account. Depending on their skill, a tester can get a significantly greater performance from a sword than another can: for this reason, in ancient Japan, being a "sword tester" was a profession. Another point is the "lemons," which even occur among swords. Sometimes you can also find complete production lines (especially the first batch in mass production), which are deficient—often, the problems can only be corrected in the second series.

Therefore, if you want to purchase a battle-ready sword, there is only one way: think carefully what your requirements are for your sword. Find out as much as possible. Ask for detailed documentation (in particular production methods, return policy, and guarantee) from retailers and manufacturers. Use the Internet forums to obtain specific information on particular models. Think about exactly how much money a sword is worth to you.

To conclude this chapter, I would like to give sword fighting expert Guy Windsor the last word: "The most important thing, is to buy a sword that fulfills its purpose and has an appearance you really like. If you like it and want to play with it all the time, you will spend more time practicing," (Windsor, p.38).

No historically
exact replica,
but a modern,
workable new
interpretation
(created for the
film *Kingdom
of Heaven*).

Photo: Museum Replicas

Cutting tests on a
rolled-up straw mat.

Photo: Wally Hayes

The Different Types of Swords

So you like to learn, work with skill and fight back.
If you are easily frightened, you shall never learn fencing.
— (From Master Liechtenauer's verses,
according to Sigmund Ringeck)

It is usual in the field of historical weaponry, to categorize medieval swords either chronologically or geographically. I am against using this classification for several reasons. First, because of the lively trade in swords and the few region-specific types, it is only possible to make a limited geographic classification. Secondly, many sword types were in use for several centuries, so that chronological classification is not always easy.

I instead opted for a mixed form of classification. The "prologue" comprises the swords of the Early Middle Ages and the Viking period; the "epilogue," the heavy sword types—these two represent, in a sense, the ancestors and descendants of the knightly swords. The main body of swords, however, is divided

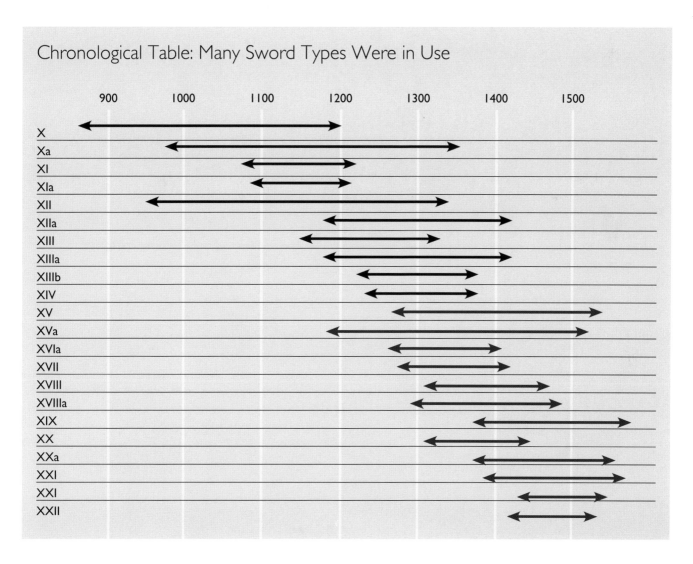

Chronological Table: Many Sword Types Were in Use

In the Early Middle Ages, a large fighting knife, the Sax or seax, played the role of a sword (reconstruction by Jens Nettlich).

Photo: Jens Nettlich

We can distinguish three main forms of the Germanic seax blade.

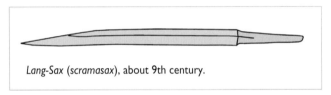

Lang-Sax (scramasax), about 9th century.

Warrior with seax (drawing from gravestone from Niederdollendorf, about 7th to 9th centuries AD).

based on different aspects, primarily according to the method of wielding them. Thus, I arrived at the categories of:

- one-handed swords
- two-handed swords
- curved swords

This classification is justified in so far as these sword types are wielded in fundamentally different ways from one another. One might even say that it was the appearance of the long-sword in the first place, which led to the emergence of a systematic swordsmanship. Within the broad categories, the swords are sorted according to the international standard—the Oakeshott system. So that you will not be completely confused regarding the historical sequence, I have created a timeline that provides an overview, at least for the straight swords.

7.1 Swords of the Germans and Vikings

The so-called knightly swords, that is, the swords of the High and Late Middle Ages, are the direct descendants of the Viking swords. And these go back to the Germanic long-sword (spatha) of the Early Middle Ages. In this context, "long" is a way to distinguish them from the Roman short sword, the *gladius*. In order not to confuse this type of sword with the completely different type of long-swords of the Late Middle Ages, you should consistently use the Latin expression spatha, which, since Plutarch (46-120), has been handed down as the term for the two-edged long sword of the northern "barbarians" (more information on etymology in Menghin, pp.15ff). This Roman name was also used among the Germanic tribes until the Merovingian period. The term spatha is also the origin of modern terms in some Romance languages, such as the Spanish *espada* and the French *epee*. The German word *Schwert* and the English "sword," however, are taken from the Old Norse word *sværd*.

Although the spatha only really attained widespread use among the Germans, it is not originally Germanic. During the era from the first centuries AD over the Migration Period until the Early Middle Ages, we find that the Germanic tribes primarily used a *Hiebwaffe* [bladed or cutting weapon] besides the ax and spear: the seax. The seax is both a sword and a combat knife. The distinction is only by its length. The seax's blade length usually varies between 15.7-25.5 inches (40 and 65 centimeters), but later—in the Viking period—types were made with blades up to 33.4 inches (85 centimeters) long. Thus we see that the range reaches from combat knife, to a short sword, to the "matured" sword. During the Migration Period, the seax was increasingly replaced by double-edged swords. Probably only leaders and high-ranking warriors were initially armed with a spatha, while the common soldiers had to be content with the long seax. When the spatha later came into general use, a large diameter seax still remained part of the armaments.

Before we get to the weapon itself, I would like to make some remarks on linguistic matters. According to many historians, the term seax derives from the Saxon tribe, namely, the "men who are armed with a *Sax*." Thus, we find that in the *Res Gestae Saxonicae*, the chronicler Widukind remarks that the Saxons are known for the use of "big knives." Another word also derives from the *Sax*: The modern German term *Messer* [knife] is a corruption of *Mezzi-Sax*, which means something like "*Messer zum Essen*" ("knife for food"). A technical term that we often encounter in the wrong context, is *Scramasax*. We find the first documentary mention of this term in the *Historia Francorum* of Gregory of Tours (538-594). Commonly, *Scramasax* is translated as "*Wunden schlagender Sax*" ("wound-striking seax"). This was, therefore, in contrast to the knife-length seax, purely a combat weapon. Unfortunately, nothing else is known about this weapon. Thus, we come to the vague conclusion that a *scramasax* is a Frankish type of seax, of sword size.

Seaxes had simple horn or wooden grips, simply pushed over the tang and secured with clamps. A seax typically had no pommel; pieces with pommels were the exceptions. Seax blades were often constructed from several panels of twisted and un-twisted Damascus steel. Thus, they represent a very high-quality cutting weapon. The scabbards consisted of two slabs of wood, held together with iron bands.

The blades of the basic single-edged seax can be divided into three main types:

- One is a single-edged symmetric blade.
- The other has a cutting edge with a distinct curvature at the point.
- The last has a bent back (as opposed to the later Bowie knife, and not sharpened).

Seaxes were often decorated with inlay and engravings. There were two dominant techniques for decoration: coating with precious metals such as gold and silver, and damascening or inlay. For coating or plating, the iron or steel base surface was scored in a fine diamond pattern. Then a thin layer of precious metal was hammered onto this diamond-patterned surface. For damascening, a pattern is engraved into the base surface. A fine wire of precious metal was then hammered into the resulting grooves. Finally, we should note that on seaxes, in contrast to most spathas, we also often find ornamentation in the form of runic inscriptions, which probably have some magical character for the weapons.

As we see, the seax was the Germanic warriors' original cutting weapon, not the two-edged sword. The spatha only became part of their armaments later, while the seax shrinks in size and supplemented the sword as a kind of multi-functional survival and combat knife. There is much speculation about the origin of Germanic spatha, and historians sometimes contradict each other very emphatically. It could be that the Germans learned to make them from the Celts or from the Romans, who in turn had copied them from the Celts. I do not want to lead the discussion to this issue—this has already been done elsewhere (Seitz, vol.1, pp.69, 87; Menghin, p.12; Davidson, p.36). In any case, this matter is completely irrelevant to our topic.

In the 1st century, the Romans took over the spatha from the Celts, and by the 2nd and 3rd centuries, it has become the standard weapon of the cavalry. Some historians see the introduction of high-quality iron from the province of Noricum as the reason for this, since it compensated for the qualitative shortcomings of the Celtic long-swords. The Roman spatha had a blade 23.6-29.5 inches (60 to 75 centimeters) long and 1.18-1.57 inches (three to four centimeters) wide. There is little preserved of the mountings, but, as we know from pictorial representations (such as the cavalry legionnaire Romanius Gaius Capito from the 1st century), the grip of the Roman spatha usually corresponded to that of the Gladius short sword.

The spatha seems to have increasingly come into use among the Germanic people from the 3rd century AD. In the beginning period, you can sometimes barely distinguish between Germanic and Roman weapons, but from the 4th and 5th centuries, independent types of the Germanic spatha emerge. This type of sword is in use up to the 8th century, when it then slowly develops into what we now call the "Viking sword." The Germanic spatha is on average almost 35.4 inches (90 centimeters) long, with the blade about 29.5 inches (75 centimeters) long and 1.9-2.3 inches (five to six centimeters) wide. One characteristic of the blade is a wide and shallow fuller (sometimes there are also two narrow fullers). The grip design is just as typical: It is basically one-handed; the pommel and cross-guard mainly form horizontal bars, with the cross-guard much shorter than those of High Middle Ages swords. The grips are often decorated with precious stones (such as garnets), gold and silver. The blades are very well made; these were often what were called "worm-colored" blades (see Damascus steel).

In contrast to the swords of the Age of Chivalry, the types from the Migration Period and the swords of the Vikings are not classified according to their overall shape, but "only" based on the grips. The basic typology of early medieval sword grips was elaborated in 1939 by Elis Behmer in *Das zweischneidige Schwert der Germanischen Völkerwanderungszeit* [*The Double-edged Sword of the Germanic Migration Period*]. This work was expanded in 1962 by Hilda Ellis Davidson in *The Sword in Anglo-Saxon England*, and in 1983, Wilfried Menghin contributed his own approach to classification in *Das Schwert im frühen Mittelalter* [*The Sword in the Early Middle Ages*]. In the international sword community, however, Behmer's

Even after the introduction of the spatha, the knife-sized seax remained part of German armaments, along with the spear and throwing ax (*Franziska*).

Photo: Del Tin

The longswords of the Early Middle Ages were generally straight and one-handed; they had double-edged blades with a wide fuller.

Photo: Del Tin

Late Roman cavalry sword (spatha) with ring pommel, 300 AD. Reconstruction by Patrick Barta.

Photos: Patrick Barta/Tomas Balej

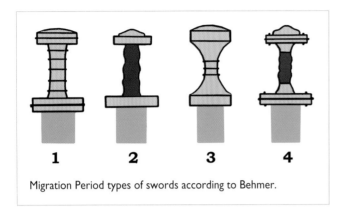

Migration Period types of swords according to Behmer.

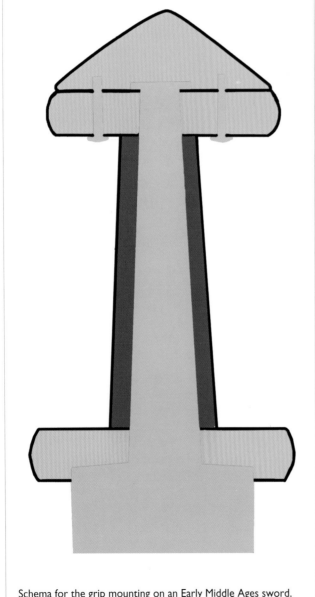

Schema for the grip mounting on an Early Middle Ages sword.

Forging a pommel crown.

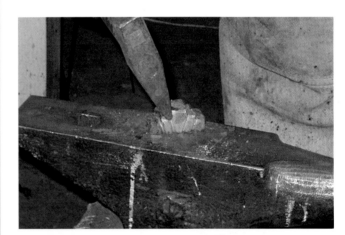

The rough shape of the crown is created using a hammer.

The forging process is completed. Finally, the details of the pommel crown are worked out using a file.

simplified typology has prevailed: Behmer differentiates among a total of nine different types, although his classification was later reduced to four types, for practical reasons.

A characteristic detail of Early Middle Ages swords is the composite pommel, which was used until late in the Viking Age. This pommel is made of two parts: a horizontal pommel bar (international term: "upper guard") riveted to the pommel crown. The pommel crown was often made of individual lobes or round pieces; at times, it was made as a single, triangular piece. In these swords, the tang—in contrast to later weapons—is not riveted over the pommel or pommel crown, but over the upper guard. The pommel crown is set on the tang and riveted with the upper guard on the other side.

What is particularly interesting is that we find most of the legends about special or magical swords originating in the Migration Period and among the Vikings, and not in the High Middle Ages. Whether it is Sigurd's Gram, Arthur's Caliburn (Excalibur), or the bloodthirsty sword Tyrfing: the pagan Germanic legends are full of these special swords. In addition to their sumptuous decoration and the high quality of the swordsmith's work, this is further proof the important role the sword played in Germanic culture.

Perhaps the most elegant and most highly crafted sword of the Migration Period is the type 3. It has a characteristic inwardly curved "biconical" bronze grip. One of the most beautiful examples is the 5th-century Kragehul Sword, which was found in a Danish bog of the same name.

The type 4 is the most important type of spatha from the Germanic Migration Period; this is sometimes called the "Vendel type" after the Swedish Vendel boat graves. In these, the pommel and cross-guard are assembled of separate disk-shaped pieces. The sword makers frequently riveted organic materials such as horn or bone, or other metal alloys, between these precious metal disks. The pommel crown is shaped like a triangle or "upturned boat." Most of these grips are superbly hand-engraved in a braided pattern.

Many Vendel type spathas have an interesting detail: the so-called ring-knobs. This is a small ring attached to the pommel by a bracket. In the Edda, we find a passage in the song of the hero Helge Hjorvardsson,

An Early Middle Ages pommel consisted of an individual pommel bar, or upper guard, and pommel crown.

Photo: Armart Antiquanova

The tang is riveted to the pommel bar and this in turn with the crown.

Photo: Armart Antiquanova

The Kragehul Sword is one of the finest examples of Behmer's type 3.

Photo: Albion Armorers

Swords of Wheeler-Oakeshott type III were widespread throughout Europe.

Photo: Armart Antiquanova

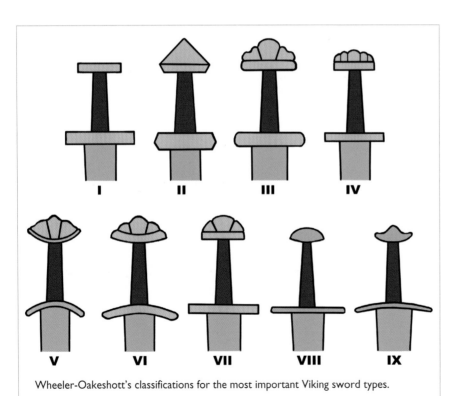

Wheeler-Oakeshott's classifications for the most important Viking sword types.

The magnificent Viking swords are the direct ancestors of the knightly sword.

Photo: Del Tin

in which the Valkyrie Swawa describes Helge's sword: "On the pommel is a ring, in the blade courage, the edge conveys fear of the bearer, a bloody worm sits on the blade, a viper is coiled around the back." The precise meaning of these ring-knobs has been lost in the mists of the past, and present-day historians usually regard them as a badge of rank. On the early ring-knobs, the ring can be moved freely, but in the later versions the ring is often fused with the bracket, which excludes any practical function. This is probably a detail of the swords of particularly high-ranking warriors. It was common during the Migration Period for a chief or prince to pledge his allegiance with a sword or ring. Since all surviving ring-knob swords are very sumptuously decorated, it seems likely that these were gifts from a prince to a warrior, which were to make clear and reinforce their special relationship and symbolize the warrior's rank. However, it was apparently also expressly provided, where appropriate, that they could be used to degrade the warrior again: "The pommels above all indicate that the rings could be awarded on a temporary basis, since the design provided for affixing a ring rivet, or where traces of material demonstrate the former existence of such sword rings," (Menghin, p.145).

The Sword of Sutton Hoo is the most important type 4 spatha. In 1939, a magnificent, well-preserved ship grave was discovered in Suffolk, England, in the Sutton Hoo mound. According to archaeologists' findings, this is the grave of the Anglo-Saxon king Raedwald, who died around 625. One of the most important grave finds is Raedwald's sword. The blade is welded together from several bands of Damascus steel (more on this in the relevant chapter). The grip is almost entirely made of gold and decorated in the cloisonne technique. While the gold cells are usually filled with colored enamel, in the Sutton Hoo Sword, polished garnets were inserted. This is truly a king's weapon, which represents the high standard of craftsmanship of the Migration Period. The replica (photo on page 68), is a total 35.0 inches (89 centimeters) long, with a blade 29.9 inches (76 centimeters) long, and weighs a little over one kilogram.

The "Viking sword" is the direct descendant of the spatha and the direct ancestor of the knightly sword. Actually, these should be called "swords of the Viking Age," because these swords belong to a specific era—they were used by all the warriors of the Viking era and not just by the Vikings themselves (the beginning of the Viking era is usually set in the year 793, with the assault on the Lindesfarne monastery; it ended with the Norman conquest of England in 1066). Nevertheless, the term "Viking sword" has been adopted into the language, among other reasons because the sword was a typical Viking weapon. Although the ax perhaps played a bigger role as a weapon, the Vikings valued the sword most highly. The pagan Viking sagas teem with references to special swords. In addition to magical swords, we often find famous family swords: swords which had their own names and special properties.

The swords of the Viking age are usually longer, stronger, and heavier than their predecessors. Viking swords are distinguished according to the shape of the hilt. However, this issue is somewhat more complicated than for the swords of the Migration Period, since several scientists have invented competing classification systems. In 1919, Jan Petersen presented in his *De norske vikingesverd*, the fundamental typology, including twenty-six different grip shapes (interested readers are here referred to the excellent monograph, *Swords of the Viking Age*). In 1927, R. Wheeler consolidated the most important types into seven categories (denoted, in contrast to Behmer, with Roman numerals). Wheeler's typology was expanded by Ewart Oakeshott in the 1960s. Oakeshott added two categories that characterize the transition from the Viking sword to the knightly sword. In 1991, Alfred Geibig presented another, well-thought-out system in *Beiträge zur morphologischen Entwicklung des Schwerts im Mittelalter* (*Contributions to the Morphological Development of the Sword in the Middle Ages*). From an international viewpoint, however, the systems of Petersen and Wheeler-Oakeshott are the standard classifications (see chart at left). Since this book concentrates mainly on the knightly sword—and especially its properties as a weapon, rather than as a subject of art history—the Wheeler- Oakeshott system is absolutely sufficient for our use, and we only reference Petersen in some isolated cases.

One of the most importing Viking swords is the type II. This sword, with its simple, triangular pommel, represents the standard weapon of the ordinary Viking soldier. They originated in Norway, but, in the period from 800 to 950, were widespread from the British Isles to Switzerland. The type III is typical of Viking swords. These are very valuable weapons of the latter Viking period: The blades are usually from the European continent (in many cases, Ulfberht blades), while the grips come from the north and are usually decorated with precious metals and engraved. During the 9th and 10th centuries, the type III is widespread through the entire northwestern area of Europe into Russia. The sword pictured (top right page 64) is based on a specimen from the 10th century, which was found in Norway.

One of the most characteristic preserved Viking swords is a type VI (page 69 top left). This type dates from the 10th and early 11th centuries, and was mainly found in Denmark and those parts of England occupied by the Danes. Therefore, we can speak with some justification of a "Danish type." This is the Leutlrit Sword—this name is welded into the fuller on the blade in Damascus steel letters (not in the replica). The sword probably dates from the 10th century and was found at the bottom of the River Witham in Lincoln. The ornamentation of the pommel and cross-guard is absolutely remarkable. Diamond-shaped pieces of brass are set in a layer of silver, creating a wonderful contrast. This simple and beautiful decoration, which does not deprive the sword of its functionality, is typical of Viking swords. With a total length of 38.1 inches (97 centimeters) and a blade 30.9 inches (78.5 centimeters) long, the replica's dimensions differ from the original 36.0 inches (91.5 centimeters) total length and 30.5 inches (77.5 centimeter) blade length. The weight is about 2.6 pounds (1.2 kilograms).

As we have already heard, Wheeler's system is greatly simplified and based mainly on findings in the British Isles. As a result, some characteristic and remarkable Petersen types are not included. These

Vendel type sword grips (Behmer type 4).

Photo: Del Tin

A ring-knob on the sword grip probably indicates a high-ranking warrior.

Photo: Del Tin

The Sword from the Blucina tomb

In 1953, a grave dating from the 5th century was discovered in Blucina, the Czech Republic, near Brno. All indications are that this was the tomb of a Germanic prince of the Migration Period. Besides a few pieces of jewelry, glass bottles, bows and arrows, and a short seax, the grave contained a magnificent spatha, decorated with gold. This weapon was recently reconstructed by the Czech swordsmith Patrick Barta.

The first step in making a reconstruction is to carefully analyze the preserved remains. The Blucina sword is a variant of Behmer's type 2. The mounting of the 35.4-inch (90-centimeter) long sword is made of gold-covered wood. The leather scabbard is also decorated with magnificent gold fittings.

The blade is especially interesting. The core is of high quality Damascus steel. Various types of steel were welded together to give elasticity to the blade, resulting in a characteristic pattern, which often had magical significance (more on this in the chapter on Damascus steel).

The remnants of the original sword were carefully studied.

The finished reconstructed Blucina sword.

Photos: Patrick Barta/Tomas Balej

The parts of the mounting before they were riveted together.

Photo: Patrick Barta

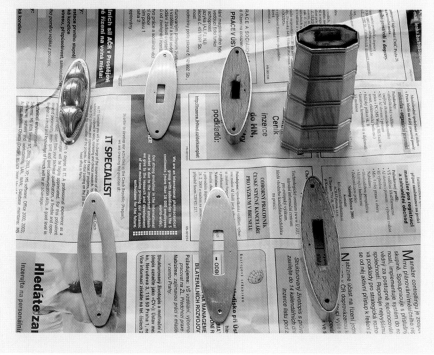

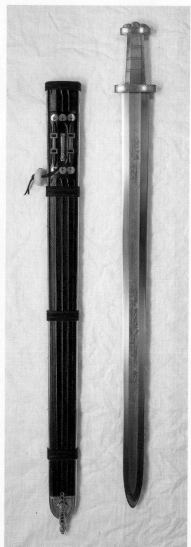

A king's weapon, the famous
Sutton Hoo Sword.

include types Z and A: they come from the end of the Viking age and are found primarily in Scandinavia.

The blades of Viking swords changed little, in contrast to those of knightly swords. Geibig divided this development into five finely distinguished types. First, the edges remain fairly parallel, but later, the blades are tapered. The initially more symmetrical fullers are also more tapered in later swords. Types 1 to 4 have blade lengths varying from 24.8-33.4 inches (63 to 85 centimeters). At the end of the development of these swords, they had a long, strongly tapered point on a significantly longer blade—33.0-35.8 inches (84 to 91 centimeters).

According to Geibig, the first type of blade was characteristic of the transition from the Migration Period to the Viking sword. Types 4 and 5 indicate the transition to the knightly sword.

In simplified terms, we can extract the following evolutionary sequence:

Type 1: 7th and 8th centuries
Type 2: about 750 to 950
Type 3: End of the 8th century to the
        end of the 10th century
Type 4: about 950-1050
Type 5: Mid-10th to the end of the 11th centuries

In types 4 and 5, we can recognize a significant tapering of the blade profile. This change to the blade is accompanied by a significant improvement in balance: "But by 900 AD, there was an alteration in the blade, and swords of this time proved to be better balanced— the center of balance was no longer halfway down the length of the blade, but closer to the grip—so that they must have become more efficient weapons, both for the cut as well as the thrust," (Davidson, p.39).

Some historians attribute this development directly to the work of the Frankish master swordsmith Ulfberht. In principle, Geibig's types 2, 3, and 4 represent refined gradations of Oakeshott's type X, while type 5 is somewhat similar to type Xa—but Oakeshott's and Geibig's classifications are not entirely congruent. When applied to the Viking swords. Geibig's system becomes increasingly interesting, while for the knightly swords, Oakeshott's classification remains unchallenged.

Type VI Viking sword.

Photo: Museum Replicas

Type III Viking sword. The solid execution of pommel and cross-guard is typical.

Photo: Museum Replicas

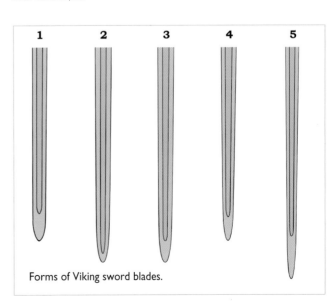

Forms of Viking sword blades.

Although most Viking swords are double-edged, contrary to popular belief, this was not always the case. There are also single-edged specimens. In contrast to the later sabers, these blades are basically straight, and rather cutlass-like. These blades are usually from the transition phase from the Migration Period to the early Viking Age. Mostly they are found in type II swords. Blades of single-edged Viking swords characteristically have no fuller. With blades 31.4-33.4 inches (80 to 85 centimeters) long, they are significantly longer than those of contemporary two-edged swords. However, the single-edged sword could not prevail against the double-edged. In the fighting style of the Early Middle Ages, two cutting edges offered a unique advantage: if a blade was dulled and nicked, the sword was turned in the hand and the fresh edge put into use.

Types VIII and IX are found in the transition period from the Viking to the knightly swords. While they are found in 10th-century Viking graves, there are also finds from areas where no Vikings had advanced. With their slender, long cross-guards and Brazil nut- or tea cozy/mushroom-shaped pommels, they display the first elements of what is commonly known as a "knightly sword."

Efficiency of the Seax

Medieval image and text sources are not always reliable, so that often – if the question has not been verified by experimental archeology – we can only come to speculative conclusions about how effective a sword is. As a complement to the medieval sources and modern experiments, however, we can also draw on more recent evidence. Therefore, reports on how cutting weapons were used during the Napoleonic Wars also allow us to draw conclusions about medieval swords. The Light Cavalry Trooper's Sword 1796 Pattern – known as the *Blüchersäbel* in German-speaking regions – was a heavy, short cutting weapon with a broad fuller, intended primarily for the cavalry. It had a blade about 32.6 inches (83 centimeters) long and blade curvature [*Pfeilhöhe*, literally "arrow height," is the German technical term here, referencing the "brace height" of a bow] of five to six centimeters. Fortunately, many eyewitness reports about the use of these Trooper's Swords have come down to us. Most are from British officers who fought under Wellington against Napoleon in Spain.

William Tomkinson of the 16th Light Dragoons later described the battle at Villa Garcia (1812): "A French Dragoon had his head nearly cut off – thus far I had never seen anything like it; it happened by a saber stroke in the neck."

There were many more such experiences of just how effective this cavalry saber was. The *Courier* reported as follows about the Battle of Campo Mayor (1811) and a duel between a French colonel and a British corporal: "[…] the corporal was well mounted and a good swordsman, as was the colonel. Both were able to maintain themselves against the other for a while; then the corporal struck him twice in the face, his helmet cracked open and at that moment the corporal delivered a blow which split his skull to the nose."

Perhaps the most impressive report on the performance of this saber comes from George Farmer, who, with the 11th Light Dragoons, took part in a skirmish by the Guadiana, where he was able to witness the impact of this saber on a brass helmet: "At that moment, a French officer […] struck a blow to the body of the unfortunate Harry Wilson, and did it successfully. I'm certain that Wilson was immediately struck dead, but he had already launched a saber cut. With characteristic self-control, he kept his enemy in sight, stood up in the stirrups, and delivered such a blow to the head of the Frenchman, that brass and skull were split apart and the head gaped open to the chin. I think this was the most terrible blow ever struck, and both – he who delivered it, and he who

Blade cross section of a Viking sword.

Many Viking era swords were sumptuously decorated. Reconstruction of a Dybeck sword (Petersen type Z).

Photo: Traumschmiede/Eckhardt

Single-edged swords emerged in the transitional period from the Great Migration to the Vikings.

received it – fell dead together. The helmet was later examined by order of a French officer. Both he and I were surprised by the result: The cut was as clean as if the saber had cut through a turnip, and there was not the slightest dent on either side."

Although a medieval steel helmet would certainly provide a different resistance than that from a modern brass helmet, we can still conclude from reports, from medieval image sources representing a helmet being split open are not as exaggerated and absurd as was long believed.

Image source of how swords were used (sketch from a 12th-century miniature).

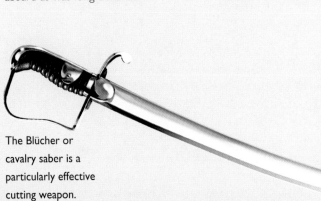

The Blücher or cavalry saber is a particularly effective cutting weapon.

Photo: Cold Steel

7.2 Types of One-Handed Swords from the Age of Chivalry

Although the long-sword represents the pinnacle of medieval swordsmanship, the lion's share of swords were one-handed. Their tradition extends from the swords of the Germans and Vikings, through the knightly sword, to the early forms of the broadsword and rapier.

Swords against Shield and Chainmail

Form follows function: for a sword, this means that its functional design is determined by the enemy's armor. In the Early and High Middle Ages, this consisted, as a rule, of shield, helmet, and some form of body armor. If the common soldier had any body armor, it was usually leather armor: "Boiled and cured in a hot wax bath, it offered adequate protection from enemy weapons," (Arens, p.180).

Soldiers of higher rank also often wore an armored coat or shirt. This could be made of either scale armor or the famous chainmail. Chainmail is an effective protection, but it does not make the wearer invulnerable. The earlier thesis of historians, that a sword stroke—in contrast to a thrust from the point—could not penetrate chain mail, has now been clearly refuted by practical tests: a direct cut from a properly hardened sword will definitely penetrate chainmail.

A helmet is also an important piece of equipment. Even a superficial head wound is fatal, so a helmet is vital for a soldier. Up to the 11th century, medieval helmets were made of hardened leather reinforced with iron. Later, they were mainly made of iron or steel. Although a skilled stroke, correctly aimed, can penetrate a helmet, we know from written accounts of modern warfare that the round surface of some types of helmets can often deflect a blow.

A medieval warrior's most important body protection was his shield. A skillfully used shield offers an effective screen (it can also be used as an offensive weapon), and in addition, common solders who could not afford armor, were equipped with a shield. The shape of these shields was relatively secondary—in sword fights, they all fulfilled their purpose. What was important was the design and construction. Medieval shields were usually made of an about two-centimeter-thick layer of hardwood, which was often covered with leather and partly reinforced with iron rivets, strips, and frame.

Such a shield had a solid construction, and, in contrast to the shields described in fantasy novels, cannot be destroyed by a single sword stroke. Since a shield (optimized by additional body armor) gives effective protection, the opponent must use a specific tactic: "[…] the idea is to force the opponent to react, and thus, as he moves his shield to defend himself, to create a gap in its protective cover," states sword fighting expert John Clements.

The Battle of Visby

In 1361, a battle was fought in Visby, Gotland, Sweden, in which more than 1,200 men were killed. Because of the very hot weather, they were buried in mass graves on the spot, without – as was usual – their armor being stolen. Archaeological investigation of the remains produced very interesting findings.

- All types of armor were represented: Leather shirts, hardened leather armor, scale armor, and chainmail.
- Many bodies showed signs of wounds in the back, meaning they were killed on the run.

- Almost all the bodies had injuries to the limbs.
- About half of those killed died due to severe head injuries.
- About 70 percent of the fallen had serious leg injuries.
- In many cases, there were no serious bone injuries, which indicates that the men died due to loss of blood (from deep flesh wounds).

From this, we can conclude that both the head and limbs, especially the legs, were the enemy's preferred targets.

Only high-ranking warriors could afford a shirt of armor
(Scene from *Kingdom of Heaven*).

Photo: 20th Century Fox/Museum Replicas

A practical test of "sword against chainmail." A direct cut penetrates,
the chain links are split apart, and the blade itself shows almost no
damage. Conclusion: Even wearing chainmail, you aren't safe
from a sword.

Photo: Museum Replicas

Knight wearing chainmail (drawing from the tomb of
Sir Johan d' Aubernoun, 13th century, after Demmin).

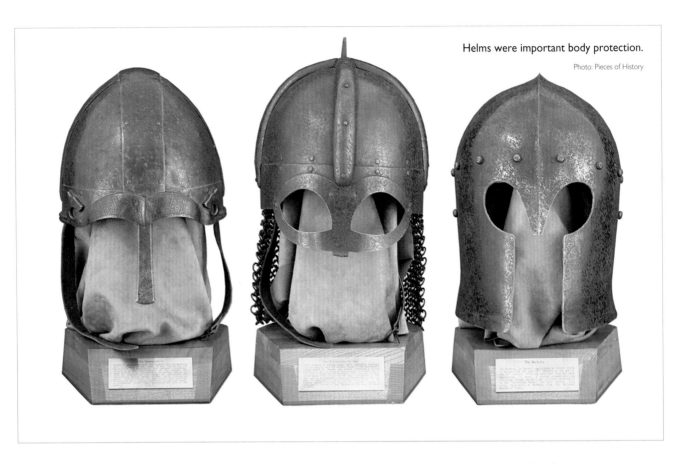

Helms were important body protection.

Photo: Pieces of History

A shield gives the body broad protection against attack (drawing from the Sigurd carvings in the church at Hyllestad, around 1200).

Warriors of the Early and High Middle Ages normally had a shield for protection, and often also a helmet.

Photo: Del Tin

Swords of the Early and High Middle Ages usually had rounded, thus convex, edges to deliver a cleaving stroke.

In sword fighting of this period, your targets are the parts of the opponent's body that are not covered by the shield; then you must use your sword to pierce his body armor. These requirements set the following design factors for a sword:

- The sword must be short and light enough to be wielded with one hand (the other arm holds the shield).
- The cutting edge must be made so that it can penetrate the armor and also bear the impact of a shield.

With these objectives, most swords of the High Middle Ages were made based on the following criteria:

- They were one-handed.
- They had an average total length of 35.4-37.4 inches (90 to 95 centimeters).
- They had a straight and two-edged blade.
- The blade must be polished round (convex) to enable a cleaving stroke.
- They weighed an average of 2.2 pounds (one kilogram), maximum 2.8 pounds (1.3 kilograms).

All High Middle Ages swords—or, more precisely, group 1—look fairly similar. Nevertheless, we can distinguish eight different types.

TYPE X: This is the knightly sword, which most resembles the Viking sword. The grip averages four centimeters; the blade about 31.4 inches (80 centimeters) long. The blade is broad and only slightly tapered. The fuller is also very wide (at least one third of the blade width), shallow, and usually extends the entire length of the blade to just before the point. The point is usually somewhat rounded, but we do see some specimens that have a distinct point. Type X existed from the end of the Viking period, up to the 12th century. Within type X, we can, in principle, distinguish Giebig's types 2, 3 and 4.

The type X sword shown far left, is a replica of a Ulfberht blade from the 10th century. The Ulfberht swords were not only associated with the transition from Damascus steel to all-steel swords, but also with the development of the type X. Thus, they mark the

transition from top-heavy Viking swords to the better-balanced knightly swords. All the swords of this group have the name of the swordsmith, Ulfberht, welded into the fuller in majuscule letters of iron or Damascus steel (in the replica, these markings are only etched in).

The sword shown is dated at about 950, meaning it was not made by the original Ulfberht, who probably was working a century earlier, but by one of his successors or imitators. All Ulfberht swords are of excellent quality, and this example is one of the most beautiful. The cutting edges extend almost in parallel along two thirds of the length of the blade, and then are gently tapered. The pronounced Brazil nut pommel is large enough to balance the blade. The total length is about 35.4 inches (90 centimeters), with an almost 30.3 inch (77 centimeter) blade; the replica weighs 2.8 pounds (1.3 kilograms).

TYPE XA: This type closely resembles type X, although the blade is slightly longer and the fuller much narrower type Xa was in use mainly from the 11th to 13th centuries, and some from in the 14th century, and roughly corresponds to Geibig's type 4. The Pieces of History replica shown on page 77 is just 39.7 inches (101 centimeters) long, with a blade length of 33.4 inches (85 centimeters), and weighs a little over 2.2 pounds (one kilogram). The original probably dates from the 12th to 13th centuries.

Right next to it is a very interesting Xa sword. This 12th-century piece has a classic mushroom-shaped pommel, which often occurs in this time period (in English, this form is called a "tea cozy").

The sword at bottom left on page 77 cannot be definitely associated with type Xa, and it also has type XI elements. The sword comes from the first half of the 13th century and has interesting features. First, the 37.7-inch (96 centimeter) blade is unusually long. In addition, in both fullers we find fine inscriptions inlaid in silver, whose meaning is unknown. On one side, we can decipher the letters +NRADNRADNRADNRADNRADNR+ and on the other +NREDAREDX+. Both the meaning of the five-fold repetition of NRAD, and the importance of the other inscription, have remained a mystery until now. Finally, the sword is a very beautiful example

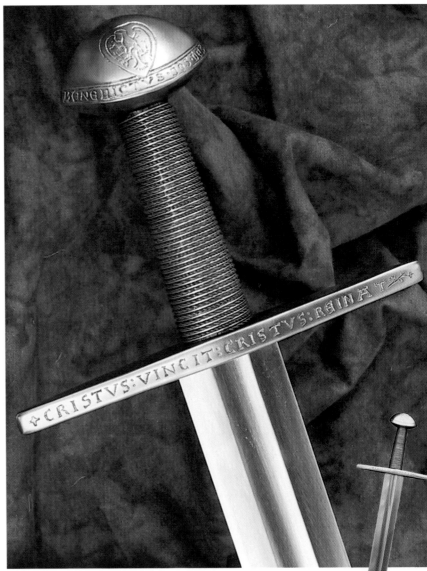

The St. Mauritius (St. Maurice) Sword: the engravings on
the pommel and cross-guard complement each other.

Photo: Arms & Armour

St. Maurice Sword blade
cross section.

Type X swords most
closely resemble
Viking swords. Swords
marked "Ulfbehrt" were
especially in demand.

Photo: Museum Replicas.

The famous
St. Maurice
Sword is
one of the
most beautiful
examples of
a type XI.

Photo: Arms & Armour

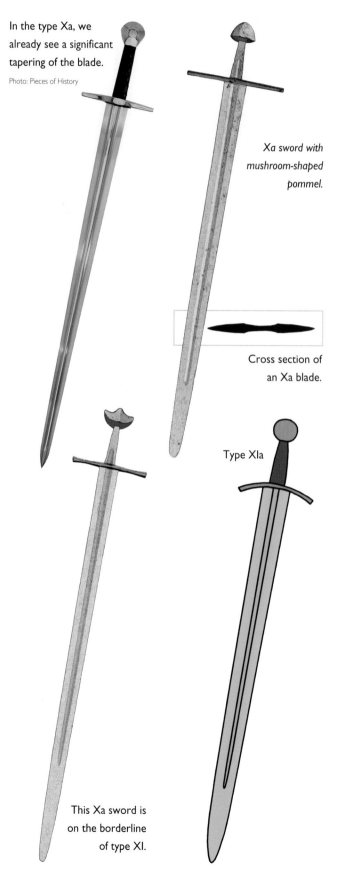

In the type Xa, we already see a significant tapering of the blade.

Photo: Pieces of History

Xa sword with mushroom-shaped pommel.

Cross section of an Xa blade.

Type XIa

This Xa sword is on the borderline of type XI.

of the "cocked hat" pommel (pagoda roof pommel in German), which we find more frequently in the 12th and 13th centuries. The grip and its cocked hat pommel (Wheeler-Oakeshott type IX) is characteristic of some swords in the transition period from Viking era weapons to the knightly sword. The sword is 44.0 inches (112 centimeters long) and weighs about 3.0 pounds (1.4 kilograms).

TYPE XI: The blade of this type is slender and averages 33.4-37.4 inches (85-95 centimeters) long. The fuller runs the whole length of the blade, is narrow, and often very shallow. The blade tapers moderately and ends in a distinct point. Type XI occurs mainly in the 12th century.

The most famous XI sword is the Imperial Sword of the Holy Roman Empire: for over 800 years, this was the coronation sword of the German or Austrian Emperor. It was last used for this purpose in 1916, when Karl I of Austria was crowned King IV of Hungary. According to legend, Saint Maurice (Mauritius in German) was killed with this sword, which is why it is named for him (the same is claimed for another, far less well known sword).

In short: there is not the smallest grain of truth behind the legend. If St. Maurice really lived, it was in the 2nd or 3rd centuries AD—and the sword comes from the High Middle Ages. As far as we know, the legend of the St. Mauritius sword dates from the 14th century. Today, we have no idea how this came about.

Apart from the actual sword, the magnificent, gilded scabbard is important in itself, as demonstrated by its provenance of use by fourteen medieval rulers—from Charlemagne to Henry III. The blade of the St. Mauritius sword is 37.5 inches (95.3 centimeters) long and 1.7 inches (4.4 centimeters) wide at the base. Apparently, the sword was not only used in ceremonies, because the blade was sharpened many times. The St. Mauritius sword is an extremely elegant and beautiful weapon. With a length of 43.3 inches (1.10 meters), the Arms & Armor replica pictured corresponds exactly to the original and weighs about 3.0 pounds (1.4 kilograms). The pommel and cross-guard are made of gilded silver and decorated with engravings in a characteristic style. "On the front and back sides of the Imperial Sword's gold-plated cross-guard, a verse of Lauds is engraved, the three-part Lauds used to pay homage to the newly crowned ruler in the Middle Ages," (Schulze-Dörrlamm, p.27). If the Imperial Sword is held with point upwards, you can see on one side the following inscription:

+ CRISTVS • VINCIT • CRISTVS • REIGNAT • CRIST' (VS) • INPERAT

"Christ is victorious—Christ reigns—Christ has dominion."

With the point downwards, we find on the side opposite the abbreviated version:

CRISTVS : VINCIT : CRISTVS : REINAT

The pommel displays the coat of arms of Emperor Otto IV (1198-1218) on its first side, which is mounted to correspond to the inscription on the cross-guard—thus, you can see it only when the blade points upwards. On the other side of the pommel, the imperial eagle is engraved in reverse, so that it accords with the inscription on this side of the cross-guard. Around the bottom of the pommel, runs the inscription:

BENEDICTVS • DO(MINV)S • DE(V)S • QUI • DOCET • MANV(S) +

"Blessed (be my) Lord (and) God, who teaches (my) hands (to fight)."

The actual age of the sword was the subject of fierce debate for many decades. Many historians argued that a 10th-century blade was newly mounted for the coronation of Otto IV. Historian Mechthild Schulze-Dörrlamm conducted an extensive investigation in 1995 and came to a very different conclusion:

Detailed analysis of the Imperial Sword leads to the conclusion that all individual parts of this weapon originated at the same time—that is, towards the end of the 12th century […] The Imperial Sword thus is a typical weapon of the late 12th century—which can be securely dated by the coat of arms of Emperor Otto IV (1198-1218). Very probably, it was used in the coronation of Otto IV on July 12, 1198 in Aachen instead of the old Imperial Sword from the Salian period, which at that time—as well as all the other insignia—were found in the possession of King Philip of Swabia […]. Due to the linguistic peculiarities of the inscriptions, we can conclude that Otto IV, as Count of Poitou and Duke of Aquitaine, had brought the sword with him from France. The scabbard, however, did not originally belong to the Imperial Sword, but was probably already made in 1084 for the coronation of the Salian Emperor Henry IV in Italy. The fourteen portraits of German kings and emperors on the scabbard thus deliberately also represent "an early form of political propaganda. The succession of

Espada Jineta – Boabdil Swords

From the 8th to the 15th centuries, large parts of the Iberian Peninsula was dominated by the Moors. The mixed Spanish-Moorish culture created achievements in art, architecture, and literature unparalleled to this day. Only a few weapons from this culture have been preserved. The magnificent swords from the 15th century are an exception. The grips are made of gold and decorated with cloisonne inlay; the blades are straight and double-edged. Grip and pommel are somewhat reminiscent of

a tower with an onion-shaped roof, or a minaret. In German, such swords were known as Boabdil type, after the last Emir of Granada; in international parlance, they are referred to as Granada-style, while the actual technical term in Spanish is espada jineta. According to some researchers, these swords are primarily status symbols that were deliberately given an archaic design.

rulers is likely intended to identify King Henry IV, whose power was widely disputed during the years of the Investiture Controversy, as a descendant of Charlemagne, and thus the sole legitimate ruler of the Empire. Therefore, this scabbard, as both an insignia of the late Salian period and mark of royal self-display at the same time, is an historical document of a period of very bitter conflict between Church and Empire, (Schulze-Dörrlamm, p.89).

TYPE XIA: This type has the same narrow fuller as the XI, but the blade is shorter and wider. Like the type XI, the XIa also mainly occurred in the 12th century (see picture on page 77).

TYPE XII: The first departure from the purely cutting blades derived from the Viking period, begins with type XII. The blade tapers more sharply, and the fuller is shorter than on the older types. As a result, XII swords are well suited for both cut and thrust. Due to their versatility, type XII swords were also very widespread—it is the most important sword type of the High Middle Ages. Type XII is one of the most difficult types to identify in general. Its individual characteristics are also found in other types, but it is distinct in the totality of its features. The type XII blade averages just 31.4-33.4 inches (80 to 85 centimeters), with the grip about 4.7 inches (12 centimeters) long (basically, never of the length of a bastard sword). The blade is broad and tapers evenly, to then end in a sharp point. The fuller is usually no longer than two-thirds of the entire blade. Type XII is found mainly in the 13th and 14th centuries.

The XII sword pictured above right is the second St. Maurice sword, of Turin. Unlike its namesake in Vienna, we can here establish a clear link to the legend: Since the High Middle Ages, the sword has been preserved along with relics attributed to St. Maurice. The sword itself dates from the 13th century, and the fuller is unusually wide for type XII. With a blade length of about 35.8 inches (91 centimeters), the sword is 41.3 inches (105 centimeters) long and weighs 2.8 pounds (1.3 kilograms).

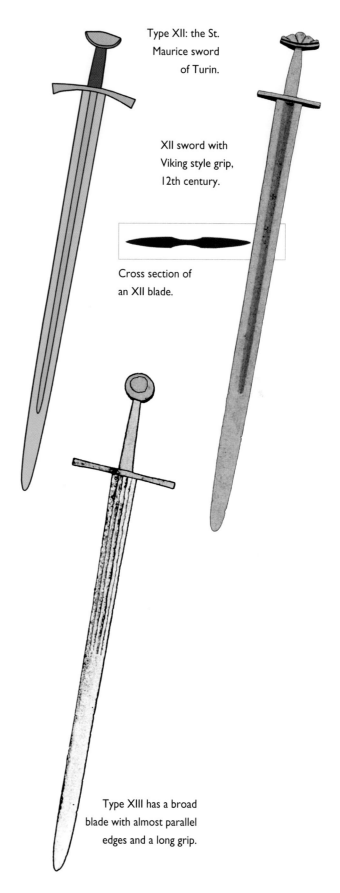

Type XII: the St. Maurice sword of Turin.

XII sword with Viking style grip, 12th century.

Cross section of an XII blade.

Type XIII has a broad blade with almost parallel edges and a long grip.

The XII sword right next to it is unusual in several respects. Although the sword dates from the 12th century, thus from the High Middle Ages, the pommel clearly displays the design of a typical type VI Viking sword. The "Viking style" survived for a very long time, in isolated examples. As on the weapon on page 77 bottom left, we also find enigmatic inscriptions in the fuller here:

+NRISSDIADG+SBENSIS+ and
+MEHDXOEHRNISDX+

With a blade 30.3 inches (77 centimeters) long, the sword overall is 35.4 inches (90 centimeters) long and weighs 2.0 pounds (920 grams).

TYPE XIII: Here we find a wide blade with a lenticular cross section, with almost no tapering, and a point that is usually slightly rounded. The fuller normally extends over one half to two thirds of the blade.

The grip is significantly longer than those of the other one-handed types: With an average 31.4-33.4 inch (80 to 85 centimeters) blade length, the grip is 5.9 inches (15 centimeters) long—thus balancing the slightly heavier blade. Type XIII was in use mainly from the mid-13th to the end of the 14th centuries.

The sword pictured on page 79 below, is almost a classical example of an XIII swords, but the three short fullers are fairly rare, making this sword stand out from the crowd. With a 31.1 inch (79 centimeter) blade, the weapon weighs just 3.3 pounds (1.5 kilograms). It can be dated to the 13th century.

Type XIIIB: These swords are almost indistinguishable from type XIII. The only difference is that they are much shorter, especially in the grip area. As we have seen, the grip of a type XIII sword is usually somewhat longer. Like the XIII, the XIIIb comes mainly from the mid-13th up the end of the 14th-century period (the XIIIa is a long battle sword).

A very fine specimen of this type is the so-called Tritonia Sword (photos page 81), which was reconstructed by the swordsmith Peter Johnsson. It was found in a district of Stockholm that was called Tritonia in the Middle Ages. Particularly interesting is the relatively rare spherical pommel with a rosette-shaped cap, which is found in other contemporary Scandinavian swords. Tritonia type swords were widepread in the late 13th and early 14th centuries.

The Tritonia sword is a tall order, with a 33.0-inch (84 centimeter) blade and weighing a little over 3.3 pounds (1.5 kilograms). However, despite the high total weight and very short grip, the sword is well balanced, thanks to its fuller, flat blade cross section, and distal taper.

TYPE XIV: These swords are relatively short, with an average blade length of 29.5 inches (75 centimeters) and grip length of 3.9 inches (10 centimeters). The blade is very broad and tapers sharply to a sharp point. We note here a tendency towards a thrusting sword, so to speak, transition to Group 2. The fuller runs approximately half the length of the blade. Type XIV is equally good for making a cut as well as a thrust, and was in common use from the end of the 13th to the mid-14th centuries.

The piece pictured to the right of the Tritonia Sword, with a 32.0-inch (81.5 centimeter) blade and weighing about 2.6 pounds (1.2 kilograms), is relatively large for a type XIV, but has more elements of this type than of the type XII. This sword, reconstructed by Peter Johnsson, is very "biddable" or guidable, and agile—it almost becomes alive in the hand. The faceted round pommel is very rare.

The sword on the far right is a very interesting specimen. It dates from the first half of the 14th century; the 31.8-inch (81 centimeter) blade, which displays the remnants of some inscriptions, is estimated to be older. The mounting is not made of iron or steel, but of bronze, decorated with a coating of silver.

On the pommel is a silver ring with the Latin inscription *"sunt hic etiam sua precune laudi"*—"Here are the messengers of his glory" (some books on the subject state erroneously that this sword bears a similar-sounding quote from Virgil's *Aeneid: "sunt hic etiam sua praemia laveli"* = "here also virtue finds its reward").

We can see the characteristic features of a type XIV especially well in the sword shown at left. The original dates from the first half of the 14th century; the mounting is gilded. A cross-shaped cloth relic is set under a rock crystal cover in a hollow in the

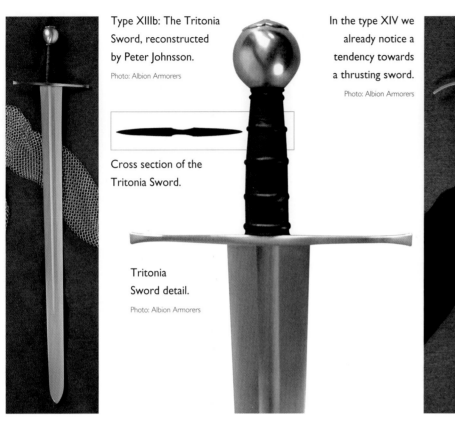

Type XIIIb: The Tritonia Sword, reconstructed by Peter Johnsson.

Photo: Albion Armorers

Cross section of the Tritonia Sword.

Tritonia Sword detail.

Photo: Albion Armorers

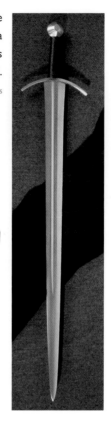

In the type XIV we already notice a tendency towards a thrusting sword.

Photo: Albion Armorers

Very rare XIV sword from the 14th century.

The *Katzbalger*

The *Katzbalger* is the typical sword of the German and Swiss *Landsknechte*, [lansquenet or mercenary foot soldier]. They originated towards the end of the 15th century and existed until the mid-16th century. It is quite difficult to classify this sword – it has features characteristic of the type XIIIb, but also has a flat, diamond-shaped cross section like that of the late medieval type XVIII. Overall, the *Katzbalger* is classified more as a late Renaissance form of the XIIIb sword.

It features a sharply curved, horizontal S-shaped cross-guard, which developed later into an actual figure eight.

A common misconception is that this name comes from a scabbard made of cat's fur. It is claimed that these cat-fur sheaths had no tip, so that you could stab with the sword without unsheathing it. As original

as this explanation for the name is, it is also highly unlikely. Image sources clearly show that *Katzbalgers* were indeed carried in a scabbard. It seems that the sword's name can be traced back to an archaic term for close combat: To *katzbalgen* or "*wie-die-Katzen-balgen*" ["how cats tussle"].

Katzbalger sword grips.

Photo: Lutel

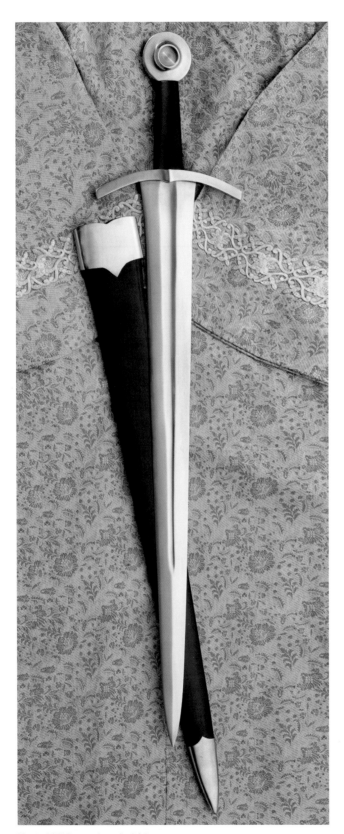

Typical XIV sword, early 14th century.

Photo: Museum Replicas

pommel, and on the blade is the inscription *"nulla de virtutibus tuis major clementia est"* ("none of your virtues is more important than grace"). The replica does not include these ornaments, but its proportions are correct (blade length 26.3 inches [67 centimeters], total length 33.4 inches [85 centimeters], weight just under 2.8 pounds [1.3 kilograms]).

Swords against Plate Armor

"At the end of the High Middle Ages, there was a serious change in armor. Around 1240, rectangular iron plates were developed, which were sewn inside a tunic to make it protective. This armor, also called Spangenharnisch ["clasped harness" or armor], created the first reinforcement of the traditional mail shirt: The development of plate armor had begun," (Schlunk and Giersch, p.45).

In the first half of the 14th century, ring or chainmail was increasingly reinforced with additional plates, which then finally developed into full plate armor in the 15th century. Although modern tests have proven that a sword point can penetrate even stronger steel (such as car hoods), it requires a very forceful and well-aimed stroke to do this. When dealing with rounded plates of armor on a fast-moving opponent, things look quite different. Here, the fighter has to rely on thrusting his sword into the weak points of his opponent's armor. This change, from cut or stroke to a thrust, leads to a fundamental alteration in the form of sword blades. This included altering the shape of the blade sides. The blades taper more sharply, and the point is much more pronounced. The blade cross section is also changed. The blade is no longer so much weighted on the cutting edges, but more forward, at the point. The rounded cutting blades of the High Middle Ages are replaced more and more by much thicker, relatively rigid blades with a diamond-shaped cross section, and also in part by blades with a central rib, or six-edged blades.

In contrast to the earlier swords, which all appear relatively similar, we now find a greater differentiation, leading to obvious differences. Although this is the heyday of the long-sword, we also find seven different types of one-handed swords.

Transitional form between chainmail and full plate armor.

Photo: Del Tin

The biggest challenge when facing an opponent in armor is to find the gaps in his armor and covering.

Photo: Agilitas.tv

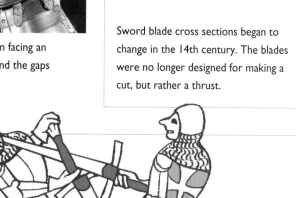

Sword blade cross sections began to change in the 14th century. The blades were no longer designed for making a cut, but rather a thrust.

Fully trained plate armor.

Photo: Del Tin

When fencing in armor, your tactical objective is the gaps in your opponent's armor – this requires a blade suitable for thrusting (drawing after the *Codex Wallerstein*).

The oldest known depiction of Joan of Arc (and the only one from her lifetime), shows her with a classic thrusting sword type XV (drawing after a drawing from the court transcripts of 1431).

TYPE XV: This has a sharply tapering blade with diamond cross section, or a blade with a middle rib and almost straight cutting edges—clearly designed primarily for making a thrust between sections of armor. Excepting only the tucks, or armor piercing swords, XV swords have the most pronounced thrusting blades. The grip length is on average 3.9 inches (10 centimeters), the blade length, 29.5 inches (75 centimeters). There are almost no fullers, and the cross-guards are frequently slightly curved downwards. The type XV was common from the late 13th to the end of the 15th centuries, but was still in use at the beginning of the 16th century.

The sword in the large illustration at right is, so to speak, the archetypal sword, the paradigm for type XV. Noteworthy here is the simple, yet elegant form of pommel and cross-guard. With a blade 31.8 inches (81 centimeters) long, the replica is 38.1 inches (97 centimeters) long and weighs one kilogram. The XV sword next to it at top right, is one of the rarest types at all—the "ear sword." These curious weapons are to some extent the "big brothers" of the ear dagger, which is found already in the Bronze Age. The pommel of these daggers is formed of two "ears" slanted towards each other—some historians think that grips made of femur bones were the models for this particular design. In the Late Middle Ages, ear daggers were popular throughout the Mediterranean region, but the ear sword, in contrast, are limited mainly to Italy, in particular Venice. Unlike the daggers, these swords have a second pair of ears on the cross-guard. Ear daggers were considered the hallmark of the Stradioti, the light cavalry of the Venetian Republic, and were also called *Pugnale alla Stradiotti*. Based on this name, an ear sword is also known as *Spada alla Stradiotta*. Ear swords almost always have type XV blades. They were most widespread at the end of the 15th and early 16th centuries.

TYPE XVI: This sword is very similar to type XIV, since the blade is broad and flat and the fuller generally runs only about halfway, rather than two-thirds of the way down the blade. However, in the lower section, we find a characteristic blade with diamond-shaped cross section, which runs to a sharp point.

The blade length is 27.5-31.4 inches (70 to 80 centimeters), and grip length 3.9 inches (10 centimeters). XVI swords developed at the beginning of the 14th century, when chain shirts were increasingly reinforced with armor plates. They are both broad enough to deliver a hefty cut, but also pointed enough to make a thrust into gaps in the armor. The XVI sword at right dates from the first half of the 14th century, and has a 37.7-inch (96 centimeter) blade.

TYPE XVIII: The blades of these weapons are equally suitable for delivering a cut or a thrust. They are wide (four to five centimeters at the base) and flat and taper elegantly to a sharp point. Blade lengths vary from 27.5-31.4 inches (70 to 80 centimeters), and the grip is about 3.9 inches (10 centimeters) long. Type XVIII occurs mainly from the middle of the 14th to the beginning of the 15th centuries.

The XVIII sword shown on page 85 probably dates from the end of the 14th or early 15th centuries. The blade is nearly 27.1 inches (69 centimeters) long, and this weapon weighs about one kilogram. There are some indications that this sword hung for a long time over the grave of the English King Henry V. Whether it was really among his possessions can now no longer be determined.

Irish Swords

In Ireland, a special type of grip was developed, in use well into the 16th century, and found nowhere else. It features a ring pommel, through which the tang is visible, and a horizontal, S-shaped curved cross-guard, which is spatulate at the end.

These special Irish types are usually one-handed swords with a blade about 31.4 inches (80 centimeters) long, but we sometimes find large bastard or two-handed swords.

Type XV cutting edges are almost straight.

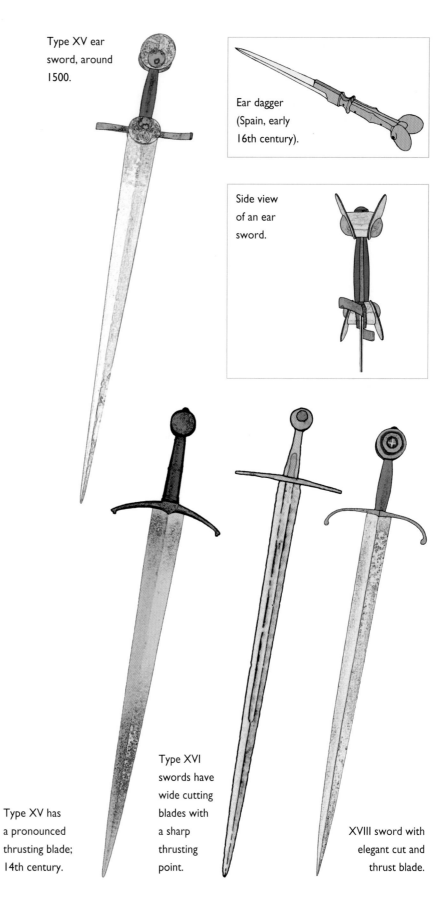

Type XV ear sword, around 1500.

Ear dagger (Spain, early 16th century).

Side view of an ear sword.

Type XV has a pronounced thrusting blade; 14th century.

Type XVI swords have wide cutting blades with a sharp thrusting point.

XVIII sword with elegant cut and thrust blade.

The XVIII sword on page 87, top left, is a typical example of a sword with a fish-tail pommel. One-handed swords with this pommel usually have a short grip—approximately 3.9 inches (10 centimeters)—and short, straight cross-guards. In addition, fish-tail pommel swords almost always belong to types XVIII or XVIIIa. The original of the copy shown here dates from the second half of the 15th century.

TYPE XIX: The blades of XIX swords are all so similar that the majority of them probably come from the same workshop. The blade is about 31.4-33.4 inches (80 to 85 centimeters) long, with almost parallel edges that suddenly run to a sharp point. The blade cross section is hexagonal, and a narrow, deep fuller runs down more than half of the blade. All blades have a pronounced, five to seven centimeter long ricasso. Two grooves are engraved in the ricasso, which flank the fuller. Most of these blades seem to be of Arab origin and can be dated to a period from about 1350 to 1450.

The XIX sword shown at right below comes from the Arsenal in Alexandria. The blade bears an Arabic inscription, with the notations of the reigning Sultan al-Malik al-Ashraf Barsbey (also known in the West as Baybars), the Arsenal of Alexandria, and the year 836 (1432 European era). With a blade length of 33.8 inches (86 centimeters), the sword is overall a meter long and weighs just 1.7 pounds (0.8 kilograms). According to some historians, it is of Italian origin and was sent as a tribute to the Turks, along with other armaments of King John II of Cyprus. Two nearly identical swords were found in Istanbul. Very interesting in this copy is the finger ring forged on the cross-guard (actually a finger guard, since the "ring" is not completely closed).

The ring allows the sword to be used for a fighting technique that actually reached its perfection only in the Renaissance, with the rapier or broadsword. They are very rare on medieval swords. Sword fighting expert Guy Windsor commented: "It is not wrong to hook a finger over the cross-guard and thus shift the grip closer to the center of balance. This allows you to control the sword more easily. However, it also puts the finger in potential danger and should be reserved for the moment when you are so tired that you need this support," (Windsor, p.68).

To reduce risk to the finger, starting in the 14th century, sometimes a finger ring was attached to the cross-guard for protection. This type of grip passes directly into the cross hilt dagger knuckle bow guard: The origin of using a completely different hand position for broadsword or rapier fencing. The earliest evidence of index finger rings dates from around 1340 to 1350. In the diptych "The Crucifixion and Lamentation" by the Masters of the Codex of St. George in Siena, you can see a falchion with a finger ring. The earliest surviving finger ring dates from the same period—surprisingly, on a type XIIa battle sword.

The weapon at center, below, is an XIX, so-called Spanish type sword from the second half of the 15th century. We find here a sharply down-curved cross-guard which widens at the end, and two finger rings that were not added later, but are an integral part of the cross-guard. Typically, the rings are joined together by a bow. Spanish types normally have disc pommels, but they also have distinct pommel shapes. Often the mounting is gilded and finely engraved. A beautiful example of such a weapon is the sword of King Fernando of Aragon, in the Armeria Real in Madrid.

TYPE XXA: These swords have a very broad blade, which narrows quickly to a sharp point. The blade generally has three fullers, with the longer third either lying under two shorter ones, or is flanked by them. Type XXa was used mainly in the 14th and 15th centuries (see picture on page 87).

The last two types in the Oakeshott classification—types XXI and XXII—play a special role. These are actually no longer purely medieval swords, but rare types from the transitional period to the Renaissance. In principle, types XXI and XXII correspond to the Italian sword known internationally as the *cinquedea*. The name comes from the fact that the blade is about five fingers (*cinque dita*) wide at the base. In the vernacular, they were also known as the "ox tongue" (*lingua di bue*) because of the shape of the blade. Most *cinquedeas* are short swords with blades 19.6-21.6 inches (50 to 55 centimeters) long (but there are also daggers of this shape, as well as slimmer, longer swords). The blade width is between seven and eleven centimeters. The usually quite short grip is generally made of ivory and heavily decorated with precious

XVIII sword with
fish tail pommel.

Photo: Del Tin

Classic XIX sword from
the 15th century

XIX sword blades have a
hexagonal cross section.

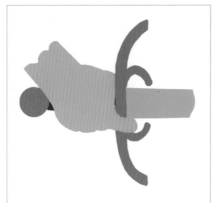

A finger over the cross-guard allows
greater control of the weapon.
To protect the finger, rings
were forged on the guard.

XIX Spanish type sword.

Type XXa.

The Renaissance
cinquedea has many
small, flat fullers.

metals. Another characteristic of this sword is the short, sharply down curved cross-guard.

The *cinquedea* was a fashionable weapon, mainly in use in the second half of the 15th century in the Mediterranean region. In contrast to the transitional types XXI and XXII, we generally do not find the usual fullers in a real Renaissance *cinquedea*, but rather many very short and shallow fullers (*sgusci*) arranged in a pyramid design (see picture on page 87).

TYPE XXI: Type XXI were in use mainly in the late 15th century. It generally had an average length of about 29.5 inches (75 centimeters), and very broad, sharply tapered blade. We generally find double fullers, which also taper sharply and run down to the point. The XXI sword shown at right (inset) is a relatively late piece and was probably made around 1500 in Bologna. The blade is 20.0 inches (51 centimeters) long and thus more representative of a true Renaissance *cinquedea*. The width at the base is 3.5 inches (9 centimeters). The sword's total weight is almost 1.9 pounds (0.9 kilograms).

The large photo at right shows a classic Renaissance type XXI sword, made in Italy in 1520. It has a characteristic highly decorated disc pommel and downward curved cross-guard. The infamous Cesare Borgia owned an amazingly similar sword from the second half of the 15th century. The blade of the replica is 31.8 inches (81 centimeters) long, just 1.1 inches (3 centimeters) shorter than the original; the rich engraving on the blade was omitted on the replica. It weighs almost 3.0 pounds (1.4 kilograms).

TYPE XXII: These swords do not differ very much from type XXI—here the blade is also broad and flat, but does not taper as sharply and abruptly, but rather more moderately, and then runs into a gentle curve at the point. The fullers are short and narrow, in pairs at the base of the blade. XXII swords are mainly from the 14th and 15th centuries. The specimen pictured at right is from the period around 1500; the blade is 25.9 inches (66 centimeters) long.

As indicated elsewhere, medieval swords are all unique pieces; accordingly, we find examples that cannot be precisely assigned to any particular type. Some specimens do not justify establishing a new type. A fine example of such an unclassifiable sword is shown in the illustration below right. The two short fullers on the blade base clearly correspond to type XXII. The blade profile and the hexagonal cross section, however, are characteristic of type XIX. The mounting is the so-called Spanish type: A sharply downward curved cross-guard in combination with double finger rings. Overall, the sword corresponds more to early 16th-century weapons rather than to type XIX, but not exactly.

Type XXI is in principle a
Renaissance rather than
medieval weapon.

Photo: Museum Replicas

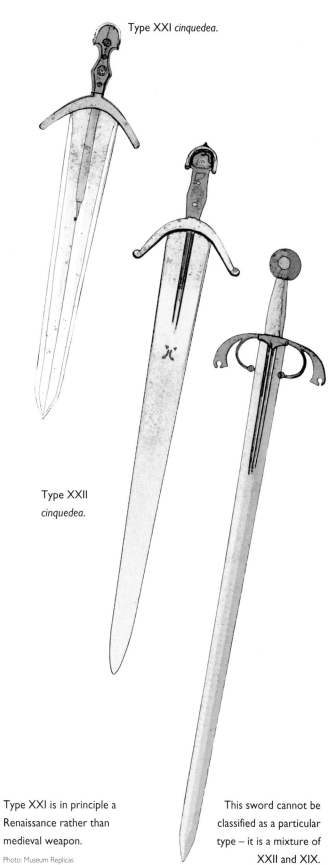

Type XXI *cinquedea.*

Type XXII
cinquedea.

This sword cannot be
classified as a particular
type – it is a mixture of
XXII and XIX.

7.3 Long-Sword, Battle Sword & Co.

I pray you, is Signior Mountanto [Schlachtschwer: battle sword] return'd from the wars or no?
— (Shakespeare, *Much Ado About Nothing*)

At the beginning of the 14th century, some drastic changes were made in military fighting methods. Armies of foot soldiers had dealt some crushing defeats to armies of knights. Slowly, profound upheavals occurred: at times, infantrymen proved themselves to be militarily superior to the noble horsemen. During this period, therefore, infantry weapons began to develop rapidly. Previously, warriors always fought each other with sword and shield. Due to improved body armor, it was possible to make the shield much smaller, or fight without it altogether. As a result, completely new opportunities opened up for the swordsman. For the sword itself, this meant one thing above all: it became longer!

While the term "long-sword" generally only describes a sword longer than a one-handed weapon, we can identify two special categories: the bastard sword and the battle sword. The problem we have today, is that there is some overlap among all three swords, and sometimes we cannot classify a sword exactly. In the re-enactment scene, it is often customary to classify the battle sword and bastard sword as subcategories of the long-sword, but this does not reflect exactly the complicated facts and circumstances. However, we can agree on a "lowest common denominator": Long-swords, battle swords, and bastard swords are weapons mainly used with both hands.

In 20th-century historical and archaeological literature, we almost never find the term "long-sword" used for long swords. However, we know from medieval sources that swordsmen used this term. We find the long-sword in world literature—in Shakespeare's *Romeo and Juliet*, Lord Capulet exclaims: "Give me my long sword, ho!" Despite—or perhaps because— it is mentioned frequently, it is not easy to determine what exactly is meant by a long-sword. We only know this much: warriors distinguished between the (short, one-handed) "sword" and the "long-sword." From an Old English text from around 1450, we can learn that in single combat, you should carry your dagger on the right side, your (short) sword on the left, and your long-sword in your hand.

Based on contemporary sources, we can also determine something else: The long-sword was the most important weapon for medieval swordsmanship. Several facts demonstrate the long-sword's special importance:

- Although other weapons play a role in the fencing books—pole arms, daggers, short swords—long-swords occupy the largest place.
- The long-sword is shown in most of the few surviving depictions of medieval fencing masters.
- The title conferred by the fencing societies was "master of the long-sword."

The bastard sword is the intermediate step (hybrid or bastard) between one-handed and two-handed swords: A sword that can be wielded as well with one as with two hands. However, for an in-depth definition of a bastard sword, there are two criteria which, so to speak, compete with each other:

- grip length
- size/weight

It is characteristic of many bastard swords that the grip often barely has space for two hands—the left hand grasps the last part of the grip, as well as the large, usually oblong pommel. In the scientific world, the term "hand-and-a-half sword" is often used for the bastard sword—among more unconventional sword fans, most stick with the internationally used "bastard sword." The latter term was first used in Europe in the 15th and 16th centuries. There is a 17th-century French document, which portrays a duel which took place before King Henri II of France in 1549. The fighters used *epées bâtardes*, or more precisely: "Bastard swords, which can be used with both one and two hands." It is not known what bastard swords were called before this time—likely, people simply said long-sword. We often find bastard swords with a waisted grip, which supports both one-handed and two-handed use (see Figure 91, below center).

Due to reinforced armor, it was possible to fight without a shield – the sword could be held with both hands.

Photo: Agilitas.tv

The long-sword of the Late Middle Ages is an elegant weapon that led to the blossoming of medieval swordsmanship.

Photo: Museum Replicas

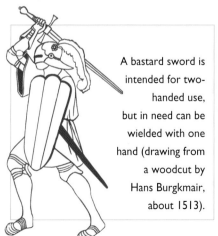

A bastard sword is intended for two-handed use, but in need can be wielded with one hand (drawing from a woodcut by Hans Burgkmair, about 1513).

Bastard swords often have a waisted grip, for hand-and-a-half use.

Photo: Herbert Schmidt

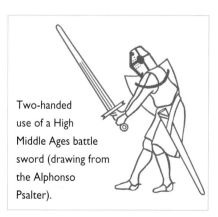

Two-handed use of a High Middle Ages battle sword (drawing from the Alphonso Psalter).

The Executioner's Sword

Execution swords have a special role in the history of edged weapons. They cannot be easily placed among the other categories. In the Middle Ages, people were usually beheaded with an ax. If swords were ever used, the condemned were nobles or princes. Besides the special social role of the sword (compared to the "peasant" ax), there were more practical reasons for this: A sword has a different blade geometry from an ax; the cut is clean, the condemned suffers less pain, which is why nobles were executed with a sword. This special situation changed in the 16th century: At latest from mid-century, bourgeois offenders were also more frequently beheaded with a sword. At this time, a special type of sword was developed for executioners. The earliest surviving executioner's sword comes from Germany and can be dated at around 1540. Most existing execution swords come from the 17th century; by the beginning of the 19th century, it was out of use. In Germany, a sword was last used in 1893 to behead a poisoner.

Execution by sword requires a very different technique than when using an ax, where the condemned had to lay his head and shoulders on a chopping block. The procedure has been accurately handed down through countless medieval illustrations.

When the sword was used, the condemned kneels on the floor. The executioner raises his sword far over his shoulder and performs a horizontal stroke, which cuts the head off the shoulders.

In England, there was no one who could use the executioner's sword since beheadings were mostly done with an ax. Accordingly, the small number of executions using a sword is good testimony of the significance of this instrument and of the skill necessary to wield it. When King Henry VIII of England wanted to have his second wife, Anne Boleyn, executed in 1536, she was beheaded by a sword.

Since there were few specialists who could use an executioner sword in England, the executioner from St. Omer near Calais was brought over specially. He beheaded Anne Boleyn with a single blow.

How important it was to have a specialist to deliver a painless death, was shown by an incident in France in 1626: a clumsy volunteer required a total of twenty-nine blows of his sword to execute the Comte de Chalais

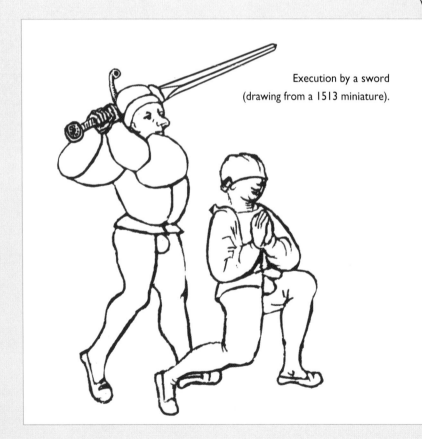

Execution by a sword
(drawing from a 1513 miniature).

An executioner's sword had no point, the blades were topped at the tip like a screwdriver.

(!). In contrast, in 1501 a professional executioner beheaded two condemned he had tied back to back, with a single stroke.

Execution swords basically have two-handed grips and usually straight cross-guards. Unlike combat swords, they do not require a point, so this is eliminated completely. The front part of the blade is topped off almost horizontally, resembling a screwdriver – due to their parallel cutting edges, execution swords could be characterized as "type XIIIa without a point." Typically, execution sword blades are very broad (six to seven centimeters); total length is equal to that of a bastard sword. In terms of weight, execution swords, weighing between 3.7-5.0 pounds (1.7 to 2.3 kilograms), are between a bastard sword and a very heavy two-handed sword.

Execution sword blades often have one or more shallow fullers. Very often, the blades are furnished with representations of jurisdiction (ranging from the goddess Justitia, to murder and manslaughter). There are also characteristic moral sayings, such as "Fear God and love justice, then the angel will be your servant." On a 1676 sword made by the Solingen swordsmith John Beugel, we find rhyming inscriptions on the sides of the blade:

"When you want to practice in virtue,
this execution sword should not touch you."
"When I do pick up the sword,
so I wish the poor sinner eternal life."

Apart from the length of the grip, we can also define a bastard sword by size and weight: Although its appearance is like that of a two-handed sword, it is light and "short" enough to be wielded with one hand. Thus, you can also hold a shield or a dagger as an auxiliary weapon in your other hand. Bastard swords have an average overall length of about 43.3 inches (110 centimeters) and a blade length of about 35.4 inches (90 centimeters). In contrast, a "real" medieval two-handed sword, with an overall length of about 47.2 inches (120 centimeters), has a blade that is one meter or more long. While the length and shape of the grip are important criteria, to me, size and weight appear to be crucial, because if the sword is too big and too heavy, then even a suitable grip would not help you wield it with one hand. At this point, we should again clarify that, according to the teachings of the old masters, bastard swords were basically used with two hands. The sword was only used with a single hand if that could not be avoided.

The "battle sword" is much more difficult to classify than the bastard sword. We definitely know that it was a great sword for use in war. In contrast to the "civilian" long-sword, used by citizens for defense in everyday life, the battle sword is purely a weapon of war. Battle swords are generally broader, heavier and larger than "civilian" long-swords. Overall, it appears that the battle sword was more designed for a cut than a thrust (although it was naturally suited for both).

Battle swords also have a very representative character. If nowadays you find a "hero sword" in a museum, that is, swords attributed to either fictional or historical heroes like Guy of Warwick, Bevis of Hampton, and William "Braveheart" Wallace, these are usually battle swords. These massive weapons are suited to the halo of heroism: only a true hero could have used such a huge weapon—a "dragon slayer." Usually, it turns out that no connection to the heroes can be established, and the swords themselves are much more recent than the heroic story.

While the categories long-sword and battle sword relate more to these weapons' purpose, the categories bastard sword and two-handed sword say something about their length. Long-swords and battle swords can therefore include both hand-and-a-half and two-handed types.

Battle Swords of the High Middle Ages

Although large swords first became really popular in the time of plate armor, we already find types in group 1, i.e., in the period when the sword was still used mainly against chainmail and shield. A significant source on the use of the early battle sword is a miniature from the *Alphonso Psalter* of 1280 (also known as *Tenison Psalter*). It shows a knight with pot helmet and chainmail, who has thrown his shield protectively around his right shoulder so that he can wield his great battle sword with two hands. These long swords were always broad battle swords in the period of the 13th to 14th centuries—pure weapons of war. The slimmer long-sword as a bourgeois self-defense weapon, emerges only later.

In the German weapons literature, it was long common to use the term *Schlachtschwert* [battle sword] only for the gigantic two-handed swords of the Renaissance. In contrast, recent results show that it is also used for the two-handed swords of the High Middle Ages. In the Old English literature of the Middle Ages, we find terms such as "Grete Swerdes," "Grete War Swerdes," and "Swerdes of Werre"—in French "*epées de Guerre*"—i.e. "war or battle swords"—being used for these swords. The contemporary French knights also referred to battle swords as "large German swords," suggesting that they were either developed in German-speaking regions or were most widespread there. In the English language, the High Middle Ages battle swords are called "great swords," but the term "*große Schwerter*" in the German language is simply too undifferentiated to use. In this respect, here, "battle sword" is the sensible choice. Among High Middle Ages battle swords, we can distinguish between types XIIa and XIIIa.

TYPE XIIA: Blade length is usually from 35.4-37.4 inches (90 to 95 centimeters) but there are specimens with blades more than a meter long, the grip length is 5.9-9.8 inches (15 to 25 centimeters). This sword weighed 3.3-4.4 pounds (1.5 to 2 kilograms). The blade tapers evenly and ends in a sharp point, and the fuller runs about two-thirds down the blade. Type XIIa is mainly found in the 13th and 14th centuries.

The XIIa sword shown on page 95 (top right) is particularly interesting. First, here we have a flat, hexagonal blade with a short fuller (blade length: 37.7 inches [96 centimeters]). It is also likely the oldest sword with a finger ring (about 1300-1350).

There are no great differences between types XIIa and XIIIa. XIIa swords are slightly narrower, more tapered, with a more pronounced point. At times, you have to look very closely to notice the differences, such as with the sword shown bottom left on page 95. It dates from around 1400, and has a 37.4-inch (95 centimeter) blade. With a total length of 47.6 inches (121 centimeters), the weight is just under 3.9 pounds (1.8 kilograms).

The Scottish Two-Handed Sword

One of the most famous long-swords was developed in Scotland in the 15th century: The *claidheamh da laimh* (= two-handed sword), later known as the Claymore (a corruption of *claidheamh mor* = great sword). The Scottish two-handed sword has a long grip and a broad blade, which is usually 41.3-43.3 inches (105-110 centimeters) long. It can be found in both types XIIa and XIIIa. The shape of the cross-guard is characteristic: straight and pointed sharply downwards, becoming narrower towards the ends. It generally has long, narrow languets and often has open-work, four-leaf clovers on the ends. Usually the pommel is shaped like a small disk, but there are some spherical versions. The Scottish two-handed sword had its heyday in the 16th century, but can be frequently found in use later. The *claidheamh beg* is much rarer than the *claidheamh da laimh*; this is a one-handed version with the typical down-pointed cross-guard. The *claidheamh beg* is usually found at the end of the 14th and early 15th centuries.

Photo: Pieces of History

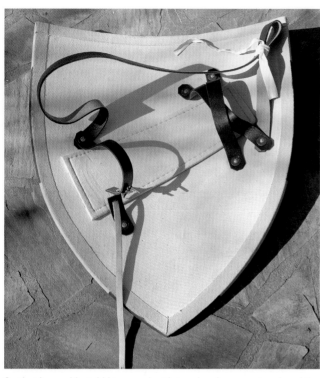

So that he could wield his sword with two hands, a warrior slung his shield on a strap around his shoulder.

Photo: Museum Replicas

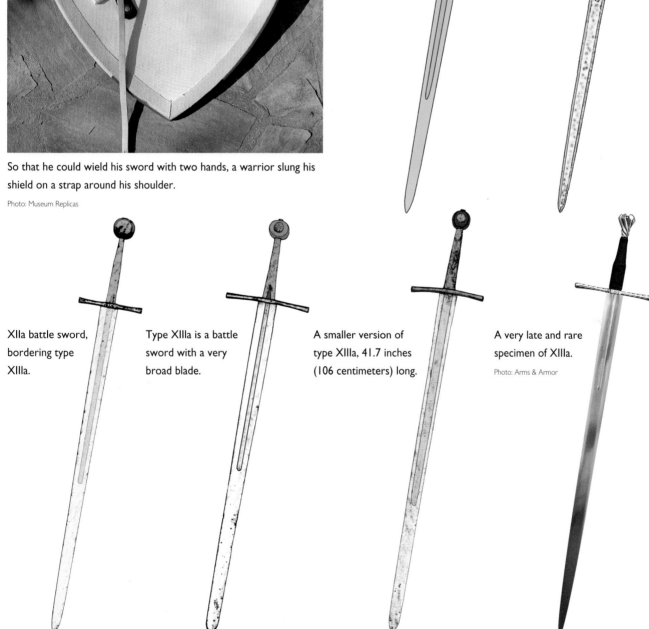

A type XIIa battle sword.

XIIa sword with finger ring.

XIIa battle sword, bordering type XIIIa.

Type XIIIa is a battle sword with a very broad blade.

A smaller version of type XIIIa, 41.7 inches (106 centimeters) long.

A very late and rare specimen of XIIIa.

Photo: Arms & Armor

Full plate armor developed in the Late Middle Ages, giving rise to the heyday of the longsword.

Photo: Agilitas.tv

In half-sword technique, the hand grasps around the blade (drawing from the *Codex Wallerstein*).

Half-sword technique aims to penetrate gaps in the armor (drawing from the *Codex Wallerstein*).

TYPE XIIIA: This can be called the "archetypal" battle sword. The blade is very wide, tapering only slightly—almost not at all, so that essentially the cutting edges are almost parallel. The fuller is usually about half the length of the blade. The point is very rounded, and sometimes almost recalls an executioner's sword. The sword lengths vary greatly; there are both very large bastard swords and actual two-handed weapons. The blade length averages between 31.4 inches (80 centimeters) and 39.3 inches (1 meter), the grip between 5.9-9.8 inches (15 to 25 centimeters) long, and the weight is 3.7-4.4 pounds (1.7 to 2 kilograms). Type XIIIa was in use in the 13th and 14th centuries.

The XIIIa sword shown on page 95 below (second from the left) dates from the second half of the 14th century. With a total length of 49.2 inches (125 centimeters), a one-meter long blade, and a weight of just 5.0 pounds (2.3 kilograms), this mighty battle sword is among the larger specimens of type XIIIa.

The sword next to it (3rd from left) is unusually small for an XIIIa. With a blade just 33.8 inches (86 centimeters) long, the weapon is 41.7 inches (106 centimeters) long and weighs just 3.0 pounds (1.4 kilograms). An inscription in the fuller reads ENRICS DX NERICS (= ENRICVS DVX NERICVS), so we can date this sword to the 12th century. We see a very rare XIIIa sword right next to it. It dates from around 1500 –a very late example—and was found in Bohemia. The turned *Astknauf* ['writhen' pommel] is, however, typical of Swiss weapons, such as the *Schnepfer*—we cannot say much about its real origin. In addition to the pommel and corresponding cross-guard, the 36.6-inch (93 centimeter) blade is also very rare. It has a hexagonal cross section, which usually occurs only in group 2 swords. Thus, we have here a sword with the profile of type XIIIa (group 1), but with the grip design and blade cross section of a typical group 2 sword.

Long-swords against Plate Armor

The long-sword's real heyday was in the Late Middle Ages, the period of plate armor. As already mentioned, wearing full-scale plate armor allows you to either minimize your shield or even eliminate it altogether. As a result, you can wield your sword with both hands, so that the sword itself can be longer. Another aspect

Half-sword technique: one hand guides the blade, while the other gives the thrust powerful momentum.

Photo: Agilias.tv

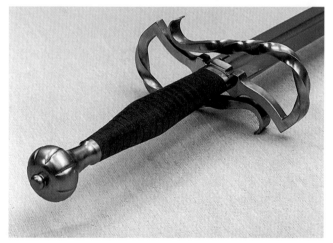

Late medieval battle sword with pretzel-shaped cross-guard.

Photo: Lutel

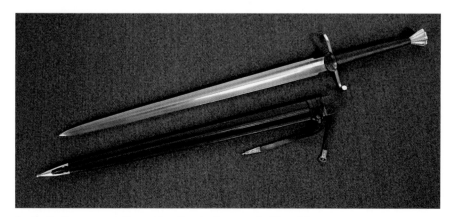

Aesthetically representative yet functional – the sword of Swedish regent Svante Nilsson Sture.

Photo: Albion Armorers

Janos Hunyadi (around 1408-1456), Hungarian regent and father of King Matthias Corvinus, in late medieval battle gear. The overlapping parts of armor can be seen clearly (drawing after a 14th-century woodcut).

"Morning star sword" with a special pommel for striking (drawing from the *Codex Wallerstein*).

of sword fighting made it almost mandatory to use two hands: the half-sword technique was especially developed for fighting an opponent in plate armor.

When fencing in armor, it is necessary to make a precisely targeted, yet powerful thrust to penetrate the gaps in your opponent's armor. To do this, the swordsman grasps the middle of the sword blade with his left hand to help guide it, while the right hand on the grip gives really strong momentum to the thrust—just as when playing billiards. Here, Master Vadi stated that a sword that is used against armor can only be sharp enough to cut near the point. The rest of the blade is less sharp, in fact, somewhat dull, so that it is relatively safe to use the half-sword technique when wearing a glove.

Master Vadi specifically mentions a length of "four fingers," although it is not clear whether he meant the finger width or length. In my estimation, it could only mean finger length: Based on my body measurements, that is about 11.4 inches (29 centimeters)—otherwise, only about nine centimeters of the blade would be sharpened.

Before we look at individual swords, there is still much to say about fencing in armor. There are a lot of preconceptions about battling it out wearing full plate armor ("you could barely move in the armor"). In truth, late medieval armor was much more flexible than you might think. For one, battle armor is widely confused with *Stechzeug*, the special armor made and used just for jousting. Jousting armor weighs between 88-110 pounds (40 and 50 kilograms), while battle armor in contrast, "only" 55-66 pounds (25 to 30 kilograms). We can consider the average weight of a suit of plate armor to be about 59.5 pounds (27 kilograms). This weight is also distributed over the whole body, so that individual parts weigh only a few kilograms. Wearing such armor, it is possible to run and twist about, roll around, and so on. In short, one can perform all major sword-fighting techniques. You use the same techniques to fence in armor as you do to fence without wearing protection—so it is not a matter of pure strength.

Group 2 long-swords can have widely different characteristics. We find both bastard swords and actual two-handed swords: most swords, however, are smaller, lighter, and sleeker than the old battle swords. "Modern" bastard swords increasingly feature waisted grips, that clearly indicated that the sword was intended for one-and-a-half hands. The bastard sword came into increasing favor from the 14th century on, and by the 15th century, it was the most popular sword size overall. Long-swords can also have a more "civilian" character, and be simpler than the models specifically designed for war. In the 16th century, the bastard sword came into fashion as representative weapons—the magnificent specimen that was laid in the grave with King Gustav Vasa of Sweden in 1560 is but one example.

Another example of such a model is the sword of Swedish regent Svante Nilsson Sture (around 1460-1512). It was found in Sture's grave in 1958 during restoration work in the Vasteras Cathedral. It is therefore one of the few swords that can be assigned exactly to a single historical individual. The Sture Sword is a two-handed weapon (or a very large bastard sword). It is well balanced and light enough to be wielded with one hand. Although the sword is a fully functional combat weapon, the fluted, tapered pommel and the horizontal S-shaped cross-guard give it its own understated elegance: the sword has a definite representative character—which is also confirmed by the fact that the sword followed Sture into his grave. The Sture Sword is unique in its combination of features. We can only find similar models in image sources, such as in a woodcut representing St. George by Lucas Cranach the Elder. The Sture Sword replica pictured, made by swordsmith Peter Johnsson (page 97) reflects the original sword down to the last detail. With a blade length of 33.4 inches (85 centimeters), the sword is 46.0 inches (117 centimeters) long and weighs 3.9 pounds (1.8 kilograms).

The battle sword also re-appeared in the Late Middle Ages—but now looking different than it did in earlier centuries. From the 15th century on, blades became increasingly narrower and the swords larger. Total length is now often 51.1-57.0 inches (130 to 145 centimeters), and blade length 39.3-43.3 inches (100 to 110 centimeters). Especially long grips are typical (at times 15.7 inches [40 centimeters]). These battle swords very often belong to types XVa, XVIa, XVII and XVIIIa—unlike the battle swords of the High Middle Ages with their broad cutting blades, we generally find blades designed for thrusting. This circumstance lets us conclude that a warrior was increasingly facing an opponent in full plate armor on the battlefield (although we still find XIIa and XIIIa swords in the Late Middle Ages).

Some fencing books show a special style of battle sword. These include types XVa or XVIIIa swords with pommels—and sometimes cross-guards—that are fitted with spikes. Such swords make techniques such as thrusts with the pommel or the "death stroke" particularly effective. In *De Arte Gladiatora Dimicandi*, Master Vadi even explicitly recommends adding spikes to the cross-guard. There is a particularly interesting form of such a sword in the *Codex Wallerstein*. While "ordinary" long-swords are used for un-armored fencing, the depictions of techniques

Longsword with knuckle bow guard.

Sword with guard ring and shell guard.

The Sword Turns Gothic

Although the disc pommel was still popular, in the late Middle Ages, other shapes began to increasingly catch on. This had to do with fashion: The Gothic style created a design that was sleek and focused on soaring upwards. There were also practical reasons for the change: A pommel that is elongated, frequently pear-shaped – the international term is scent-stopper shape – or facetted makes it easier to wield a bastard sword using a second hand that also grasps around the pommel. While there were more cross-guards given a slight downward curve, the straight cross shape remained the most popular design. The sword pictured here has a so-called *Fiederknauf* [pinnate or feather-design pommel] and slightly down-curved cross-guards. Original examples of this type of sword date from the late 15th century and have been preserved in such museums as the Zurich Landesmuseum. The detail on the grip of this replica represents St. Knut, based on an altarpiece from Trinity College (about 1479). Also very interesting here is a sword painted by Albrecht Dürer. On one wing of the Paumgartner Altarpiece, Dürer represented St. Eustace as a Late Middle Ages mercenary soldier captain, holding a bastard sword and kidney dagger. Slender and clearly of Gothic design, the sword has a double-curved cross-guard, whose ends point to the pommel. Very few original swords with this form have been preserved.

Photo: Arms & Armor

A Gothic bastard sword with an unusual cross-guard (artwork from an altarpiece by Albrecht Dürer, around 1504).

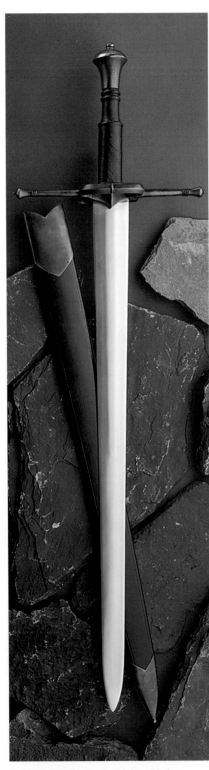

A rare bastard sword with knuckle bow guard that does not fit into the system – at just one meter, its small size is striking.

Photo: Museum Replicas

The so-called Black Prince's Sword is a classic example of type XVa.

Photo: Arms & Armor

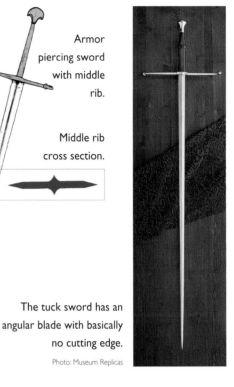

Armor piercing sword with middle rib.

Middle rib cross section.

The tuck sword has an angular blade with basically no cutting edge.

Photo: Museum Replicas

Cross section of a tuck sword blade.

At times, swords were used to effectively bore through (drawing after the *Codex Wallerstein*).

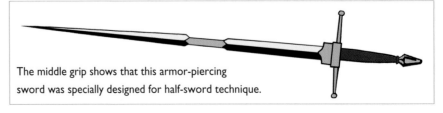

The middle grip shows that this armor-piercing sword was specially designed for half-sword technique.

used for fencing in armor show a sword with a spherical pommel, which has additional barb. This is essentially a sword with a "morning star [spiked] pommel" (page 97). The differences between fencing with or without armor, suggest that these weapons are specifically designed to be used against armored opponents. To my knowledge, unfortunately, no real examples of such sword have been preserved, so that reconstructing a swords and practical test are required to find out whether they offer any advantages over normal fencing swords for dueling in armor. It is worth mentioning that such a sword would contradict the teachings of Master Vadis, who expressly recommends a rounded pommel, which you can also grasp.

Towards the end of the Late Middle Ages, during the transitional phase to the Renaissance, we see more and more small details on medieval swords that actually already belong to the Renaissance. One such detail is added elements to the cross-guard, such as bows, rings, or small shell guards (internationally designated a "complex hilt"). When the swordsman fights without a shield, these pieces function as additional protection for the sword hand. Later, swords were developed with a more complicated bow guard system—these transitional swords represent the connecting link (page 99) to the modern broadsword. In addition to the types with additional guard rings, in 1500 some special pieces appeared, such as battle swords featuring the figure eight cross-guards of a *Katzbalger* or pretzel-shaped knotted guards.

The sword on page 100 (left) is a very rare and interesting specimen. The original was probably made around 1510 in Germany and is—at least as far as the grip is concerned—a classic bastard sword with two symmetrical knuckle bow guards. The pommel has a flattened pear shape (in international parlance, this is called a scent-stopper). But any similarity to other swords from this era ends here. The blade is very broad and has a flat, lenticular cross-section with a partial, very shallow fuller. Basically, it conforms

to a High Middle Ages cutting sword from group 1, rather than the usual late medieval design. The second difference is in the proportions. With a total length of 38.7 inches (98.5 centimeters), the blade is only 29.9 inches (76 centimeters) long—so it corresponds to the blade of a one-handed sword (the blade of an average bastard sword is at least about 35.4 inches [90 centimeters] long). This sword is a fine example of how, despite all the categorization, specimens are found which don't fit into any system.

In the heyday of the long-sword, we can distinguish eight different types, as presented below.

TYPE XVA: This narrow bastard sword is perhaps the most striking long-sword type in group 2. The blade tapers sharply—the cutting edges are almost straight—and has a diamond-shaped cross section without a fuller: this is primarily a thrusting blade.

Using either the hand-and-a-half or two-handed grip, the second hand could make a forceful thrust; you could basically bore into your opponent. Therefore, this sword type is sometimes referred to as a *Bohrschwert* [literally, "boring sword"; armor piercing sword]. The blade length averages 31.4-35.4 inches (80 to 90 centimeters); grip length 7.0-9.0 inches (18 to 23 centimeters). Type XVa was most widely used in the 13th to 15th centuries, but remained relatively common up to the beginning of the 16th century.

A classic example of type XVa is the so-called "Black Prince's Sword" (page 100). Edward Plantagenet (1330-76), the Prince of Wales, was known as an outstanding military leader; he earned his sobriquet, the Black Prince, at the Battle of Crecy (1346) because of his dark armor. His sword, which hung over his grave in Canterbury Cathedral, was stolen during the Cromwell's rule. Shortly after World War II, a sword appeared which showed various indications that it might be the missing sword. However, in contrast to the case of the sword of Edward III—the Black Prince's father—this cannot be established exactly.

XVIa sword.

Photo: Albion Armorers

The sword blade is about 33.8 inches (86 centimeters) long; it almost qualifies as an archetypal XVa sword. In addition, the hilt is a beautiful example of family D: it has a disc pommel and tapering cross-guard with rhombic cross section and slightly up-turned ends. The *Bohrschwert* or armor-piercing sword to its right is a very late example of an XVa (early 16th century). The blade has a pronounced middle rib. With a blade length of just 35.8 inches (91 centimeters), the total length is less than 45.2 inches (115 centimeters), and it weighs 2.7 pounds (1.25 kilograms).

A *Panzerstecher*, tuck sword in English, is a special kind of armor-piercing sword. These weapons have a very narrow, three- or four-edged blade that has almost no cutting edge—you can only use it to pierce into the gaps in your opponent's armor. The specimen pictured on page 100 probably dates from the first half of the 16th century. This replica is about 50.0 inches (127 centimeters) long and weighs 2.4 pounds (1.1 kilograms). These armor-piercing swords include special sorts, with a handgrip in the middle of the blade, specifically designed for half-sword technique. Armor piercing swords appear towards the end of the 14th century and continue in use in Eastern Europe until the 17th century.

TYPE XVIA: This bastard sword has a blade designed both for cutting as well as thrusting. The fuller usually runs about a third to halfway down the blade: This part of the blade has the cross section of a cutting sword. The other part is a flat diamond cross section blade. In contrast to the one-handed type XVI, these often also have hexagonal blades. At the bottom, the blade tapers much more sharply than at the top. The blade averages 31.4-33.4 inches (80 to 85 centimeters), and the grip 5.9-9.0 inches (15 to 23 centimeters), long. XVIa swords occurred mainly in the 14th century, in the period of transition from chainmail to plate armor.

The XVIa sword pictured at left dates from the mid-15th century. While the blade comes from the famous Passau workshops, we can see from the mounting that it was made by an Italian sword-finisher. It has a faceted scent-stopper pommel with octagonal cross section. The original shows signs of much use, but also careful polishing and care. With a total length of nearly 45.6 inches (116 centimeters), the blade is about 35.4 inches (90 centimeters) long, and it weighs 3.5 pounds (1.6 kilograms).

The XVIa sword at right above, comes from the first half of the 14th century; its six-edged blade is barely 33.0 inches (84 centimeters) long. While the pommel has a more or less normal disc shape, the cross-guard is especially exotic. It is both very short, and has very rare cone-shaped ends.

TYPE XVII: Here we include bastard- or two-handed swords with slender, very sharply tapered blades. The blade cross section is very thick and almost always hexagonal; often there is also a shallow fuller in the upper part of the blade. Blade length averages 31.4-37.4 inches (80 to 95 centimeters), but specimens are also found with blades more than 39.3 inches (1 meter) long. Due to their massive blades, XVII swords are very heavy, with some large specimens weighing 5.5 pounds (2.5 kilograms). The weight, combined with the rigid and solid blade, suggests that they were used specifically against heavy plate armor—the sword is intended to deliver a forceful stroke against the opponent's armor.

Most XVII swords are pure weapons of war, thus, "battle swords." Type XVIIs were in use from the mid-14th until the middle of the 15th century.

The XVII sword pictured on page 103 (center) was forged in the late 14th century. In a total length of 53.1 inches (135 centimeters), the blade is 41.7 inches (106 centimeters) long. It weighs just under 4.8 pounds (2.2 kilograms).

Below, we find an especially typical type XVII. This sword, from the late 14th century, belongs to the Sempach family. A characteristic Sempach type feature is a faceted, triangular pommel. It is named after a find made in the cloister church in Königsfelden, near Aarau, Switzerland. Swords of this type were found in the tombs of two Austrian knights, Friedrich von Greiffenstein and Friedrich von Tarant, who both fell in the Battle of Sempach in 1386.

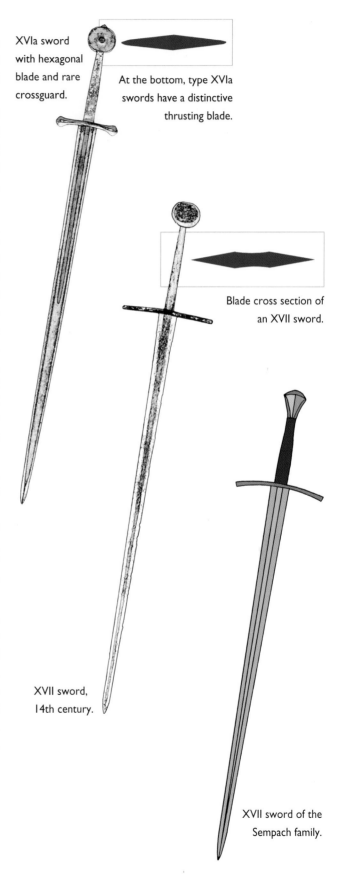

XVIa sword with hexagonal blade and rare crossguard.

At the bottom, type XVIa swords have a distinctive thrusting blade.

Blade cross section of an XVII sword.

XVII sword, 14th century.

XVII sword of the Sempach family.

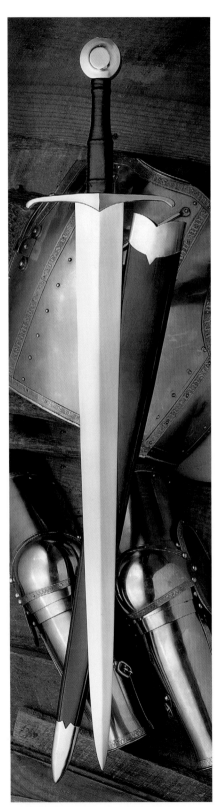

A very broad and solid type XVIIIc sword, late 14th century.

Photo: Museum Replicas

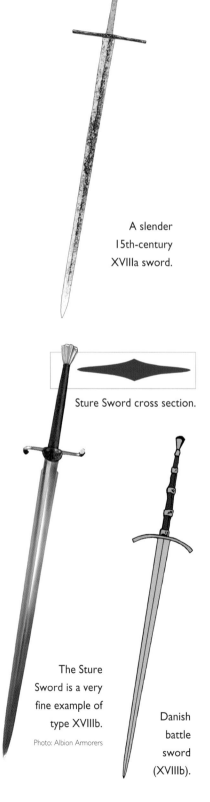

A slender 15th-century XVIIIa sword.

Sture Sword cross section.

The Sture Sword is a very fine example of type XVIIIb.

Photo: Albion Armorers

Danish battle sword (XVIIIb).

This very rare type XIX long-sword is distinguished by a long ricasso with two deep flutes.

Photo: Museum Replicas

TYPE XVIIIA: The blades of the type XVIIIa are very well suited for delivering a cut as well as a thrust, and these swords were very popular and widely used. XVIIIa is usually a bastard sword with a blade averaging 31.4-33.4 inches (80 to 85 centimeters) and a grip of about 5.1 inches (13 centimeters) long. The cross section is a flat diamond shape, and many specimens have a short fuller in the upper third area. Type XVIIIa was in use mainly from the mid-14th to halfway through the 15th centuries. Besides the XVIIIa, we can also differentiate between two subcategories, XVIIIb and XVIIIc (in his original outlines from the 1960s, Oakeshott had also distinguished between types XVIIId and XVIIIe, but these were eliminated in his revised typology).

The sword on this page is one of the most striking and beautiful examples of an XVIIIa. The original was initially in a private collection, but is now stated to be missing. We have here a perfect example of an elegant weapon for a higher-ranking warrior, which dates back to the beginning of the 15th century. The blade is engraved with two wolves—the mark of the famous Passau blade smiths—and the disc pommel is engraved with a lion crest. Some scholars conclude, because of its Bavarian origin and coat of arms, that this sword belonged to a member of the Hapsburg dynasty, specifically, Albrecht II (1397-1439), Duke of Austria and King of Hungary and Bohemia. The replica is 44.0 inches (112 centimeters) long and weighs about 3.0 pounds (1.4 kilograms).

The XVIIIa sword on page 104 (top center) is very slender (with a slightly longer grip, it would fall into category XVIIIb) and thus very light, despite its size. This weapon has a blade length of 35.8 inches (91 centimeters), is overall 46.4 inches (118 centimeters) long and weighs 2.4 pounds (1.1 kilograms).

As already stated, we actually have to distinguish between categories XVIIIb and XVIIIc: "XVIIIb is a bastard sword with a very long grip, while XVIIIc is one with a shorter handle," (Oakeshott, 1994, p.171).

The grip length on type XVIIIb swords is about 9.8-11.0 inches (25 to 28 centimeters); blade length 35.4-41.3 inches (90-105 centimeters).

The blade is very narrow and generally has no fuller. XVIIIb swords were in use during the transition period from the 15th to 16th centuries; a very good example is the Sture Sword, already described.

Another XVIIIb sword is Danish, from the second half of the 15th century. In contrast to the elegant Sture Sword (shown on page 104, bottom center), right next to it, here we find a pure battle sword: this sword is definitely meant only for war.

As is more common on battle swords with such long grips, we find a number of iron reinforcement rings on the wooden grip. Highly unusual, however, are its dimensions, which make this specimen stand out even among battle swords: The blade is 44.8 inches (114 centimeters) long, the sword in total 63.7 inches (162 centimeters) long (in the 1960s Oakeshott typology, this is type XVIIIe). Although this sword's size matches the already purely ceremonial Renaissance two-handed specimens, it is clearly specifically designed for use as a weapon. Some similar swords have been found in Denmark, and we can justifiably speak of a "Danish" type.

Type XVIIIc have blades on average 33.8 inches (86 centimeters) long, and the grip is 5.9-7.8 inches (15 to 20 centimeters) long. The sword in the large photo at left on page 104 is a very interesting type XVIIIc. Its origin is unknown, but it is likely that this sword dates from around the second half of the 14th century. The blade is very wide and solid. The replica is overall a meter long (31.4-inch [80 centimeter] blade length) and weighs about 2.6 pounds (1.2 kilograms).

Type XVIIIa swords were obviously very popular and in widespread use.

Photo: Pieces of History

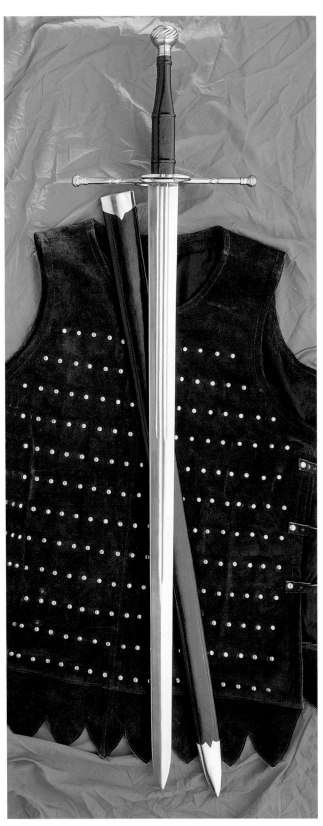

A late example of type XX, beginning of the 16th century.

Photo: Museum Replicas

A special variant of type XX. We have here five instead of three short fullers, in staggered arrangement. Probably German, beginning of the 15th century.

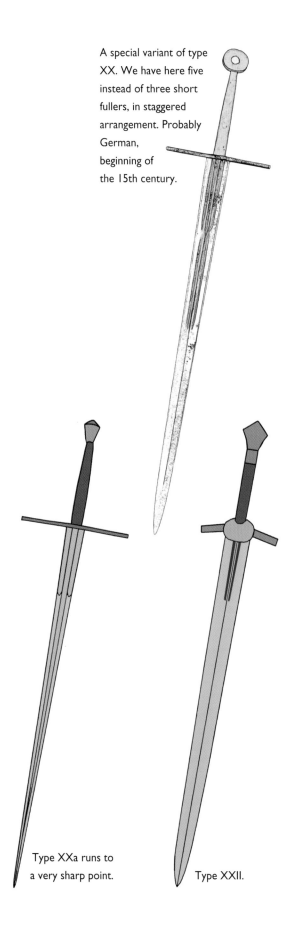

Type XXa runs to a very sharp point.

Type XXII.

TYPE XIX: XIX long-swords are among the rarest types of all. For some time, even Oakeshott himself assumed that this type included only one-handed swords. We can differentiate two versions of the XIX long-sword. One is an elongated version of the "short" swords: The blade cross section is hexagonal; the cutting edges almost parallel: it has a short ricasso. The surviving examples of this version come mostly from the first half of the 16th century and have different types of knuckle bow guards. These are essentially transitional forms to the broadsword, and the XIX sword at right on page 124 is an excellent example.

The second version dates from the first half of the 15th century; it is distinguished as type XIX by its ricasso with two flutes (page 104, right). In contrast to the other versions, however, the ricasso is very long, and extends almost a quarter of the way down the blade. The flutes in the ricasso flank a narrow fuller, which is about half as long as the blade. The blade is narrow and tapers slightly; length is about 37.4 inches (95 centimeters). In contrast to one-handed type XIX swords, here the blade cross section is not always hexagonal, but often a four-sided rhombic shape.

The long ricasso lets the swordsman grasp the weapon with his left hand, as for a Renaissance two-handed sword, making it possible to guide it more accurately. The replica shown is based loosely on two Italian originals. Overall length is just under 48.0 inches (122 centimeters) and the blade is 37.7 inches (96 centimeters) long; its weight amounts to 3.0 pounds (1.4 kilograms).

After the death of Ewart Oakeshott, there was a parting of the ways about the latter version. Although he assigned this piece to type XIX in his last work, *Records of the Medieval Sword*, it really does not match the criteria he laid down for type XIX. Some views assigned it meanwhile to type XXa, but the flutes in the ricasso do not correspond to a typical XX or XXa fuller, while the blade also does not taper sharply enough. Unfortunately, Oakeshott left no explanation for his classification as XIX. It is probably most useful to consider it a very "exotic" variant of type XIX.

Companion Knives and Awls

Mercenary soldiers and *Landsknechte* ["land servitors," another term for mercenary] travelled light. Their equipment had to be practical and multifunctional. Many plain battle swords had scabbards fitted with holders for a set of tools. These tools were primarily a small, very sharp companion knife for fine cutting work and an awl, as a kind of universal tool. Sometimes we also find a small sharpener instead of an awl.

It is interesting that we also find holders for a complete set of tools in the Japanese *buke-zukuri* mounting. There we also find a companion knife (*kogatana*), however the sword needle (*kogai*) has a different function than an awl, although these two pieces of cutlery appear strikingly similar (see Japanese swords).

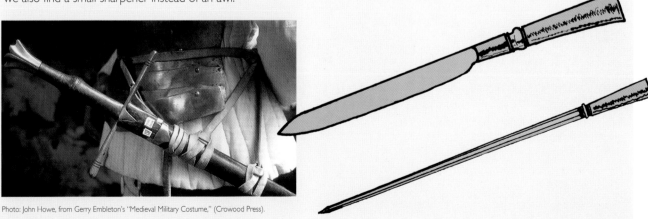

Photo: John Howe, from Gerry Embleton's "Medieval Military Costume," (Crowood Press).

TYPE XX: These are large bastard swords, but real two-handed weapons are also included here. Grip length is usually 7.8-9.8 inches (20-25 centimeters), blade length between 35.4-39.3 inches (90-100 centimeters). The blade is broad, relatively straight, and ends in a sharp point. The swords usually have two short parallel fullers or three staggered ones, with the third lying either below the other two or flanked by them. XX swords were in use mainly in the 14th and 15th centuries. The XX sword shown here (page 106 top right) was forged at the beginning of the 15th century. The blade has five instead of three staggered fullers. Total length is 49.6 inches (126 centimeters); blade length 38.5 inches (98 centimeters). This two-handed weapon weighs 4.8 pounds (2.2 kilograms).

The sword in the large picture at left on page 106 is a fine example of a late type XX. The original is probably of German origin and dates from the first quarter of the 16th century. There are two oval guard rings on both sides of the cross-guard to better protect the hands—the first indications of a transition to Renaissance design. The replica is 47.2 inches (120 centimeters) long and weighs 3.5 pounds (1.6 kilograms).

TYPE XXA: On type XXa blades, the fullers are arranged as on type XX. However, XXa blades run to a sharper point. XXa swords occur mainly in the 14th and 15 centuries. The sword pictured on page 106 is from the first half of the 15th century.

TYPE XXII: Long-swords of this type are extremely rare; they are mostly symbolic bearing swords from the beginning of the Renaissance. The blade is wide and flat, it tapers rather moderately, and then runs to a gentle curve at the point. The fullers are short and narrow, in pairs at the base of the blade.

Distinctive Forms

Again and again, individual swords appear, which are difficult or impossible to categorize and often represent extreme designs. You could classify the sword pictured right, for example, as a two-handed, almost 49.2-inch (125 centimeter) long *cinquedea* because of its blade profile. The blade is a remarkable 6.6 inches (16.8 centimeters) wide at the base.

Even if this blade resembles that of a *cinquedea* and the sword originated in Italy, the total design is so rare and extreme, that it can only be classified as an absolutely special case.

Distinctive Forms

The *Bidenhänder*, the two-handed sword of the Renaissance, can be clearly distinguished from the battle swords of the Middle Ages (although the term battle sword is often used also here). The differences lie not only in details of the design, but especially in length and weight, as well as how it is wielded in battle.

The two-handed sword has a total length of 62.9-70.8 inches (160-180 centimeters) (the sword shown at right, at 58.0 inches [147.5 centimeters] long, is among the smaller specimens). These swords had no scabbards; they were carried over the shoulder like a pike. The upper part of the blade is not sharpened, but usually covered with leather. This makes it possible to grasp the blade with your hand, making the sword at least somewhat easier to handle (or indeed possible at all). Very often the blade has additional *Parierhaken* or parrying hooks at the end of the unsharpened portion. It is clear that the Renaissance two-handed sword could not be used like a medieval battle sword. If it were still used in battle at all, this was done by foot soldiers (*Gassenhauer*, units of light armored swordsmen) to make a breach in the ranks of the enemy spears. Because these were essentially suicide missions and only the strongest men could really use a two-handed sword, they got double pay [Sold] which is why they were also called *Doppelsöldner*.

During the 16th century, two handed swords were used less and less for military purposes; they become more ceremonial weapons. Honor guards were equipped with them, for example, because these massive swords made a big impression. The two handed sword was carried at the front as a bearing sword. These swords became larger (often two meters long) and ever more pretentious, with the cross-guards fancily curved and ornamented, with the blades sometimes given a wavy polish (called *Flamberge*).

The bearing swords carried by Prince Edward of Wales' attending guards while he was Earl of Chester (1475-1483), hold the size record. These swords are no less than 88.9 inches (2.26 meters) long – there is no question that such monster swords could have any practical purpose.

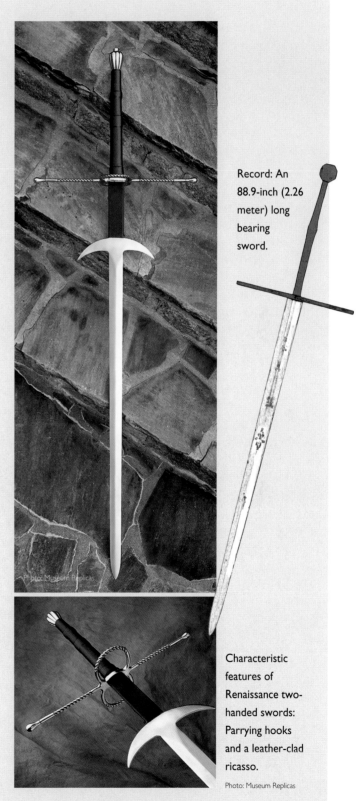

Photo: Museum Replicas

Record: An 88.9-inch (2.26 meter) long bearing sword.

Characteristic features of Renaissance two-handed swords: Parrying hooks and a leather-clad ricasso.

Photo: Museum Replicas

7.4 Sabers and Scimitars

"Take note and know, that you really cannot say, write or explain anything really meaningful about fencing, as you can likely show it and point it out as well as possible by hand. So use thy senses, and this way see it better, thus practice it more for pleasure, this way thou art mindful of it all the more in earnest. For practice is better than skill, thy practice is worth something, even without skill, but skill is not worth much without practice."

– (Anonymous 14th-century sword master)

Sabers and scimitars are only a marginal group among medieval edged weapons. In contrast to the later centuries, when the saber represented a major weapon, it was rather insignificant during the Middle Ages. I will introduce below the few curved swords which played a role in the Middle Ages.

Before we deal with the individual types, we first require a few basics. The first question is: How to actually distinguish between saber and scimitar?:

- A saber has a curved, single-edged blade and an asymmetrical grip that usually curves opposite to the blade.
- A scimitar characteristically has a curved, single-edged blade and a straight, symmetrical grip. The blade is usually wider and heavier than a saber's.
- According to this definition, samurai swords are actually sabers (in French, the term "samurai sword" is actually used). However, the term "samurai sword" is here so firmly anchored in our consciousness, that it would be ridiculous to insist on the correct scientific name.

At this point we must note a few special characteristics of a curved blade which are important for fighting with a saber:

- A curved blade cuts significantly better than a straight edge. This is because a curved cutting edge is longer, with the same blade length. Due to the curvature, even a direct stroke has a dragging or pulling, and thus cutting, effect. With one blow, a curved blade "eats" its way into the body more forcefully than a straight sword.

- Most sabers have a pistol grip handle, which is slightly curved opposite to the blade. This type of grip allows for a better transfer of force from the wrist to the weapon.
- The curved blade either greatly impedes, or even makes it impossible, to deliver a thrust (depending on the curvature). Therefore, sabers are primarily classified as weapons for cutting rather than thrusting.

Unlike other types of swords, the saber has one principle deployment: the saber is a cavalry weapon. This seems a bit contradictory, because the Western knight's main weapon was certainly a straight, double-edged sword. Therefore, we should be specific: the saber is a weapon for mounted men, for a light, only lightly armored cavalry. Although a light saber can do little against heavy steel body armor, it is very effective against lightly armored opponents. As already mentioned, it creates primarily a pulling-cutting effect. This can be put to excellent use while riding a very fast horse. We must also mention here, however, that this effect can also reach its limits. Making the blade too curved is counterproductive, and such a saber is only of very limited use. A gentle curve is ideal to get the best effect.

Another effect is that if you swing a saber at a gallop, the curved blade compensates better for any errors in precision due to the high speed, than a straight blade can. The excellent cutting action also ensures that you can make a saber lighter than a sword—this weight reduction is of enormous importance for equestrian peoples. Given these facts, it is no wonder that the saber developed into a cavalry weapon.

In the Middle Ages, the saber was used mainly in the East and in Eastern Europe; it was not actually used in the rest of Europe, because of the heavy armor worn there. This changed in the Late Middle Ages and early Renaissance. The European population became increasingly involved in conflicts with mounted warriors from the East. In action against these mounted fighters, often wearing only light chainmail, the saber proved to be surprisingly effective. The more that body armor was abandoned as the use of firearms became more common, the more widespread use of sabers became, until by the 18th century it became the most fashionable weapon throughout Europe.

To understand a saber properly, it is necessary to introduce some new concepts. It is logical that a saber's curved blade cannot be measured in the "normal" way. Therefore, a special system was developed to do this. Two measurements are important:

- Blade length (sometimes also known, in contrast to straight swords, as "bowstring length") is measured by a straight vector from the base to the point.
- Blade curvature: Measures the longest distance of the blade from the vector.

These two figures make it possible to specify a blade's curvature fairly accurately (for Japanese swords, there are many other important details beyond these two dimensions, which have an entirely separate nomenclature). In addition to blade length and curvature, the *yelman* or *yalman* is also an important detail: this Tartar expression refers to the broader, double-edged section of the blade at the point. In addition, sabers with pistol grips usually have no pommel, but a so-called grip cap.

As already noted, few types of sabers were used during the European Middle Ages. If at all, it appeared in the Eastern regions. The saber was first brought to Europe by southern Russian or Tartar equestrian peoples, such as the Avars. The earliest archaeological finds of sabers in Europe come from Avar graves in Pannonia, dating from the 7th century. However, the Avars were soon supplanted by Frankish warriors. In the 8th century, another equestrian people invaded the Danube plain and settled there: the Hungarians. The typical 9th or 10th-century Hungarian saber has a long, slightly curved blade with more or less pronounced *yelman*. The grip is curved pistol shape, the cross-guards often slightly curved down, and some are made thicker at the end. This pagan type of saber was called the *gladius hunnicus* by Western Christians, and in the German translation of the *Waltari-Lied* (*Song of Walter*) the term "*hunnisches Halbschwert*" (Hun half-sword) is used.

It is interesting that Charlemagne's saber—also known as Attila's saber—could be considered the prototype for this type of sword. However, things are not quite so simple, because the origin of this weapon is still an unsolved mystery. According to legend, the sword was taken from Charlemagne's tomb in the Aachen Cathedral in the year 1000 by Otto III. There is, however, no reliable historical evidence for this. Another legend is reported by historian Lambert von Hersfeld in the 11th century: the saber once belonged to Mars, god of war. A shepherd found it and gave it to Attila the Hun (406-453). Later, it came to the German King Henry IV, who gave it to a friend named Luitpold von Meersburg. He had an accident and fell from his horse right onto the blade. The king was saddened by the death of his friend, took back the sword, and added it to the Imperial regalia, for the king to use to dub his knights. Apart from the accident at Meersburg, nothing from this story can be proven. Other theories are much more down to earth: that the saber was a gift from Harun al-Rashid to Charlemagne, or that Charlemagne captured it during his campaigns against the Avars. The only certain conclusion is that, at some point, the weapon appeared among the Imperial regalia in Aachen and later simply became a part of them.

As is so often the case, myths and legends cannot be carried over into reality. The fact is that the saber is neither of Avar origin, nor dates from the time of Charlemagne (742-814). Its origin can be dated to the period around 900 to 950. In addition, this weapon combines completely different style elements, making it unique. The gilded grip is decorated in typical Western style with a braid motif, which is also interpreted as Hasidic-Arab work. The jeweled band on the grip was added much later and has no significance for determining its origin. In contrast, the gold-inlaid blade has a typical oriental shape—also found in rare Turkish and southern Russian blades. The grip covering, however, is not of leather but made of skate or ray skin. Charlemagne's saber is thus a unique mix of East and West, and its mysteries will occupy science for some time to come. However, its basic form corresponds to those of the previously described Hungarian sabers as well as some 10th-century Russian weapons. As a result, we can at least classify this saber as "Eastern European-Russian".

These early Hungarian sabers fell victim to rapprochement with the West. After their disastrous defeat at the Battle of Lechfeld (955), the Hungarians

The curved blade gives the sword stroke a pulling-cutting effect. In the photo, the so-called "Charlemagne's saber." Easily recognizable: the broader, double-edged point (*yelman*).

Photo: Pieces of History

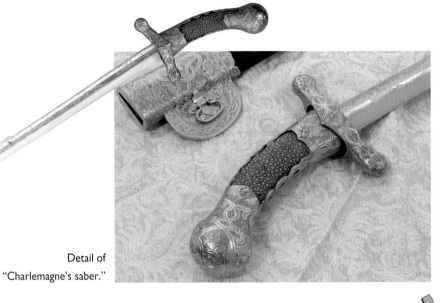

Detail of "Charlemagne's saber."

Blade cross section of a falchion from the period around 1500. The high, flat wedge sharpening makes this scimitar an effective cutting weapon.

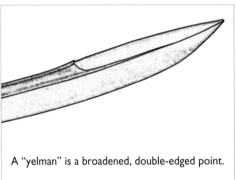

A "yelman" is a broadened, double-edged point.

Hungarian saber – *gladius hunnicus* – from the 10th century.

The curved blade shape is measured in two dimensions: The length is measured in a straight line from the point to the base of the blade (red), and the blade curvature shows the degree of curvature (green).

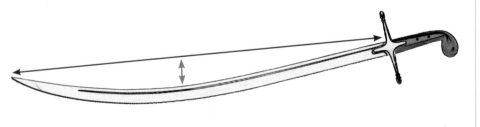

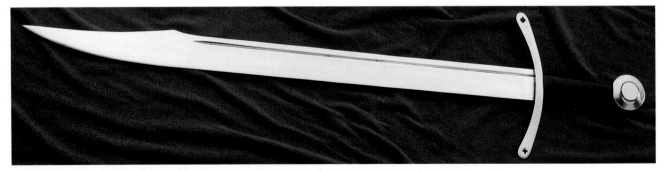

A falchion is a heavy, short scimitar of the High Middle Ages. The piece shown here is a replica of the so-called Thorpe Falchion, a type I weapon from the 14th century.

Photo: Museum Replicas

were Christianized and have since been a nation with a mixed Western and Oriental culture. In particular, the Hungarian nobility very rapidly acquired Western weapons, especially the straight, double-edged sword, gradually displacing the saber among the Hungarian armaments. This situation changed when, in the Late Middle Ages, a new equestrian people, the Turks, pushed into Hungary.

While the saber played only a small role throughout the European Middle Ages, in the High Middle Ages, we come across a fascinating scimitar in Europe, internationally known as the falchion. This probably derives from the Latin *falx* (sense). In French, it is called a *fauchon* (also *baudelaire*), and in Italian a *storta*. The German name is *Malchus* (after John 18:10):

> Then Simon Peter having a sword, he drew it out and struck the high priest's servant, and cut off his right ear. And the servant's name was Malchus.

The falchion is a scimitar with a short, heavy cutting blade. The center of balance is shifted much more towards the point, and the edges are polished either to a slightly rounded (convex) or flattened wedge shape. The grip corresponds to those of contemporary one-handed swords. We can distinguish two main categories based on the blade:

- Falchion type I: Curved blade with a convex point (clip point in English), with a section of the back edge sharpened. This type corresponds to Oriental sabers and is presumed to have come to Europe through the Crusades.
- Falchion type II: Blade with a straight back and asymmetrical, curved cutting edge. This type is quite rare and is actually only found in the British Isles. According to one hypothesis, this is a cross between type I and the early medieval seax.

There are of course various mixtures of types I and II, but these are much less common than the two main groups. The falchion always remained a "footnote" compared to the double-edged sword, but there are pieces of particular significance. One example is the Conyers falchion. According to legend, in the 11th century, Sir John Conyers used it to slay the Sockburn

Worm. This deed brought his family a hereditary fief in Durham County, and the falchion was the symbol of their feudal power. Well into the 18th century, the tradition persisted that the inauguration of the new Bishops of Durham was celebrated in a ceremony including the Conyers falchion. The falchion itself is 35.0 inches (89 centimeters) long with a blade length of 28.7 inches (73 centimeters) and weighs 2.8 pounds (1.3 kilograms). Contrary to the legend, the shape and the crest on the disc pommel allow us to accept the 13th century as the period of its origin—this is not the original weapon of Sir John Conyers. What kind of sword he actually used, and why a falchion of all things was chosen as the family sword, is unknown.

The type I falchion was found throughout Europe after 1100, but only achieved some amount of popularity beginning in the 14th century. In particular, the falchion was used by painters and artists because of its characteristic appearance. However, real, existing fighting weapons and passages in the fencing books show that this scimitar was also a popular combat weapon. The falchion remained rare in Western Europe, but in the Mediterranean countries (especially Italy), it was very popular, and developed during the Renaissance into a fashionable weapon for the upper class bourgeoisie and the nobility. These "modern falchions" differ from their High Middle Ages predecessors—which were weapons for common soldiers—especially in the complicated design of the cross-guards and lavish ornamentation.

The "long knife" is closely related to both falchion and seax: this is a cutting weapon that only appeared in the Late Middle Ages, and was in use in the German speaking countries (especially southern Germany and Switzerland). The long knife is primarily a weapon for the general population (farmers, teamsters, craftsmen), which is why historians also call it the *Hauswehr* or *Bauernwehr* [household or peasant defense weapon]. Later, however, these weapons also crop up in the fencing books (some fencing masters even specialized in their use)—these sources make clear that during the Middle Ages, these weapons were simply known as a "(long) knife" (in Switzerland, they were also called a *Rugger*). The background for the creation of these weapons, is that only the nobility, knights, and free privileged citizens were allowed to wear a real sword.

The *Dussack*

The *Dussack* (not to be confused with a *dussage* or *Dussäge* [tesack]) was used as a long knife mainly in German-speaking countries. This is a short, clumsy looking cutting weapon that basically consists only of a blade – that is, a flat piece of steel. The grip is a hole for the finger forged into the piece of steel, and it has no guard at all. The *Dussack* pictured is from Bohemia (probably early 16th century), it is just under 24.4 inches (62 centimeters) long.

Although the *Dussack* apparently had no special significance, from the 16th to the 18th centuries, German fencing masters taught their students how to wield it, as evidenced by the fencing books, and was an integral feature of the fencing schools.

Fighting with a Dussack
(drawing from a medieval picture).

However, the peasantry also required some defense against robbers. Therefore, they carried a more or less long knife, which the same laws, which prohibited them from carrying swords, expressly allowed them to possess (such as the *Bayrischen Landfrieden* [Bavarian ordnances] of 1244).

The size of the knife varies considerably—we find blade lengths of just over 7.8 inches (20 centimeters) to about 23.6 inches (60 centimeters). Thus, it can be considered either a large combat knife or a weapon in the form of a "short saber". It is not always easy to distinguish a "long knife" from a type I falchion. The main difference is the design of the grip. While a falchion has the same grip as a sword, on the long knives, the design is completely different. They are usually asymmetrical and have no pommel. The tang goes right through the grip, and the wooden or bone grip panels are riveted on. Blade shapes vary widely. The short saber almost always has a broad and slightly curved blade. Sometimes you see a short cross-guard, and in some cases a small shell-shaped second guard or guard ring. There is also a two-handed version of the long knife, known as a *Kriegsmesser* or "war knife" (more on this in the next chapter).

A typical British weapon is closely related to these long knives: the hanger. The hanger is a short, broad-bladed saber, which became popular among the landed gentry of the British Isles beginning in the 17th century. Initially, a hanger was considered a hunting weapon, which was also used in the country as a weapon for civilian self-defense. But later, they found their way into military armaments. It is possible to consider the hanger a precursor of the cutlass, but it was almost certainly the ancestor of the *Hirschfänger* [deer hunting knife].

In contrast to the German *Messer* [knife], the hanger is not a much-needed self-defense weapon for the peasantry, but a weapon of the higher ranking, landed gentry. Therefore, in addition to relatively plain pieces, there are also many highly decorated examples. We could say much more here, but since the hanger is not a medieval weapon, this is sufficient at this point.

The falchion and long knife are exceptions in a world dominated by the straight double-edged sword. This situation would change slowly due to the Turkish

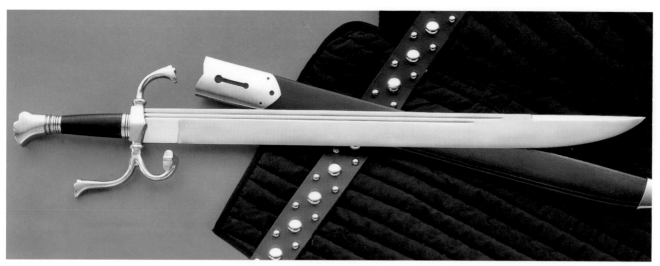

The falchion was a fashionable weapon during the 15th and 16th centuries, as the medieval cross hilt was progressively altered.

Photos: Museum Replicas

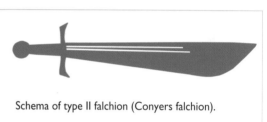

Schema of type II falchion (Conyers falchion).

Dueling with
long knives.

Photo: Agilitas.tv

The "common" man was only
allowed to carry a more or
less long knife for self defense.

Photo: Traumschmiede/Eckhardt

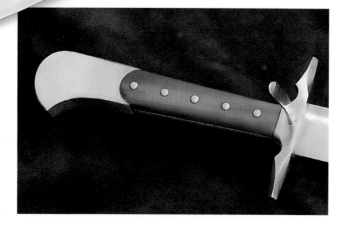

On a long knife, the grip panels were
riveted to the tang. The small shell
guard, the *Wehrnagel* or defensive
needle, was also characteristic.

Photo: Traumschmiede/Eckhardt

Hanger, around 1610,
English or Scottish.

The saber of
Mehmed II, the
Conqueror.

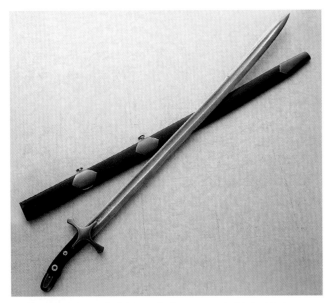

Early form of the Turkish *kilij*, with almost straight blade. Modern
interpretation of Damascus steel, by swordsmith by Vince Evans.

Photo: Vince Evans/Point Seven

Initially Straight

Contrary to popular belief, the "original" Islamic sword
was not curved, but straight and double-edged, like those
of Western knights. The saber only appeared in the 9th
century, and then became increasingly more common.
In the 14th century, straight swords and sabers were
about equally widespread, but then the saber increasingly
became the trendsetter in the Islamic world.

expansion. Although it may be hard to imagine today,
Turkey was a world power during the Late Middle
Ages and Renaissance. Since the 14th century, the
Ottoman Empire had penetrated ever farther into
Europe by way of the Balkans. In 1453, Constantinople
fell to Mehmed the Conqueror, and in 1529, Turks
were at the gates of Vienna for the first time. They
brought the saber with them, and here for the first
time, the advantages of this weapon were recognized
by the European countries outside the immediate
neighborhood of Turkey.

This was further aided by another factor: in the
late 15th and early 16th centuries, the introduction
of firearms radically changed military technology
(more on this in the chapter on the broadsword). The
effect was that body armor was worn less and less,
until, at the end, only the cuirass (breastplate) and
the helmet remained. Due to this development, the
light, one-handed cavalry saber all at once represented
a weapon to take seriously, and so, the various types
of Oriental sabers began to spread across Europe.
Although the saber mainly prevailed in Poland and
Hungary, it is also found in the western and northern
European countries. These were mostly captured
weapons, but also sabers forged in Europe itself,
sometimes with European hilts on genuine Oriental
blades. These sabers were mostly custom-made
weapons for fashion-conscious aristocrats—often
Turkish blades were fitted with new grips and scabbards
forged by European ornamental metalsmiths. Weapons
of this type were often decorated with gold, silver
and precious stones. "The saber was at that time no
general European military weapon, but usually only
an exclusive treasure," (Seitz, vol.1, p.353). In contrast,
the saber virtually became a part of the national dress
in Poland and Hungary.

Two Oriental saber types became particularly
widespread in Europe: the Turkish and Persian types.
The Turkish saber had the greatest impact on Europe.
We will not discuss here whether this is due to the fact
that the Turks are geographically Europe's closest
regional neighbor, or whether the Turkish type of saber
is more practical for use against European armor than
the other types. Both types have pistol-shaped curved
grips, with straight cross-guards with widened or
spherical ends. The cross-guard usually runs in two

tongues along the base of the blade—these tongues fit into a recess on the scabbard opening and hold the saber tight in the scabbard. There is no pommel, but instead the grip is more or less angled at the end. The tang does not extend through to the end of the grip, but is relatively wide and riveted two to three times to the grip panels (usually bone or ivory). This style of grip was known as the Mameluke grip during the 18th and 19th centuries.

The Turkish *kilij* saber has a broad, curved blade, usually with a distinctive *yelman*. The blades often have a wide fuller—sometimes the cross section is also T-shaped—and are 23.6-27.5 inches (60-70 centimeters) long. If the curvature was greater and/or the *yelman* very broad, the scabbard was slit down its back, which made it possible to draw the saber at all. The chape was flexible, and after the saber was drawn, it fell back over the slit to cover it.

The Persian *shamshir* (lion's tail) saber, also called a scimitar, is superficially very similar to the Turkish saber. However, the blade is usually much narrower and more curved, and it has no *yelman*. The blade cross section is wedge-shaped and flat (page 119). The term "scimitar" is now used incorrectly to mean all kinds of curved sabers and scimitars. To avoid misunderstandings, it is better to use *shamshir*.

As already stated, the saber began to spread into Europe beginning in the 15th century. Although it had a special status as a ceremonial weapon, there were also more and more relatively simple sabers, intended as weapons for common soldiers. Another group from the 16th and the early 17th centuries is known as the *deutschgefasster Säbel* ("German-mounted saber"). This was a saber with fully developed broadsword or basket hilt (see basket-hilt sword). These plain weapons were manufactured in Germany; the nobility liked to buy

Wootz – Damascus Steel from a Crucible

Many Oriental swords are made with a special kind of Damascus steel: Wootz. Wootz was (and is) often considered the only true Damascus steel, although today it is clear that the European forge or pattern welded steel was known much earlier than wootz, which can be dated earliest to the 14th century. This is because wootz does not have to be first welded together from different metals, but is already formed as the steel is melted, and therefore appears more "original" than pattern welded steel does.

Due to the way it is produced, wootz is also known as crucible or crystalline Damascus steel (sometimes also cast Damascus steel). Otherwise, it is known as *bulat* (Russian), *fulat* or *jauardar* (Arabic), these being only the most famous names. Wootz was produced mainly in India and the Persian or Arabian countries, and later in the Caucasus and Russia. Some of the exact details of how wootz was made remain unclear today, and for this reason there is still a certain atmosphere of mystery attached to this steel.

Wootz characteristically has an extremely high carbon content of 1.2 to 2.0 percent. This is the result of a melting process which probably looked like this: Small chunks of charcoal and pieces of two different sorts of iron were mixed with various plant products and heated in a closed crucible of fireproof clay for a day and a night. This then smelted into high-carbon wootz. The high carbon content made it necessary to take great care when forging objects from this steel.

There are a number of conflicting views on how hardening and tempering were done, so I will say nothing on this question. Etching was then done to create a blade of a color ranging from gray to black (the "black steel of Khorassan" was the most desirable).

them to arm their common foot soldiers. They were most widely used in Germany and Scandinavia. In Norway, they are also known as "Sinclair sabers." According to the story, they were seized as war booty from a troop of Scottish soldiers under the command of Captain Sinclair, who was fighting in Norway as a Swedish mercenary. The *Dussag* or *Dussäge* (not to be confused with the *Dussack*) comprise a special group of these Germam-mounted sabers. These have a hilt with a triangular shell guard, which is bent upwards towards the pommel (page 119).

The Two-Handed Saber

Although in our times, the concept of a curved, two-handed sword is associated almost exclusively with Japanese swords, there were also some typical two-handed sabers in late medieval Europe. Numerically, they represent one of the smallest sword groups, but are, in my opinion, one of the most fascinating. A very interesting specimen (shown on page 121, above) has, for example, a symmetrical grip and downward curved cross-guard (thus, actually a scimitar) and a blade whose profile has an almost startling resemblance to that of a samurai sword. This saber was probably made in Germany at the beginning of the 16th century. Total length is about 52.7 inches (134 centimeters), and weight about 3.0 pounds (1.4 kilograms).

The Hungarian two-handed saber is a particularly characteristic kind of weapon; it was widely used in the 15th century. In contrast to a *Kriegsmesser*, this type has a slightly curved grip and a flat rectangular or oval pommel, with a small stud at the center. The cross-guard consists of a broad flat band, in a horizontal S-curve, so that the ends form small hoops. The shape of the pommel and cross-guard correspond to contemporary Hungarian straight swords. The blades of the two-handed saber average nearly 35.4 inches (90 centimeters) long, are slightly curved and have a distinct *yelman*. The weapon shown is a total 42.9 inches (109 centimeters) long, with a blade length of 34.2 inches (87 centimeters), and weighs just 2.8 pounds (1.3 kilograms).

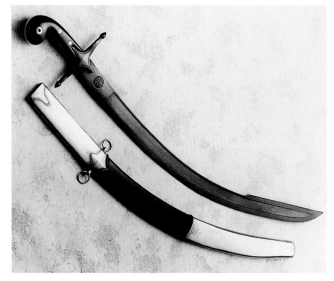

Kilij with "mameluk grip," sharply curved blade, and marked yelman. Modern interpretation made of Damascus steel with buffalo horn grip by swordsmith Vince Evans.

Photo: Vince Evans/Weyer of Toledo

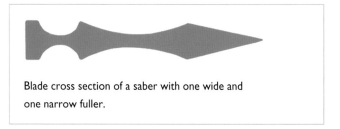

Blade cross section of a saber with one wide and one narrow fuller.

Landsknecht (mercenary) with a *Kriegsmesser* (war knife). These two-handed sabers were worn with no scabbard in a *Koppelschuh* (knife frog) (drawing after a 16th-century woodcut).

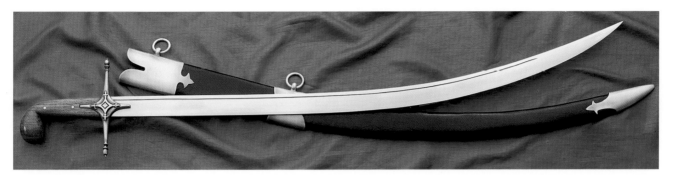

Persian *shamshir*.

Photo: Museum Replicas

Soldier with a war knife (drawing after woodcut "The 5th Commandment" by Hans Baldung Grien).

Grip section of a rather sumptuously decorated Sinclair saber.

Modern replica of a *Kriegsmesser*.

Photo: www.frankonia.de

A Turkish saber (*kilij*) from the 18th century.

Remnant of a *Kriegsmesser* (war knife) with a broken-off tang, end of the 15th century. On the tang, we can clearly see the typical rivet holes for the grip panels, while the *yelman* and slightly down curved cross-guard are rather unusual.

Dusägge – a plain saber with triangular shell guard, from the group of so-called German-mounted sabers.

Perhaps the most fascinating two-handed saber is known as a *Kriegsmesser* (war knife), or *Zweihändermesser* (two-handed knife) and was particularly widespread in German-speaking regions. This is a two-handed version of the long knife already discussed. While the latter is usually found in pictorial representations of village festivals or weddings, the two-handed knife occurs only in war situations, which is why the term "war knife" certainly is most apt.

The Chinese Saber

In the Chinese martial arts, the saber – *dao* – still has great importance. Although Chinese sabers come in different shapes, the *darn dao* (plum-blossom saber) was developed to an ideal form during the Song Dynasty (960-1279 AD).

Since that time, neither the *dao* nor the straight sword – *jian* – altered much until the 19th century. Over the centuries, the *darn dao* became the most widely distributed and used sword in China. At first glance, you might consider the *darn dao* clumsy, but anyone who has seen a demonstraton of this weapon knows that the opposite is the case. The *darn dao* is well-balanced and aerodynamically shaped, and thus is an effective weapon – technique for wielding the *dao* is fast and forceful.

The *darn dao* has a pistol-shaped curved grip with a solid metal pommel, with which you can deliver an effective backhand stroke. The hands are protected by a simple, but strongly made shell guard. Most remarkable, certainly, is the blade: The back is blunt along its whole length, so that the left hand can support the back for specific defensive techniques. The cutting edge is polished to different degrees of sharpness.

It is sharpest at the front of the point, because this is the offensive area of the weapon. The point itself is slightly rounded, but sharp. The lower, not as sharp area of the blade is mainly used for blocking techniques, while you counter using the front section. Targeting was just as differentiated: Slashing techniques were used for the large muscle groups (such as the chest), while the swordsman would use

a stroke technique against bones (such as the clavicle). The modern *darn dao* for Kung Fu training have much thinner and therefore lighter blades than the original fighting sabers.

Ancient writings have handed down how a Chinese swordsman was tested: First, he had to strike through a copper rod a thumb-width thick with his saber. To perform this stroke without breaking the blade, you not only required a good saber, but also the right technique. In addition, the swordsman had to take on soldiers with spears and halberds. If they could not fend off the swordsman, and keep him at a distance, the swordsman had passed the test.

In China, the *dao* is associated with the tiger: "The saber is wild like a tiger." This refers to the aggressive, powerful fighting style. On the other hand, the straight sword, the *jian*, is associated with the mythical phoenix. Fighting techniques for this sword embody beauty and precision. If the sword is wielded correctly, it seems to be almost weightless. For this reason, it was also the weapon preferred by women. Otherwise it was, unlike the military dao, used to equip the nobility as a typical weapon of the court. Preserved *jian* are therefore usually sumptuously decorated, while the *dao* is a plain soldier's weapon.

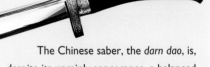

The Chinese saber, the *darn dao*, is, despite its ungainly appearance, a balanced weapon with elegant handling.

Photo: Cold Steel

Apart from its overall length, this weapon really is not much different from the long knife; only the cross-guards are proportionally larger. Typically, the war knife did not have a sheath, but was carried with naked blade in a kind of *Koppelshuh* or knife frog. War knives were plain, unspectacular weapons and were a preferred weapon of the *Landsknechte* mercenaries of the 15th and early 16th centuries. There is a considerable collection of war knives used by the Bohemian-Moravian troops in King Maximilian's army (late 15th century) in the Imperial Armory in Vienna. Although the war knives were used mostly by common mercenaries, there were individual, even high-ranking princes who preferred this weapon. One of these was George Castriota (1403-1468), the ruler of Albania—also called Iskenderbeg. He was a fighting comrade of Vlad Dracula, who made a name for himself as a resistance fighter against the Turks.

In Switzerland, a special type appeared at this time: The so-called Swiss saber, also known as a "*Schnepf(er)*" ("snipe"). In the 15th century, this was still a straight, single-edged sword. This saber got its typical slight curvature only at the beginning of the 16th century. These early weapons often have, in addition to a meter-long blade with its broad fuller, the characteristic two-part grip of the bastard sword. We can thus safely speak of a "bastard sword" in this context. In the course of the century, the hilt changes: The grip is shorter and has a pistol-shape curvature, the grip cap is often shaped like a lion's head. In addition, side guards and later shell guards, were added to the grips. These late, some smaller types were common especially among Swiss officers.

Hungarian two-handed saber, 15th century.

The blade profile of this two-handed sword has a striking resemblance to that of a samurai sword.

A "bastard saber": the Swiss *Schnepfer* (slightly simplfied, new interpretation without the typical writhen pommel).

Photo: Traumschmiede/Eckhardt

7.5 The Sword Becomes the Broadsword

In terms of history, the broadsword or *Degen* (the German military sword) is an advancement over the sword. This does not mean that the broadsword is a better weapon than the older sword, but rather, that the nature of warfare changed. A broadsword would have been useless on a medieval battlefield, but it is perfectly adapted to modern warfare. The reverse is true of the medieval sword: it would have been of little use on any Renaissance battlefield.

Broadsword Basics

Neither the art of swordsmanship nor the medieval swords themselves were the catalysts for radical new developments in the field of edged weapons. The actual basis for these changes were the ever-better and more frequently used handguns. The best armor is of no use whatever against a bullet fired from a gun. A fast bullet could penetrate most armor. As a result, wearing protective armor declined—why wear so much iron, if it could not protect you against firearms? This, in turn, meant that medieval swords, primarily designed to fight against armor, were useless. Fencing changed, and fencing weapons became lighter and more flexible. The broadsword was launched on its path to glory.

The year 1600 can be regarded as a boundary point in the development of weapons technology. Firearms were now widely established weapons, which finally delivered the "death blow" to anything left over from the medieval era. Edged weapons become ever-lighter and narrower, and were designed for delivering a thrust. Apart from that, they were increasingly specialized, differentiated as to rank and the branch of the military, and by their different primary purposes—this is especially true of the distinction between military and civilian edged weapons, respectively, broadsword and rapier.

The broadsword was mainly a military weapon. In war, soldiers still wore some body armor (such as a cuirass), and above all helmets. Beyond this, now you had to deal with ever-more opponents on the battlefield. Here you needed a heavy, broad blade, suitable for delivering a cutting stroke as well as stabbing. In English, therefore, a broadsword can also be referred to as a "cut-and-thrust" sword.

In civilian life, however, things were different: Either you had to defend your honor in a duel or yourself against bandits—in both cases, your opponents were usually not wearing armor. Therefore, civilians preferred a narrow, lightweight blade which was mainly designed to thrust: the rapier. Contrary to what is portrayed in many Musketeer films, you can only deliver a thrust with a narrow rapier; it was impossible to make an effective cut. In addition, at the time, the rapier was to some extent part of a gentleman's wardrobe—no one wanted to carry around a heavy broadsword in their daily life. There is no difference between the mountings of rapiers and broadsword, another reason why these types of weapons are often confused. A blade width of about three centimeters is considered a differentiating measure, although this is only a rough guide: in reality, the transition from one to the other is completely fluid.

The difference between rapier and broadsword is therefore "only" in the blade—and the shape of the blade indicates the method of sword fighting used. "The decisive factor with a rapier was clearly that—since it was more maneuverable and lighter—you could shift more rapidly from defensive to offensive action. After his sword point has been parried downward (parade) or the blade was struck away, the swordsman can immediately bring it right back into position. The rapier makes it possible to turn immediately back on your attacker with the point. This—combined with Ausfall [lunge or sudden counter-attack] movements—fulfill the potential for a counter-attack. It was precisely this dynamic that made the narrower, lighter rapier blade more effective in (unarmored) dueling than a broad cutting blade," according to sword fighting expert John Clements.

Here, we have to emphasize that the transition from the medieval sword to the broadsword was neither abrupt nor absolute. There are many transitional models, representing intermediate designs between the sword and fully developed broadsword (more on this below); at the same time, both sword and broadsword were in use during the same time period.

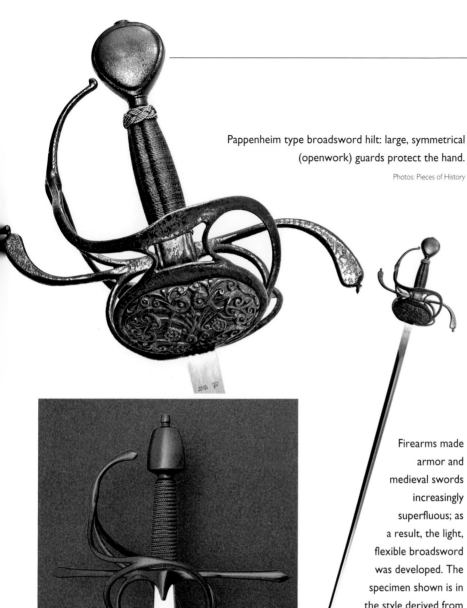

Pappenheim type broadsword hilt: large, symmetrical (openwork) guards protect the hand.

Photos: Pieces of History

Full-fledged broadsword hilt.

Photo: Arms & Armor

Firearms made armor and medieval swords increasingly superfluous; as a result, the light, flexible broadsword was developed. The specimen shown is in the style derived from the broadsword wielded by Swedish King Gustavus Adolphus, when he fell in the Battle of Lützen in 1632.

Photo: Pieces of History

This classic rapier was made around 1600. Rapier blades are usually slimmer than broadsword blades.

Photo: Museum Replicas

Fighting stance for *Degen* and left-hand dagger (drawing after Joachim Meyer's *Gründtliche Beschreibung der freyen ritterlichen und adelichen Kunst des Fechtens* [*Thorough Description of the Free Knightly and Noble Art of Fencing*], 1570).

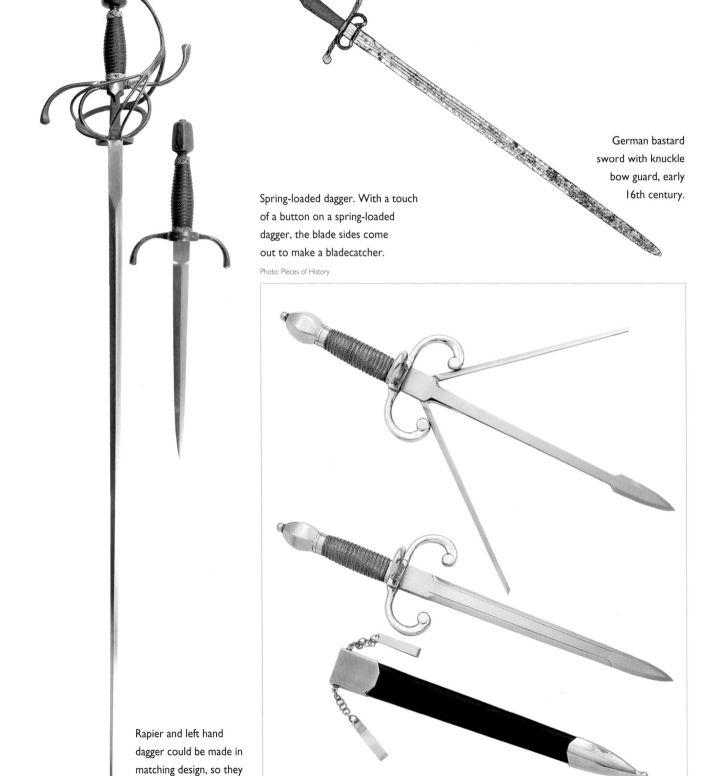

German bastard sword with knuckle bow guard, early 16th century.

Spring-loaded dagger. With a touch of a button on a spring-loaded dagger, the blade sides come out to make a bladecatcher.

Photo: Pieces of History

Rapier and left hand dagger could be made in matching design, so they formed a "set."

Photo: Pieces of History

The fighting method for both broadsword and rapier was essentially to use a thrust rather than cut or stroke.

There are three factors that influenced the development of the broadsword:

- Its blade is constantly in contact with the opponent's blade.
- The sword hand is increasingly within the opponent's range.
- To perform an effective thrust, you must use your hand to grasp the broadsword grip in a different manner than used for a cutting sword.

These factors meant that is was necessary to provide ever-more protection for the sword hand. A cross-shaped guard was no longer sufficient. Therefore, different systems of rings, clasps, and bars were designed to provide hand protection. These complex grips are called "hilts" by the experts.

As the broadsword—but especially the rapier—was developed, it became customary to fight with broadsword or rapier in the right hand and a dagger in the left. The left hand dagger was either used to help parry—that is, to deflect, block, or break the opponent's blade, and to pry it out of his hands—or to break through your opponent's guard and, "to slip by" and kill him with this blade. Broadswords, rapiers, and left hand daggers were later made in matching styles: The mountings were made in the same style by the same sword-finisher—the two weapons form a set.

To improve the effect of the left hand daggers, some special weapons—such as the *Degenbrecher* or "sword breaker"—were invented. The spring-loaded dagger is a particularly interesting special specimen (not to be confused with a modern spring knife or switchblade!). In these daggers, the blade is divided lengthways into three pieces. When a button on the ricasso is pressed, the spring action makes the two side pieces jump outwards, to form two blade catchers. In contrast to a sword breaker, a spring-loaded dagger's blade catcher is effective, since the surprise itself alone has a big effect on the opponent.

The 16th century brought significant technological innovations to the blade-making industry, such as the introduction of mechanical hammers driven by water power. This made forging carburized steel much more efficient and economical. The blade smiths would take refined ready-made steel and finished forging the blades by hand.

The average citizen knows the Renaissance mainly through such great artists as Leonardo da Vinci. The contemporary interest in art also had an impact on the blade industry. Blades and hilts were often richly decorated. There were two leading techniques for decorating edged weapons in particular: Etching a picture on the hilt or blade using a corrosive solution. This was later re-engraved as needed. The other technique was iron-cutting, used to create the wonderfully shaped hilts.

Heavy Broadsword Types: The Last Battle Swords

Although a broadsword is generally much lighter and more slender than a medieval sword, we still find various types which are heavier than the other models. These are clearly military weapons. meant for the battlefield. They are the true heirs of the medieval swords.

Although different broadswords look more or less the same to the untrained eye, we almost never find identical examples. Broadswords (or sets of weapons) are generally hand-crafted. The diversity this creates is emphasized even more because a broadsword is decorated much more than a medieval sword is. Nevertheless, despite all the diversity of the countless models, we can establish specific primary groupings based on the shape of the hilt. Although there are heavy broadswords in almost all groups, they are particularly common in two of them:

- cross-hilt with knuckle bow guard
- basket hilt

Cross-Hilt with Knuckle Bow Guard

This group could be described as the transition between the medieval sword and the broadsword. There is no hand guard, and only a relatively simple cross-guard, but it does feature a number of ring guards. Although the blades are still relatively broad and heavy, they are often already narrower than those on medieval swords. The cross-hilt with knuckle bow guard is designated

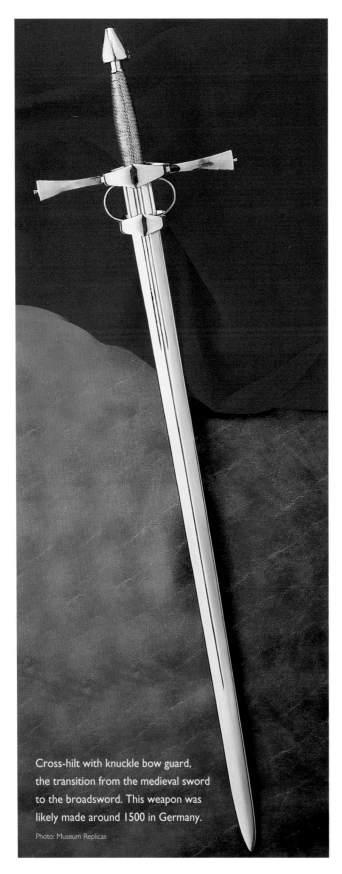

Cross-hilt with knuckle bow guard, the transition from the medieval sword to the broadsword. This weapon was likely made around 1500 in Germany.

Photo: Museum Replicas

The piece shown is virtually a mixture of medieval and Renaissance sword design.

Photo: Pieces of History

Early basket hilt for a bastard saber: The basket bars protect the sword hand, and the second hand can be used to grasp the back of the grip (detail of Swiss saber on page 121).

Photo: Traumschmiede/Eckhardt

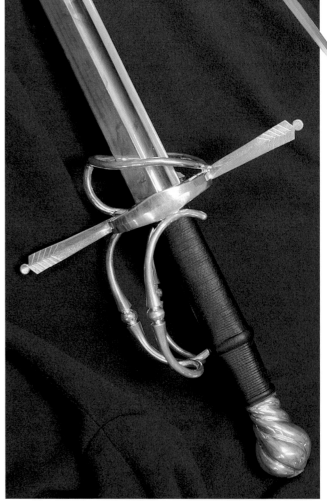

a "complex hilt" by Ewart Oakeshott and is still classified among medieval swords. From the mid-16th century, more and more specimens appear with slender broadsword and later rapier blades.

The grip on the sword on page 126 left, has all the features of a Renaissance weapon, although the blade is still a typical medieval type XX form. We see this even more clearly on the next sword (top right). The blade is relatively broad and has a definite fuller—typical features of a medieval sword—while the grip already has a very distinct preliminary form of a bar hilt. This weapon is a kind of hybrid between broadsword and sword.

The bastard sword on page 124 goes in a completely different direction. With a 37.7-inch (96 centimeter) long blade and weighing 3.5 pounds (1.6 kilograms), this sword can be clearly classified as a heavy battle sword, not a broadsword, although there are various knuckle-bow guards. Due to the shape of the blade and its overall proportions, this sword fits best into the category of the rare XIX long-sword.

The Basket Hilt Sword

It is interesting that the basket hilt—one of the most advanced broadsword hilts—almost always comes with a heavy and broad blade which often is similar to that of a medieval sword. For this reason, in German, the *Korbgefäßdegen* (basket hilt broadsword) is often also referred to as a *Korbschwert* (basket sword).

The early forms of the basket hilt sword appear around 1570, with most of them made in Germany. In contrast to other broadsword hilts, the bars are fashioned into a basket that almost completely encloses the sword hand. Already here we have the tendency to use bars with a flat rather than rounded cross-section, since these offer better protection. An old Swedish inventory lists these weapons under *Mulekorgs-Fäste* [horse-muzzle basket hilts]. Apart from the basket, these early basket hilt swords were still quite similar to other broadswords, and all still have very long cross-guards. What is striking is the long, slender pommel that protrudes well above the basket. As often is the case with Swiss sabers, this means the left hand can be used for support—it is essentially a bastard sword.

From the 17th century on, we can divide basket hilt swords into three groups. There is an overall group of such swords, and two region-based groupings: The Venetian *schiavona* and the Scottish basket hilt sword. The most famous weapon of the general group is the *Haudegen* (literally, "hewing sword") or mortuary sword in English. As the [German] name indicates, this weapon was used mainly to deliver a cut or stroke, and for this reason, most blades have only one edge. The cross-guard has finally been eliminated from the hilt, and the basket is very distinctive. The mortuary sword was particularly prevalent in 17th-century England. Many basket hilts have a decoration

The Mary Rose Sword

As what remained of the *Mary Rose* – Henry VIII's flagship – was raised from her watery grave in 1982, an elongated metal object was discovered directly beneath the ship. It turned out to be a basket hilt sword, very well preserved by the mud. The sword went down in 1545 with the *Mary Rose*. Therefore we know that it is definitely the oldest English basket hilt sword and one of the oldest of all. Although the basket was flattened by the sinking ship, it was made together with a full cross-guard. The bars are simple and elegant, completely unornamented. The 34.8-inch (88.5-centimeter) long blade is double-edged, and also unornamented. Wilkinson Sword

has reconstructed this sword in cooperation with the Royal Armouries and the *Mary Rose* Trust, and the recreation of the basket guard in particular is a brilliant achievement. Unfortunately, the blade was given contemporary Tudor period decorations. This belated addition should be considered a negative one, and lowers the quality of the otherwise excellent reconstruction. The unembellished replica *Mary Rose* sword shows the timeless elegance of a superbly crafted weapon.

Photo: Wilkinson Sword

Photo: Wilkinson Sword

127

commemorating the beheading of King Charles I. For this reason, collectors of the English swords adopted the term "mortuary swords" for these weapons, which is still commonly used internationally today.

Perhaps the best known type within this group is the Scottish basket hilt broadsword. The Scottish basket hilt broadsword—often incorrectly referred to as the Claymore—was developed in the late 16th or early 17th centuries. Versions of this hilt spread rapidly in England and Ireland, but they remained limited to the British sphere of influence.

The history of the Scottish basket hilt sword is inextricably linked with the 18th-century Scottish Wars of Independence. In 1715, the Scots rose—in vain—against English domination. Ten years later, traditional Scottish weapons (including swords, daggers, shields, and pistols) were forbidden. Now, the British drew up the Highland regiments. They were made up of Scots who had renounced Scottish independence, and taken an oath of allegiance to the British crown.

These units were given the privilege of continuing to wear Scottish weapons with their uniforms, in Scottish style. In 1745, a new Highlander uprising arose, led by Bonnie Prince Charlie, which was again brutally suppressed. As a result, the entire Highland dress was banned in 1746. However, in 1782 the ban was lifted after massive lobbying by the London "Highland Society." The passing of thirty-six years had, however, had its effects: Civilians could no longer get used to swords, shields, and guns. The Scots Guards continued to wear a sword with Scottish basket hilt, although the blade was progressively made narrower, until the only element this weapon had in common with the original basket hilt sword was the hilt itself.

The Scottish basket hilt sword is quite different from its other relatives. For one, it is rounder than the *schiavona* or *pallasch*, and the pommel is shaped like a flattened sphere. The rods of the basket are very broad and almost completely enclose the hand. A Scottish basket hilt is characteristically lined with red leather or fabric. Blades are usually about four centimeters wide and 80 centimeters long. There are some single-edged backswords, but double-edged blades are the rule.

There are far fewer of the basket hilt swords called a *schiavona* than of the Scottish basket hilt swords, because it is found only in Venice. Originally the words *"gli schiavoni"* meant the swords of the Doge's Guard (see box below), but later all Venetian-style basket hilt swords were given this name.

It is likely that the *"spada Schiavona"* is a direct descendant of the medieval *gli schiavoni*. In any case, the *schiavona* was used not only by the Doge's Guard, but also by many fighters in the Venetian region. The basic shape of the pommel vaguely recalls that of the earlier designs, but the square pommel was given two characteristic tips, and the stud on the pommel became a rosette. In contrast to the Scottish basket hilt sword, the *schiavoni* blade is double-edged, about four centimeters wide and about 35.4 inches (90 centimeters) long. The pommel is longer and narrower than those on Scottish basket hilt swords. The *schiavona* was in use from the 16th to 18th centuries.

Gli Schiavoni

In the 15th century, the swords of the Slavonian-Dalmatian Guards of the Doge of Venice were called *gli schiavoni*. They are characterized by straight, double-edged blades, horizontal, S-shaped cross-guards and a square, studded pommel.

The basket hilt protectively encloses the entire hand. A red lining of leather or fabric is typical of Scottish basket hilt swords.

Photo: Pieces of History

From the 17th century, the Scottish basket hilt sword was the Highlanders' main weapon. After the Wars of Independence, it became part of the Scots Guard's arms.

Photo: Cold Steel

English mortuary sword, attributed to Oliver Cromwell.

Photo: Pieces of History

Basket hilt of the Cromwell mortuary sword.

Photo: Pieces of History

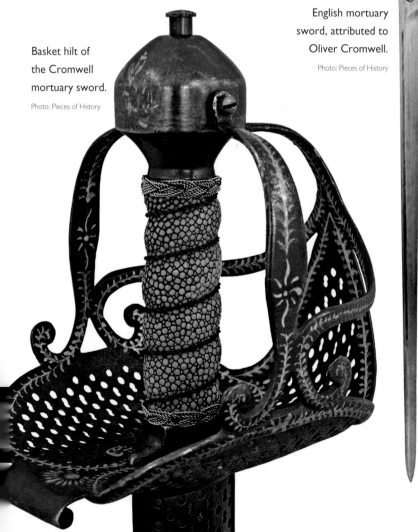

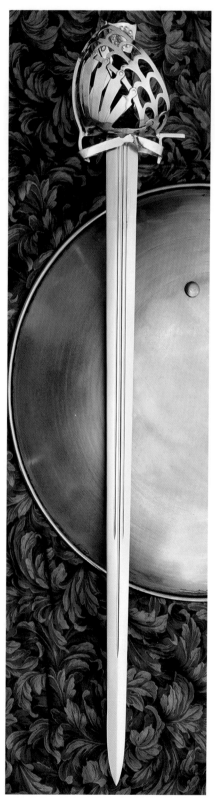

The *schiavona* is a basket hilt sword found only in Venice.

Photo: Museum Replicas

7.6 Special Swords

There are a number of specific swords that we encounter again and again, usually the swords of heroes. This does not just mean Arthur's Excalibur or Siegfried's Balmung, but swords which really existed and are associated with the life stories of warriors who also really lived. These are not about magical swords, but completely "normal" edged weapons. These swords are usually wielded by heroes, but a closer examination reveals that there is much more legend than truth behind such accounts. For lack of a better term, I will now present some of these weapons as "special swords."

One of the most famous swords ever is *Joyeuse* (Joyous), the so-called Sword of Charlemagne (742-814). The sword comes from the Treasury of St. Dénis and is mentioned for the first time in 1271 by the chronicler Guillaume de Nangis. It was used as the French kings' coronation sword from the 12th century, a tradition that continued even up to Napoleon. Contrary to all the legends, this sword did not come from the time of Charlemagne. Even a cursory inspection shows that this is clearly a classic knightly sword of the High Middle Ages. The gilded hilt displays a number of different styles. The plate in the center of the cross-guard could date from the 8th century. The pommel is engraved in Scandinavian style, as was the fashion in the transitional period between the 10th and 11th centuries. The dragon heads on the cross-guard are from the 12th century and the gilded, jeweled scabbard from the period around 1300. Moreover, it was later repeatedly refitted, such as with the new blade mounted for Napoleon's coronation.

If you look around the field of decorative swords, you will sooner or later encounter, in addition to "Charlemagne's Sword," another sword claimed to be a replica of one of the swords carried by El Cid. The Spanish knight Rodrigo Diaz de Vivar (1043-1099) gained immense fame in his lifetime. Due to his heroic deeds and just convictions, he gained the sobriquet *el campeador* (the fighter) and El Cid, derived from the Arabic "*al sajid*" (= the Lord). El Cid's life has been handed down to us in the 12th-century epic poem *Cantar de mio Cid*. The stories about El Cid repeatedly describe his two swords: "Colada" and "Tizona."

Spanish museums exhibit two swords which are supposed to be El Cid's actual swords, and thousands of cheap replicas have been made of these swords. The sword called Colada has a 16th-century mortuary sword hilt and is primarily known through the movie *El Cid*, with Charlton Heston in the lead role.

In museum archives, this sword was first called the Colada around the turn of the [20th] century. In fact, tests show that the blade is much older than the sword hilt. However, the blade comes from the 13th century, that is, about 200 years later than the time El Cid was living. It could be that the blade had belonged to a sword of Saint Ferdinand, king of Castile (1201-1252), but it certainly never belonged to the Knight Rodrigo Diaz de Vivar.

Things are a bit different with Tizona. The sword called Tizona has an ornate "Spanish type" grip from the 15th or 16th centuries. It is striking that the grip is very small compared to the blade. The blade has a finely marked ricasso and a long fuller. It is not known when this sword first turned up. Sword experts have long considered this sword a 16th-century forgery. More recent studies using a mass spectrometer, however, showed that the blade actually dates from the 11th century and was probably forged in Andalusia. This throws new light on the sword, though not nearly enough. We now know that the blade is from El Cid's time, but if it really is his sword will likely remain unclear for a long time.

Here a word about the Tizona replicas: To compensate for the unfavorable ratio of blade and grip, the replicas have grips much larger than the original. None of the replicas even remotely reflect the actual shape of the blade of the sword called Tizona.

The next sword, from the Royal Armouries Museum in Leeds, is not, strictly speaking, any famous or "hero's sword." But it meets the standard notion, or wishful thinking notion, of a 15th-century Gothic bastard sword so accurately that it is well known among sword enthusiasts. This sword gained additional popularity because a replica played a large role in the TV series *Highlander*. The market offers a variety of replicas (such as Del Tin and Museum Replicas). The replicas are very fine, but the original sword is a fake!

As with many historical falsifications, suspicions arose at first: The sword is just too good to be true. It corresponds exactly to just what we would wish a sword to be. Other criteria include the style elements, which are absolutely unique in this configuration.

The grip shows the classic two-part design of a bastard sword. The upper part is wound round with wire, the lower clad with leather. Under the leather is an X-shaped coil of wire or cord, which shows clearly under the leather. The cross-guard deserves special attention. Although open work clover leaf decoration is indeed common, the work is usually very small (see Thorpe Falchion). Here, in contrast, there are several large and very finely worked pieces of decoration, which never actually occurs in bastard swords. There are very obviously suspicious aspects of this sword.

The curators of the Royal Armouries Museum are not spreading it around, but in their view, this "Gothic bastard sword" is a forgery. While the blade might actually be 14th century, the whole grip mounting was added later. It is very likely that this sword was made in the workshop of Ernst Schmidt, the Munich forger, in the 19th century. One of Schmidt's catalogues from the early 20th century shows two swords that are very similar to our model.

After I have "dis-enchanted" some famous swords here, I would like to end this chapter by "enchanting" another sword. This is the sword of Edward III of England. Edward III (1327-1377) was a warrior king. He laid claim to the French throne and was partly responsible for launching the Hundred Years War (1393-1453). Edward won the spectacular victory of Crecy (1346), including by the aid of his longbow archers.

Just like Charlemagne's sword, the sword of Edward III is a dream come true, the ideal knightly sword. Is it just too good to be true?

The magnificent sword looks at first glance like a one-handed sword, but it has total length of 42.1 inches (107 centimeters), with a blade 33.8 inches (86 centimeters) long—type XVIIIa—the size of a long-sword. The mounting is gilded, the pommel displays Edward's coat of arms, and the blade the symbol of the famous Order of the Garter, which Edward founded. Thus, this sword's hallmarks point directly to Edward III. But as I said: it just seems too perfect to be real.

The so-called Sword of Charlemagne. While this is indeed the coronation sword of the kings of France, it unfortunately has nothing to do with Charlemagne.

Photo: Del Tin

This is reputed to be Tizona – the sword of El Cid. At least the blade actually comes from his time.

This sword showed up at the end of the 19th century, in the possession of a French dealer who had a reputation as a forger of medieval objects. For this reason, the sword was immediately considered a fake. The "experts" very quickly divided into two camps: Those who thought it was real and their opponents. The debate lasted until the 1980s.

During the 1980s, the sword changed hands several times. Under these circumstances, several studies were carried out, by, among others, Ewart Oakeshott himself. These led to the following conclusions:

- The sword is very well made and well balanced—the work of a first-class craftsman.
- Although the sword is richly decorated, it is not a ceremonial, but a real weapon for combat. This is confirmed by the existing signs of usage.
- The British Museum of Natural History identified the grip covering as snake skin.
- The light layer of rust on the blade lies above the stress marks—an indication that it was used for an extended period, was well maintained and only rusted later on.
- X-rays showed a riveted-over tang under the gold layer on the pommel, as is typical of medieval swords.
- The snake skin on the handle shows typical signs of wear, resulting from frequent contact.

As a result, Oakeshott concluded already by 1983 that the sword is genuine. In 1986, the owner of the sword had it examined by the *Bundesamt für Materialprüfung*, the German Federal Institute for Materials Research and Testing. Samples were taken from the grip and blade, and analyzed. These tests definitively confirmed that the sword was made in the 14th century. Since it was a major crime for anyone else to decorate any object with the King's coat of arms, it can only mean one thing: this is indeed the sword of Edward III.

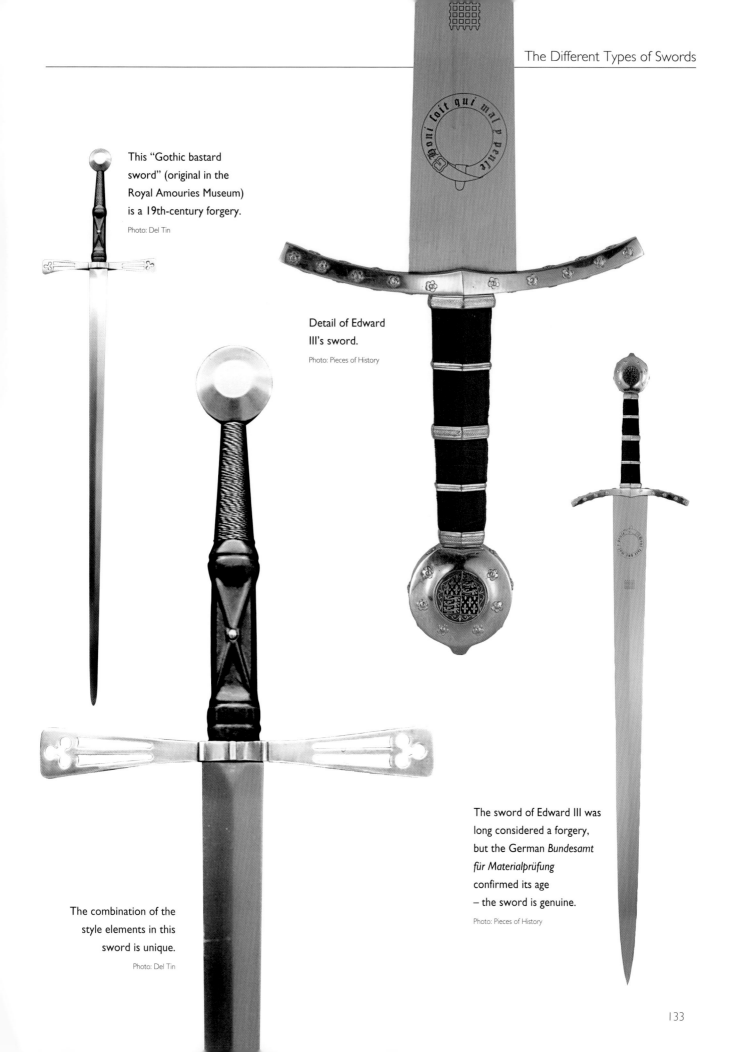

This "Gothic bastard sword" (original in the Royal Amouries Museum) is a 19th-century forgery.

Photo: Del Tin

Detail of Edward III's sword.

Photo: Pieces of History

The combination of the style elements in this sword is unique.

Photo: Del Tin

The sword of Edward III was long considered a forgery, but the German *Bundesamt für Materialprüfung* confirmed its age – the sword is genuine.

Photo: Pieces of History

Secrets of the Art of Swordmaking

Before we discuss how swords are actually forged, it is necessary to say something about the source material: steel. Although bronze and iron swords were common in ancient times, steel is the most important material in the history of the sword (Damascus steel is a special case; more on that later). All the many swordsmiths who have gone down in legend show us, not just how important a warrior's heroic deeds were, but also the skill of the swordsmith himself. Sometimes the swordsmith is not a person, but a dwarf who uses magic to make the weapons; sometimes it is a true genius, like Wieland the Smith; and in some cases a cursed sorcerer, who betrays his secrets to a simple artisan (such as the Solingen legend of Peter Simmelpusch). But in the end, all the magic can be traced back to one thing: steel.

Manufacturing a sword involves several steps:

a) refining the steel and iron,
b) welding the steel layers together,
c) forging the blade,
d) tempering,
e) making the pommel, cross-guard, grip, and scabbard.

When I discuss iron in what follows, it should not be confused with the cast iron familiar to us. Industrial cast iron from a blast furnace has a carbon content of more than two percent; it is hard and very brittle. The iron used by historic blacksmithing is different: A relatively soft iron with low carbon content, refined from ore using primitive methods.

Up to the High Middle Ages, iron was almost always refined in a smelting oven. This was a pit or cauldron, set on a slope where there was a strong air draft (later they also used large bellows). Iron ore and wood were layered over a bed of embers and the whole thing sealed up with clay. The wind or bellows generated a very high heat, so that the iron was smelted out of the ore, and would flow out through runnels made in the oven. That is why it is also called *Rennfeuereisen* (literally, running fire-iron); in English, bloomery iron. At the end of the runnel, the iron would congeal into large lumps weighing several kilograms, called *Luppen* or "blooms" of sponge iron. This iron was, however, still very impure and inhomogeneous, and was then refined or wrought by primitive means, by repeated forging. This iron was then sold in bar form—called *Zaine* in German-speaking regions in the Middle Ages.

Around 1500 BC, the Hittites discovered the techniques required to make steel, which were guarded as a state secret. At that time, steel weapons were gifts worthy of a king. Here we must note that the term "steel" was unknown in ancient times. Instead, they gave more specific descriptions to kinds of iron, with the Assyrians, for example, using the term "good iron." After the collapse of the Hittite Empire, the technology of steel making spread via the Near East to the whole world.

In contrast to iron, steel can be hardened and tempered. To do this, the metal must have a carbon content of at least 0.35 percent. Making a useable sword requires a minimum of 0.5 percent. To achieve this percentage, the raw iron must be carburized. The raw iron is brought to glowing hot using charcoal. The carbon diffuses into the iron. This carburizing (also: cementation) process is very time consuming. Creating a surface carburization two millimeters thick on an iron bar, for example, requires cementation for a full twelve hours at 900 degrees Celsius. Even after this, the carburizing is still very uneven, and the metal very inhomogeneous. Therefore, the bars must be repeatedly re-forged, before it is possible to forge the actual blade together from them. The iron's hardness has already been increased by the carburization and the higher carbon content it creates: The iron is transformed into steel.

To improve the effect of this cementation, during annealing, the steel is often mixed with organic materials. We find an excellent description of this in the saga of Wieland the Smith (also Völund, Velent,

Weland, or Wayland). Wieland receives an order to forge a "super sword" for a king. Unfortunately, he has made a wager on this matter. It literally kept running through his head. So Wieland forged a top-class sword, but used a secret trick to enhance the quality of the steel even more:

Then the king went to his hall cheerfully.

In the forge, Wieland took up a file; the sword was filed to a vain dust:

Who might have heard it, would have had his ears deafened

by the shrill file on hard steel;

the good sword's agony lasted long.

The filings lay there: the wise smith beat them together with flour and milk, he mixed the dough wonderfully.

Then he took birds to be fattened, kept till the third day in a narrow cage with nothing to eat, and threw this heavy food before the starvelings.

They ate ravenously, the eager Thor had never more bravely laid into anything when he masqueraded as Freya and showed Thyrm the giant how greedily his bride could eat:

The whole trough was emptied in a short hour

and another back-to- back in the morning, doubly weighed down.

The master put the final matter in the embers:

He stoked the fire well to smelt out the ore, then scooped the muck out from the cauldron,

and finally refined iron, loud and clear, from the slag.

As it cooled, before the seventh day he created a masterful sword worthy of a doughty warrior:

It first sharp and edged, it was strong and hard, it would be difficult to find any better on Earth.

Thus, Wieland refined raw steel from goose droppings, which still contained the undigested filings. Carburizing with bird droppings made the steel much harder, so this sword surpassed the usual—much weaker—swords. This sword was made by the secret method of Wieland's old master Mime; according to some sources, some sagas said that Siegfried also had such a sword. But this was not enough for Wieland: He

filed this sword down also and repeated the whole procedure again. Thus, he created a completely unique sword, with a steel of hardness and quality never achieved before. It was a sword of legend, that "could cut through iron like clothing." In honor of his old master, Wieland named this sword "Mimung." This process of carburization using bird droppings has been handed down to us in a number of other sources than the Wieland saga; the Arab scholar al-Biruni (about 973-1050) reports that the same manufacturing process was used for swords in ancient Rus.

What are we really dealing with in this secret of Mimung? Dr. Karl Daeves already wrote on this in 1940: "Why repeatedly break up the sword, treat, and reforge it? Droppings contain nitrogen in addition to carbon. Only since the beginning of this century, have we known that mixing in nitrogen creates a significant additional increase in hardness, so that nitrided steels have the highest degree of hardness that can be created from iron. […] The filings treated by Wieland's method thus consisted of a soft and tough core which, after hardening, got a very hard shell which cuts very well. If these filings were welded together, filed down again, treated and welded, after repeated processing and hardening, this must yield a product made very evenly of tough, hardenable iron, and extremely hard carbide (iron-carbon compound) and nitride (iron-nitrogen compound), compounded in mosaic form. The combination of this cutting quality and strength, in such a composite body, is of significantly higher quality than a thoroughly hardened modern knife; due to the greater hardness and better distribution of nitrides, it is also of better quality than a razor blade or tool steel, consisting of a hard basic measurement (martensite) with embedded carbides," (Knight, p.132). Steel is also sometimes nitrided during hardening. In summary, to make Mimung, the smith used a very exotic, almost alchemical, process to produce steel. Some historians call Mimung as the "first all-steel sword in history."

The forging of Mimung also speaks to another aspect of steel besides hardness—flexibility. Since they began to forge blades, weapons smiths had to wrestle with a a fundamental problem: If the iron contains too little carbon, it remains weak, but if it is heavily carburized and thus hard steel, it is also brittle at the same time. Both extremes create a dilemma. The historian Polybius

Fire, steel, and the smith's skill all create a good sword.

Photo: Amo Eckhardt

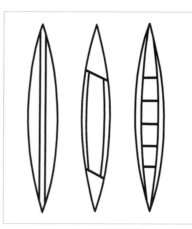

Schema of a laminated blade.

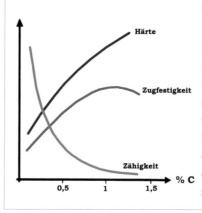

The carbon content increases the steel's hardness, but also affects properties such as tensile strength and toughness. For this reason, the smith has to determine the optimal combination of hardness, tensile strength and toughness.

If the steel is too hard and thus brittle, there is a risk the blade will break, leaving the fighter defenseless (drawing after a medieval illustration).

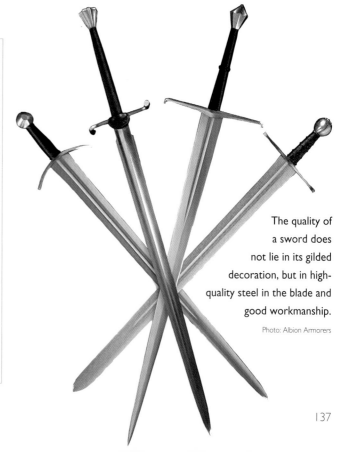

The quality of a sword does not lie in its gilded decoration, but in high-quality steel in the blade and good workmanship.

Photo: Albion Armorers

(204-122 BC) reported, for example, the following about the Celts' iron long-swords: "In the preceding battles it was observed that in the first clash, the Gauls with their aggressive spirit are extremely frightening—as long as it is still unbroken—but that their swords, because of the way they are made, can survive no more than a decisive blow or stab [...] and that they become dull after that one stroke and bend, due to their length and size, and that the warriors then have hardly any time to straighten them out with their feet, bracing it on the ground [...]." This point was paraphrased by several ancient (pro-Roman) authors, but not all Celtic swords were of such inferior quality! Such weak sword blades could of course have fatal consequences, as we know from the early medieval saga of Kjartan Olafsson: "He struck mightily, but his sword was worthless. He had always to straighten it out under his foot, until he was mortally wounded."

The opposite of such weak swords, was a hard but brittle steel blade—so brittle that, if used to deliver a powerful blow, the blade would be badly nicked, or could break entirely. Such a broken sword once almost cost no one lesser than Richard the Lionheart his life. We find another such example in the *Walthari Saga* of Walter of Acquitaine. In battle, Walter's sword breaks on the helmet of Hagan the Trojan, and the hero can only save himself because he wears a second sword:

> The helmet was forged hard. Then the sword broke with a clang,
> countless shards flew through the air and bush and grass.

Swords of Titanium?

"Actually, why steel? Surely you can make swords made of titanium." We have been hearing such comments more frequently ever since the screen adventures of Blade. Movie vampire hunters (and other video game heroes), go after their opponents to seek retribution with titanium swords. Inspired by such media, as well as by knives with titanium blades, the question arises whether, in view of our modern titanium alloys, the steel sword has not long since served out its purpose.

The element titanium has several advantageous properties: it is very tough and abrasion resistant, it is absolutely corrosion-resistant, anti-magnetic and about 40 percent lighter than steel. These qualities make titanium alloys an ideal material for knife handles. But the blade is a different story: titanium is not as flexible and strong as steel – and therefore cannot hold a cutting edge as well. Even the weakest blade steel can be brought to a hardness of about 54 HRC (Hardness Rockwell Cone), while beta titanium alloys used for knife blades are only about 47 HRC – and a sword blade should be approximately 55 HRC. If you were to make swords, with the same dimensions, one each of steel and titanium, the steel sword could literally beat the titanium sword to pieces. To obtain the same resilience as a steel sword, the titanium blade would have to be about .5-.78 inches (1.5 to 2 centimeters) thick. For this reason, titanium blades are only used for special purposes when steel is not useful – such as for an absolutely rust-free diving knife or for anti-magnetic tools for explosives experts. In all other areas, steel is clearly superior.

But even if titanium alloys would be tough enough for a sword, titanium swords have another problem: they are just too light. As we saw in the beginning, the weight of a sword is anyway often drastically overestimated, so that the benefits of using titanium for lightness are also correspondingly overestimated. Based on the assumptions of many lay people, that a long-sword weighs 22-33 pounds (10-15 kilograms), it would appear, in this theoretical case, that making them forty percent lighter would be of paramount importance, but since the actual weight is only 3.3 pounds (1.5 kilograms), forty percent would mean something completely different.

There is another much more important aspect: Ever since Albert Einstein, we know that energy has to do with mass and acceleration. The kinetic energy of a sword stroke, therefore, also depends on the weight of the sword. For a sword stroke to have an effect, the sword must not be too light. Overall, titanium is therefore an unsuitable material for swords.

Walter, when his blade splintered, harshly
proclaimed that his heart was shaken by anger,

he contemptuously threw away the grip—what
was it worth,

even if it flashes, artistically fit together of
gold?

Having a sword fail like this could be deadly, so the
blade had to be both hard and flexible. The solution
to this problem was a blade that is constructed in
layers of soft iron and hard steel, and thus laminated.
Laminated blades can be found already among the
early Iron Age Celts. In these, we find between the
sharp steel cutting edges and outer sides of steel, one
or more layers of soft iron—the blade is hard and yet
flexible (in this case, however, tempering and hardening
play a large role).

There were both laminated blades and soft iron
blades in use during the same time period. Based on
modern knowledge, only a third of Celtic long-swords
can be considered high quality. This means that the
warriors would have been able to compare both types
of swords, and the laminated blades would really appear
to them to be marvels, like magic swords. According to
modern swordsmith Peter Johnsson, laminating the
blades was more a question of cost: forged steel was
about ten times as expensive as pure iron in the Middle
Ages. According to Johnsson, a sword's flexibility is
mainly achieved by correct tempering.

It is not easy to forge a good sword. We know this
already from the old legends. The tales about Wieland
tell us that the art of sword making was a secret, for
which even kings themselves would risk much, and
some were even willing to promise the swordsmith
marriage with a princess. "Like the shaman, the smith
also is considered a master of fire. In certain cultures,
the smith is held to be a shaman's equal, or even his
superior," (Eliade, p.95).

The design is of course the beginning of a sword.
This does not mean designing the decoration, but
the functional design: "Form follows function." This
presents important questions for the smith:

- Is this to be a sword purely meant for war, or should it also have a civilian, representative character?
- Is the sword to be wielded primarily from horseback or on foot?
- What armor does the enemy have?
- Should it be a double-edged, a single-edged sword, or even a curved saber?
- Is the sword to be one-handed, hand-and-a-half, or two-handed?
- If the sword was commissioned, it should also be designed to suit the bodily dimensions of its subsequent owner as best possible.

Another design factor is the right balance. If the
swordsmith wants to proceed in the best way possible,
he matches the blade length to the arm length of his
client and follows his client's wishes on the blade
cross section and the shape of the pommel, and then
calculates the balance, the nodal points and the
required weight of the pommel for the finished blade.
"The location of the nodes is mainly decided by the
shape of the blade and then adjusted through the size
of the grip," states Peter Johnsson.

Only after taking all of this into consideration,
can the swordsmith actually start to make the weapon.
In the following description, we are assuming this is
a simple laminated blade with a soft iron core. The
raw material has three layers (steel-iron-steel). In
creating this initial billet, we must take account of
the expected material loss. Depending on the type
of steel, blade, and forging technique, this would be
25 to 50 percent of the initial billet.

First, the individual layers are welded into a solid
block. Due to the high temperature required, there
is the risk that the steel will "burn." Therefore, a
welding agent is necessary to prevent burning.

In the pre-industrial era, fine-grained river sand
was used, but at times, burning was prevented by the
natural impurities in the steel. Today, the bladesmith
has to add a special welding powder—such as borax
(sodium tetraborate).

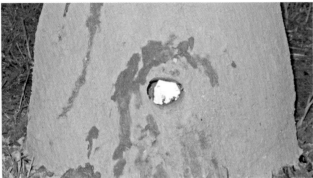

A smelting furnace used to make bloomery iron.

Photos: Stefan Roth

Robert Kazda welding individual steel layers to form a billet.

Photo: Armart Antiquanova

The smith's raw materials: Iron ore, sponge iron, and iron bloom.

Photos: Stefan Rot

The beginning of a sword: forge, anvil, the smith with his hammer, and glowing hot steel.

Photos: Amo Eckhardt

The initial billet for forming the blade is made of three layers (steel-iron-steel), which are welded together.

The raw bloomery iron is welded into a bar in the fire.

Photos: Stefan Roth

The art of welding is to achieve the right temperature. If the temperature is too high, the steel can burn despite the welding agent, and if the temperature is too low, the material will not be welded together: when such a sword is used, the individual layers of the blade could break apart. Therefore, extreme care is needed when welding. The experienced smith can recognize the right temperature from the annealing color. To forge-weld the sword blade requires a temperature of about 1,100 degrees centigrade; the steel glows yellow. So that the smith could assess the annealing color better, during the Middle Ages, forges were often darkened, which certainly contributed a lot to the mystical aura that surrounded them.

After the layers are firmly welded, the "real" forging of the sword blade begins. This step is done at about 950 degrees C, and the steel glows a bright orange. During the first phase—drawing it out—the master smith does not use the hammer himself, but he rather holds and moves the work piece. In the Middle Ages, two apprentices—the strikers—would swing the hammer. Later, the work was streamlined, and the hammers were operated by water power. During the forging, the block is first drawn out into a long, flat piece of steel. Then the tang, the lateral blade shape, and the approximate blade thickness are worked out: the blade blank is formed.

Next, the fuller is forged. So that the fuller is even on both sides, even most master swordsmiths use homemade tools. Andrew Jordan, for example, uses a die which is a kind of cookie-cutter for steel. The steel is placed between a lower and upper die which are shaped like the fuller. Then the smith strikes his hammer on the top die, thus shaping the fullers in parallel and evenly on both blade surfaces. In later centuries, the fuller was ground out—saving time, effort and cost, but this did not achieve the same quality (because grinding meant that the steel microstructure was no longer no longer adapted to the shape of the blade). As the fuller is forged, this broadens the blade. Therefore, at this point the smith must repeatedly check that he is maintaining the overall proportions of the blade.

Then comes the fine forging, to create the final shape of the blade. The more precisely you work here, the closer the blade is brought to its final appearance, all the better the steel microstructure will be, and subsequent corrections using a file will only do harm. On this, American bladesmith Don Fogg notes:

> Steel has a granular structure, and this goes in the direction it is forged. In machine-produced steel bars, the structure of the grain has already been set, since the ingot was rolled in the steel mill. The grain can therefore extend along the longitudinal direction of the blade or at right angles to it […] While this is not a serious problem in smaller dimensions, it can become a serious problem if the structure extends across a long blade. If the blade is forged into shape, the grain structure is aligned, and the steel accommodates to both the inside and outside of the blade.

Wielded by the hand of a master, the hammer shapes the blade to its final thickness. The tang is now also given a more precise form, with particular attention to the fact that the transition to the shoulders is slightly rounded, and not sharply angled. The transitional area between tang and blade is exposed to especial stress in sword fighting, so great care is needed here.

The last part of fine forging is to solidify the cutting edges. Swordsmith Tony Mansfield explains," "… This concentrates the steel layers and enables the blade to hold an edge better. To do this, the whole blade is heated until you see it just glowing red in the dark, then the edges are skillfully worked with a hammer. The hammer blows must be uniform along the entire length of the blade; otherwise they warp during tempering." Following the fine forging, the smith makes minor "cosmetic changes" using a file.

Now comes the important part: the tempering that alters the molecular structure of the steel. At this point, it must be emphasized again that it is not enough "just" to use a good grade of steel as a raw material. Only by using correct tempering is it possible to achieve the optimal, required combination of hardness and flexibility from a type of steel. The entire heat processing includes:

- annealing,
- hardening and
- tempering.

The glowing steel is shaped with a hammer.

Photo: Arno Eckhardt

If the blade cross section is right, the swordsmith makes only fine corrections using a file.

Photo: Patrick Barta

The welded steel billet is shaped by forging. The laminated layers accommodate to the later shape of the blade.

Tempering is one of the most important processes in forging.

Photo: Armart Antiquanova

When the profile is reasonably correct, the smith thins out the edges and shapes the final blank.

The forge is darkened to better assess the annealing color.

Photo: Armart Antiquanova

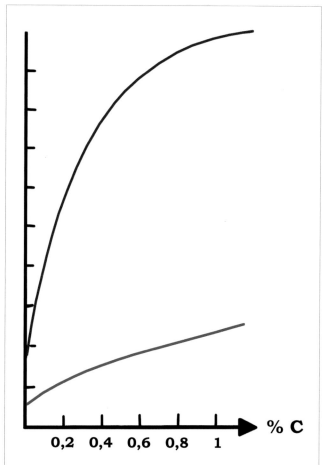

% C

0,2 0,4 0,6 0,8 1

The difference in hardness between tempered (quenched) steel (red) and air-cooled steel (blue).

"Forged, fire-welded […] steel contains tensions and a coarse-grained structure. This has unfavorable effects on the properties and hardening desired later. Therefore, you must try to correct as many of these problems as possible," states master smith Havard Bergland. These defects will be corrected by annealing. Annealing of a sword blade takes three different steps:

1) normalization,
2) molding and
3) soft annealing.

By normalizing, "the steel is to be made primarily fine-grained and consistent, thus, 'normal'," (Bergland, p.127). The blade is slowly brought (depending on the grade of steel) to a temperature of about 800 degrees. Once the correct temperature is reached—and the blade glows cherry red—it is taken from the embers and hung by the tang to cool so that it does not warp. Normalizing can be repeated a few times, depending on time and material.

Steels with a carbon content of more than 0.8 percent (hypereutectoid steel) have a structure after forging, "which is very brittle and under pressure, will break very roughly along the cutting edge," (Landes, p.113). Molding will again create a better, more finely structured steel. For this, the blade is heated to a temperature below 780 degrees (dark red annealing color) as long as possible.

This is followed by soft annealing, to resolve the tensions within the blade. "This method of annealing makes the steel workable again after forging, and the coarse structure is broken down," states Havard Bergland. During soft annealing, the blade is heated until it glows brown-red, and then is wrapped in a sheath of insulating material so that it will cool down as slowly as possible. Depending on the type of steel, this process can take up to fifteen hours.

Now comes the most critical part of the whole forging process: hardening. For this, the blade is again heated to about 800 degrees. The blade glows cherry red and then is "quenched" in a cold medium. For hardening high-carbon steels, water or oil is used. In simple terms, hardening effectively "freezes" the structure of the steel achieved by forging and annealing.

In such a complicated process, the smith can naturally make many mistakes. The blade can warp or cracks may appear. Since sword blades are much longer than knives, for example, the danger here that the blade will be twisted is especially great. "A hardening bath, with the blade point downwards is best to avoid warping. […] You slide the blade into the oil in as perpendicular a position as possible and make sure that it is totally submerged," states swordsmith Jim Hrisoulas.

Some sources indicate that blades were hardened in blood, not in water. This is no magical superstition—here again, we have a form of nitriding. The nitrogen compounds in the blood give the surface of the steel additional hardness (some alchemists recommended using urine, which works even better than blood).

In hardening, every individual factor plays a role, and a serious mistake can occur even within a few moments, so that the entire hardening process, perhaps even the entire tempering, must be repeated. It would be even worse, if the error was not noticed and is only revealed in battle, when the blade breaks. It is therefore not surprising that bladesmiths were highly paid specialists—who would want to entrust their life to a cheap but bad sword? We know that differences in quality were sometimes very great, so that already in the Middle Ages there was sword "brand piracy."

After hardening, the blade is extremely hard but brittle at the same time. Annealing reduces the brittleness to a large degree, and hardness to a lesser extent.

Tempering should follow immediately after hardening. If this is not possible, the blade should be meanwhile kept in boiling water. For tempering, the blade is heated to a temperature of about 250 to 300 degrees. Here, the blade is not in a red-hot state, but only glows brown. It is allowed to cool slowly, which takes about thirty minutes. This process is repeated a few times. During the tempering phase, any smaller errors which might recur, despite all due caution, are corrected using the hammer, until the blade is perfectly straight. After tempering, you have a hard yet flexible blade: the hardest work is done.

In English, *Anlassen* (activating, starting) means "tempering." The term "(well) tempered blade" refers to some extent to the successful completion of the entire tempering or heat treatment. In respect to tempering, we often find a translation [into German] error in historical or fantasy novels: They speak of "*getemperten Schwertern*" or something like that.

CNC Milled Swords

Due to the structural processes in steel, a professionally forged steel blade is the best choice for a sword. Many of the modern high-quality replicas are forged in a manufacturing process in "low-wage countries" such as India or in Manchuria (China), to get acceptable prices. If these swords are used for real cutting tests, however, they frequently show flaws despite the – for popular replicas – relatively high quality. However, not everyone can afford a sword hand-forged by a master. For this reason, companies such as Albion Armorers have the blades milled from industrial steel using a CNC-controlled machine – producing high quality at a good price-performance ratio.

At Albion Armorers, the blade is made from a piece of 1075 carbon steel. The product that emerges from the milling machine is a blank with the exact dimensions, blade cross section, and weight distribution. Still required to produce a finished sword blade are grinding and tempering, just like with a forged blank.

The use of machines, however, sounds easier than it actually is. "To exploit the potential of CNC machines to make blades, you have to translate the skills and insights of a swordsmith into a program to control the milling process," explains Albion Armorers. To do this, first, a detailed drawing by swordsmith Peter Johnsson is converted into a CAD graphic, from which the computer calculates the control program for the CNC machine. A first prototype of the blank is sent to Johnsson, who makes a first test cut. If necessary, the program is again corrected. At times, the machine is reprogrammed three times until serial production of the sword blanks can begin.

Actually, they would have to be called "*angelassene Schwerter*" or "*wärmebehandelte Schwerter*" (heat-treated swords). In German, we do not have this term, and traditionally use the term "*gehärtete Schwerter*" (hardened swords), although this is technically not quite correct.

On the metallurgical processes during tempering, it is best if I let swordsmith Tony Mansfield have his say:

> The merits of each steel depend absolutely on the iron-carbon ratio and the quality of the tempering. If a piece of steel was heated to different temperatures, this creates different crystal structures in the steel. At a critical temperature, the crystal lattice of the iron atoms 'opens' and the carbon atoms can be incorporated into the lattice. This is called the austenite lattice. When it is cooled very quickly, a different crystal structure called martensite forms. Martensite holds the carbon fixed in the structure and is the hardest form of steel. A slower cooling produces various softer lattices, including perlit, ferrit, and cementite. Ideally, the smith making a blade tried to obtain a structure with a body made of ferrite and perlite, with martensite cutting edges, which is known as tempered martensite. (Mansfield, *Records of the Medieval Sword*, p.250).

After tempering, the blade is polished. For the first step, we used to use large round grinding stones operated either by water or foot, or hand pedals. These stones removed the roughest traces of the forging process. Then the blade is given its angles and vertical contours by working with a file. This also removes the traces of the grinding stone. These contours are further refined with a whetstone. It is important here to keep cooling the stone with water. First, this prevents any heating (and thus any possible loss of hardness) of the blade, and second, the polished metal particles are removed from the surface of the stone.

In the Late Middle Ages, this preliminary and final polishing and the mounting were not done by the blacksmith himself, but by the "sword-finisher" (*Schwertfeger*). This occupational title comes from the so-called *Fegen* (sweeping), a rational method to remove the coarsest marks of polishing. In this process,

The blade is polished to the final shape, and details worked out.

Photo: Del Tin

The blade is ground and polished by hand.

Photo: Armart Antiquanova

A finished sword blade.

Photo: Pieces of History

Differentiated Hardening

When researching historical swords, you often encounter specimens that have a greater hardness at the cutting edge than in the center of the blade. This phenomenon is well known from Japanese swords, and the method to achieve this condition has also been carefully handed down there. In medieval swords, this was not the case. We can consider a small difference in hardness between the cutting blade and body as "natural" – the thinner cutting edges cool much faster when quenched than the rest of the blade. But modern swordsmiths also experiment with different methods to achieve a controlled differential hardening. First, the Japanese technique of using a clay shell is simply taken over (more on this in the chapter on samurai swords). On the other hand, there is historical evidence that indicates that another method was used in the European region. The blade is heated very rapidly, so that the thin cutting edges reach the right temperature for hardening, while the rest of the body of the blade has not yet done so. Then the blade is quenched for one to two seconds, pulled out of the hardening bath for the same amount of time, and then finally plunged in again.

the blade is pushed repeatedly to the bottom of a bucket containing a mixture of oil and sharp-edged iron shavings and chips—until it is fairly smooth and clean (it is interesting, that the term term *Vögeln* [archaic English: "*swive*"] for sexual intercourse, derives etymologically from the motion of sweeping [*Fegen*]). Afterwards, the surface of the blade finished with a whetstone. At the end, the blade is cleaned with oil, which also protects it against rusting. Only then is the actual sharpening done. The edges are sharpened using a whetstone.

The last step for making a sword is mounting it: Attaching the cross-guard, grip, and pommel. First, the smith or sword-finisher designs the cross-guard and pommel according to the wishes of the client, then calculates its necessary mass, based on the weight and balance of the finished blade. Then cross-guard and pommel are forged. For cost reasons, in the Middle Ages iron was often used instead of steel for this—these fittings did not require the same hardness as the blade.

When forging the cross-guard, it is necessary to create an indent on the underside for the shoulders of the blade. This indent must match the shoulders as closely as possible, or when the sword is under very heavy stress during a sword fight, the cross-guard might begin to shake. If the cross-guard was not properly fitted, the sword finisher has to fix this afterwards, such as by inserting small iron wedges. This clearly reduces the quality of the sword, and must be avoided by careful work. After forging, cross-guard and pommel are shaped using a file.

The grips on medieval swords were usually made of wood (and sometimes bone or horn), covered with leather. Frequently, cord was then wound around it. There were two methods used to mount the grip: In one, the pommel was riveted to the tang and then a grip made of two pieces of wood glued on (the "sandwich method"). The other method was to make the grip from a single piece of wood, bore through it and then insert the tang through this hole. Then the pommel was riveted on. According to Ewart Oakeshott, the "sandwich method" was used particularly during the Middle Ages to make one-handed swords with short grips, while the second method was used for the long, often waisted grips made during the Late Middle Ages. In contrast, Geibig's findings indicate that, during the Early and High Middle Ages, the boring method was generally used.

In the "sandwich" method to make the grip, cross-guard and pommel are first mounted on the tang. The pommel, with a hole bored through it, is set on the tang and hammered down. A small part of the tang protrudes through the top of the pommel. This is then carefully heated and clinched together, and forged flat into a rivet. This pommel rivet can be recessed, so that it is flush with the pommel surface, or may protrude out. In this case, it is trimmed with a file in a decorative pattern. The riveting fastens the pommel inseparably to the blade. Then, the grip is mounted on. First, two

A Viking sword, just before final mounting.

Photo: Armart Antiquanova

The top part of the tang is riveted over the pommel and hammered flat.

Photo: Del Tin

The tang is riveted through the pommel. The pommel rivet can be recessed, or jut up and be filed down.

Photos: Albion Armorers,

Torsten Schneyer

Centers of Sword-Making

A number of sword-making centers developed very early in Europe. During the 9th and 10th centuries, the blades manufactured in the Frankish Empire enjoyed a very high reputation, and were even coveted by their enemies, the Saracens. Charlemagne issued an edict to control trade in these weapons: it was strictly prohibited under penalty of law, to sell these excellent Frankish sword blades to the Normans. The main center within the Frankish Empire was likely the Bergische Land, where the city of Solingen was later built. According to some historians' theories, the famous blacksmith Ulfberth might have worked here. One likely factor, decisive in ensuring the high quality of these weapons, was the excellent iron ore mined in the region. Passau also developed a blade-making industry during the 14th century, relying on high-quality iron from Steyr in Austria (in Roman times, this province was called Noricum, and the local iron contributed to the success of the spatha).

In other European countries, it was mainly in Brescia in Italy and Toledo in Spain where excellent blades were forged. Towards the end of the Middle Ages, Solingen fought its way to the top of all these cities. Thanks to the use of water power for the hammers and *Schleifkotten* (German medieval name for the grinding workshops), and the resulting early development of a division of labor, Solingen developed into a globally recognized center of metal forging.

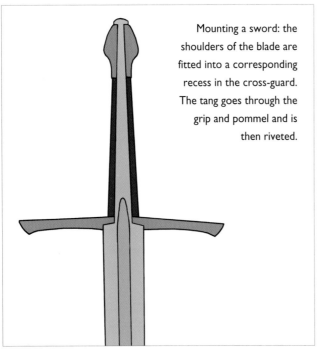

Mounting a sword: the shoulders of the blade are fitted into a corresponding recess in the cross-guard. The tang goes through the grip and pommel and is then riveted.

Decorating a sword mounting with hallmark and damascene inlay.

Photo: Armart Antiquanova

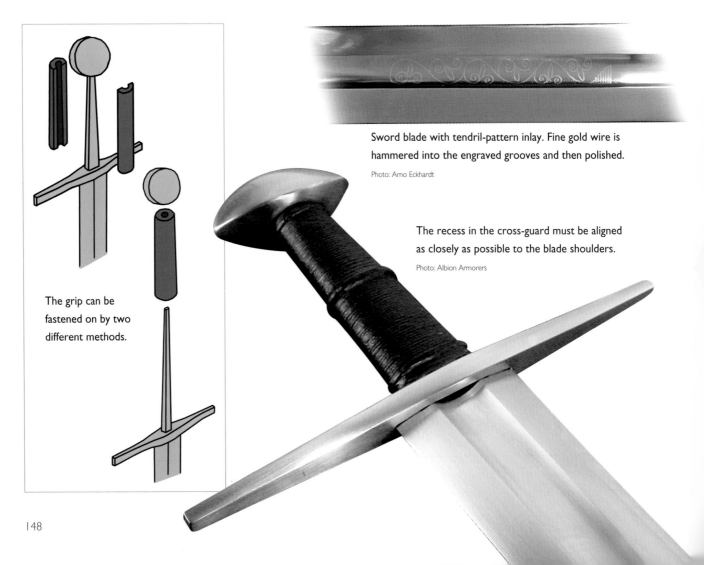

Sword blade with tendril-pattern inlay. Fine gold wire is hammered into the engraved grooves and then polished.

Photo: Arno Eckhardt

The recess in the cross-guard must be aligned as closely as possible to the blade shoulders.

Photo: Albion Armorers

The grip can be fastened on by two different methods.

grip panels are cut from hardwood and each shaped into a semi-circle or half oval. The grip panel inner surfaces are hollowed out to accommodate the tang. The two grip half sections are then shaped to fit the cross-guard, tang, and pommel and then glued to the tang using animal glue.

In the second method, the sword finisher looks for a piece of wood (linden wood was often used), which has approximately three times the diameter of the completed grip. The finisher worked with this excess size to ensure that when the hole was bored through, it would not cause cracks or fissures. A small hole was next bored lengthwise through the wood. Then the tang was heated glowing red. At this stage, Scandinavian knife smiths would customarily wrap a wet rag around the shoulders of the blade, to protect the blade from the heat. The grip is now carefully pushed over the glowing hot tang, so that its exact shape was burnt into the inner side of the grip. The grip is removed and briefly doused in water, while the tang was allowed to cool in the air. The next step was to shape the grip to ensure there would be no gaps between the grip, cross-guard, and pommel sections. The grip was then filed to the desired shape and glued to the tang with animal glue. Only then was the pommel riveted to the tang. If the craftsman's work was faulty or the grip became loosened due to the natural shrinkage of the wood, it can still be mended; the smith can chock the grip using small pieces of metal, as he could also mend the cross-guard.

In the final step, the sword finisher makes the grip cover. In early medieval swords, we find coverings made of several layers of one-centimeter-wide strips of fabric or leather, glued together, wound diagonally or cross-shaped around the grip (see page 76, picture at left). On swords from the High and Late Middle Ages, the design is often much more complicated. Here, the wooden grip is wrapped tightly with a cord. This cord sheath is coated with glue and allowed to dry for a day. Then, the finisher cuts out a leather sleeve which fits the grip exactly. It is soaked in water and glued on the grip wet. This form is again wrapped

tightly with cord. As it dries, the leather draws tight around the grip. Then the top layer of cord is unwound, and the impressions left behind in the leather give it a textured, non-slip structure.

For swords which also were used for representative purposes, the covering was often made of velvet (on Edward III's sword, as noted, it was even made of snakeskin) and then decorative coils of silk or wire were added. Some historians assumed that these decorative wire coils were only used in the Renaissance—where they are found quite often—but they can be found on special representative swords from as early as the 10th century. However, these are definitely an exception on medieval swords.

After the mounting, a matching scabbard is made. The sword maker cuts two thin shells out of hardwood. The cavity is accurately fitted to the sword blade, so that the sword will be held correctly. The shells were lined with fur or wool and then glued together. The animal fats in the fur were intended to protect the blade from rust (the fur of course also soaks up the oil on the sword blade like a brush); beyond this, some historians have even suggested that it had a different function: "The inside was lined with fur so that the lie of the fur strands [...] pointed towards the sword tip, preventing the blade from sliding out," (Menghin, p.18). This hypothesis appears rather far-fetched to me personally, but in any case, many high-quality scabbards are lined with fur.

In the Early Middle Ages, the finished wood form was then wrapped in bands of fabric or leather or completely covered with an entire piece of leather. The leather-covered scabbards are often decorated with relief carvings. During the High and Late Middle Ages, only the leather covering technique was actually used. Sometimes we also find precious materials such as velvet, decorative wire coils, and scabbard slides and chapes of precious metals. Usually the finisher would make a matching sword belt for the scabbard. Finally, the sword was sharpened for one last time and then presented to its new owner.

It can not be stressed often enough, how vital the quality of a swordsmith's work was for a warrior. A defective sword would have the same effect as malfunctioning brakes in a car today. The sword must be:

- well balanced and easy to handle,
- flexible, and
- able to hold a cutting edge.

You can find out how "biddable" or handle-able a sword is relatively quickly—simply brandish it to test it. To test flexibility, bend the blade: According to the sword fighting expert John Clements, you should be able—depending on the type—to bend it by about 3.1-5.9 inches (8-15 centimeters) and then have spring back to its original shape. In some heroic legends (for example, the Svarfdæla saga *Kalavipoeg*) and in works by some chroniclers (such as the Monk of St. Gall), there are reports of a much more ruthless test of flexibility: The sword is bent from point to pommel, forming a circle. Then it springs back perfectly straight.

While modern studies confirmed the accuracy of many historical traditions, such "test-reports" as these, based on findings of experimental archeology, should be classified as "hype." Even the best sword could not withstand such a procedure. An almost legendary test with a modern samurai sword of L6 tool steel, produced the following results:

- 60° bend => the blade springs back to the original position.
- 90° bend => the blade remains bent by about 15°.
- 160° bend => the blade breaks.

According to modern findings, the "bending tests" in these sages are of about the same level of validity as the reports about Sigurd's sword that could cleave through an anvil. A much more realistic flexibility test has been preserved for us by Philo of Alexandria (about 10 BC to 50 AD):

If one wants to test the capabilities of these [Celtiberian swords], grasp the grip with your right hand, and the sword point with the other. Lay it across your head and pull it down on both sides until it touches the shoulders. Pull both hands back quickly, to then release it. The released blade straightens out again and returns to its original shape, so that it has no trace of any curvature. Even with several repetitions of this test, it always straightens out.

Rain-Guards for Swords

To protect the precious blade from rust, 14th- and 15th-century swords often have a kind of "rain-guard" – a mini-poncho, which was intended to prevent water from getting into the scabbard. Such guards are rarely preserved on historical swords, but we can find them on the majority of the swords depicted in contemporary visual sources. These guards were made of leather or heavy cloth, usually were round and basically exactly as wide as the scabbard. Presumably they were made by the same sword finisher who had made the scabbard. It seems that most of the models, like a poncho, had a worked-in slit that simply slipped over the grip and then covered a portion of the cross-guard and the scabbard mouthpiece. However, we can also distinctly see a guard buttoned closed like a cuff, on the grave slab of knight Berchtold von Waldner, who died in 1343. Metal rain-guards which were an integral part of the cross-guard, are rare.

Photo: Albion Armourers

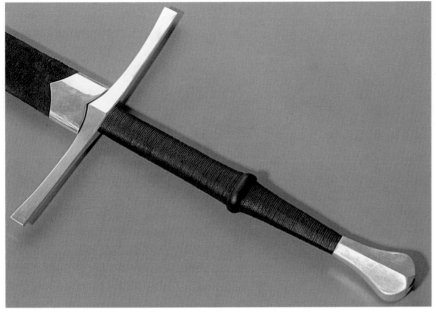

The grip is constructed of three layers: First, the hardwood core of the grip, which is then wound around with cord, and finally a leather sheath.

The uppermost layer of cord is unwound after drying. The impressions are retained by the leather as a non-slip surface on the bottom layer of cord.

Photo: Traumschmiede/Eckhardt

A scabbard usually consists of a hollow wooden form which is covered with leather and often lined with fur.

Photo: Torsten Schneyer

Some scabbards were sumptuously decorated and ornamented with precious metals.

Photo: Museum Replicas

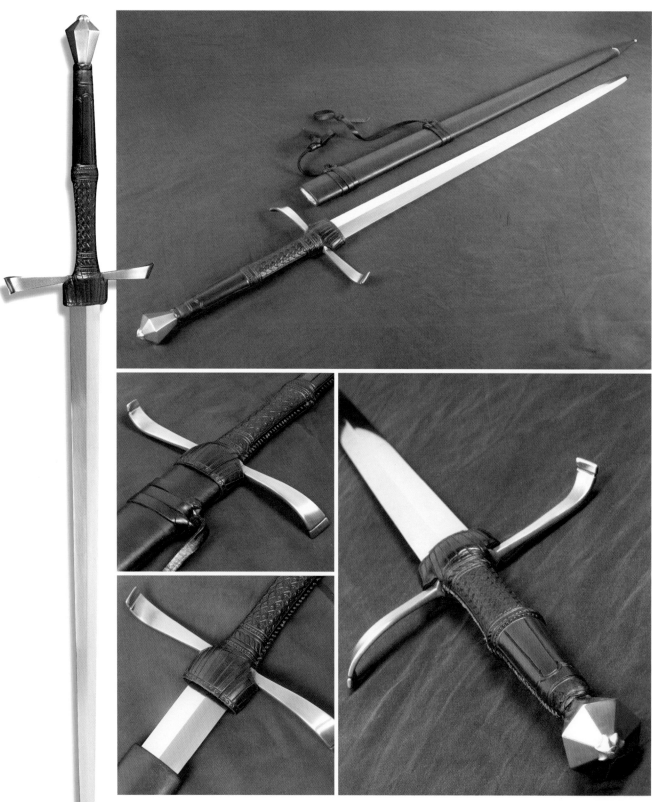

Impressions of a finished long-sword: this work of art in steel was made by the "soul swordsmith" Stefan Roth for Torsten Schneyer of the Zornhau sword fighting group.

Photo: Torsten Schneyer

Such a test puts extreme stress on the sword, and only good blades could survive it unscathed.

Unfortunately, no Middle Ages cutting tests have been handed down to us. Here also, the achievements of the legendary "super swords" do not provide us with any evidence—a sword that cuts through an anvil and remains razor sharp is a fantasy. Nevertheless, swords can perform amazing cutting capabilities. Albion Armorers test their swords' cutting edges on the rims of steel drums. The tester strikes the drum hard with the sword, and afterwards, the cutting edges should only show small nicks that can be ground away again with minimal effort. The *tameshigiri* test is another popular test, in which the sword is used to strike a rolled straw mat or thick cardboard shipping tubes.

A sword is far more than just a specially shaped piece of steel or a status symbol—in earlier times, a sword was a life insurance policy and still radiates a tremendous fascination on us today.

Bruce Brookhart, from the production department of Museum Replicas, testing the flexibility of a finished sword.

Photo: Museum Replicas

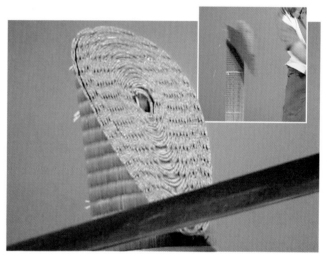

Testing the cutting ability of a bastard sword Japanese-style (on a rolled straw mat).

Photo: Cold Steel

Cutting test on a tube made of hard cardboard.

Photo: Cold Steel

Sword Trademark Piracy

Cases of sword "trademark piracy" started already in the Middle Ages, including piracy of swords made by "Ulfberht" and "Ingelri." All our modern knowledge indicates that Ulfberht (spelled in various ways) was a Frankish swordsmith who was active around 850. The first blades signed with his name, which displayed the word "Ulfberht" welded in capital letters of Damascus steel, come from this period. The Ulfberht swords are worked from superbly refined steel and are very well balanced. However, there were so many Ulfberht swords (occurring up to the High Middle Ages), that they could not possibly all have been made by this master swordsmith. In the case that these swords were not all forged by his official successors (his sons?), we have here a fairly clear case of trademark piracy. The same seems to be the case for the Ingelri swords that appear in the 10th century. In the Late Middle Ages, the Solingen bladesmiths "borrowed" the famous Passau wolf hallmark, or the names of popular smiths from Toledo. In 1464, Passau complained to Solingen about this trademark piracy — to no effect. As Solingen became famous, the hallmarks of the Bergische Land bladesmiths were, in turn, copied by other smiths.

Damascus Steel

Forging Damascus steel was always something special for me. There is an inherent beauty in this steel, evoking the feeling of a miracle.

— (Don Fogg)

Anyone interested in swords will at some time come across the term "Damascus steel." Not only by its aura of mystery, but also by its inimitable beauty, Damascus steel still works its fascination on us today. But now, what about the mystery itself?

From what we discussed previously, we already know the problems that arise due to the lack of compatibility between brittle steel and soft iron. The laminating technique was only one way to solve this problem; another is forging Damascus steel. At some point in the Early Middle Ages, a weapons smith came to the brilliant idea of welding together alternate layers of soft iron and hard steel (or softer and harder steel), so as to create a flexible and yet hard blade. This principle of composite steel welding later became known around the world as forging Damascus steel. "In the early Merovingian period, and even earlier, this finishing process seems to have been the only way that many swordsmiths had to guarantee producing usable sword blades," (Menghin, p.18).

If bare polished Damascus steel is etched with acids, the layers of steel and iron create a pattern, because the carbon-rich areas are affected more and become darker in color. Depending on the method of forging and polishing used it is possible to see these patterns without using etching, and there is evidence that medieval swords were not etched, although based on the current state of research, this matter remains quite unclear (modern Damascus blades are generally etched). In any case, these fascinating patterns and the hardness and flexibility of the blades created the legendary reputation of Damascus steel. The name comes from the city of Damascus, which formerly was regarded as the "birthplace" of Damascus steel. This theory is no longer tenable: Damascus steel was almost certainly invented in Europe.

In the Middle Ages, Damascus was only the main trading center for this type of sword.

There are several groups of Damascus steel types, as follows:

- Forge-welded (also called "artificial" Damascus steel), where the different metals are welded together during forging.
- Crystalline Damascus steel (also: real, Oriental Damascus steel, wootz), where the different metals are fused together during casting. This type of Damascus steel is discussed in more detail in the section on sabers.

The oldest and most famous Damascus steel is forge-welded. This is what is usually meant when Damascus steel is discussed. We can distinguish various techniques for forge-welding steel. The most important are:

- banded Damascus steel
- wild Damascus steel
- twisted Damascus steel
- stamped Damascus steel

Banded Damascus steel is probably the oldest and crudest kind. To forge this steel, a billet of on average four layers of iron and three layers of steel, is welded into a metal bar when it is white hot. This bar is drawn out into a rod, which is bent back on itself into a V. The V is welded around an iron core, while steel cutting edges are forged onto it. After it is etched, the blade clearly shows the V-shaped bands. Banded Damascus steel is often found in dagger blades from the first century AD, and many of the Celtic La Tene culture blades. "Roman period daggers with banded Damascus steel blades let us conclude that the makers deliberately created and made the pattern in the banded Damascus steel visible," (Hoeper, p.17).

Wild Damascus steel is made by further working the initial bar of metal. It is divided lengthways or across its width. These pieces are laid on each other and welded together, yielding double layers. Depending upon how many more times, and how finely the layers of the different types of steel are forged together, the better the different properties of these steels are distributed in the finished blade. The process of folding and doubling the layers, which can be repeated several times, is called *Gärben* (sheaf) in German; the Japanese

To forge "mysterious" Damascus steel, various types of steel are welded together to produce a blade that is tough and flexible at the same time. This forging technique produces a characteristic pattern in the steel (modern interpretation of a Viking sword by Kevin Cashen).

Photo: Kevin Cashen/Weyer

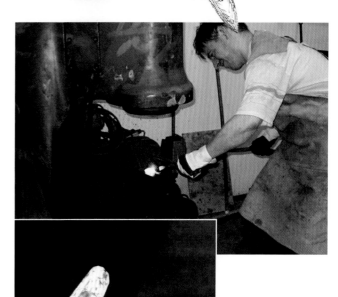

Folding over the glowing-hot steel.

Photos: Armart Antiquanova

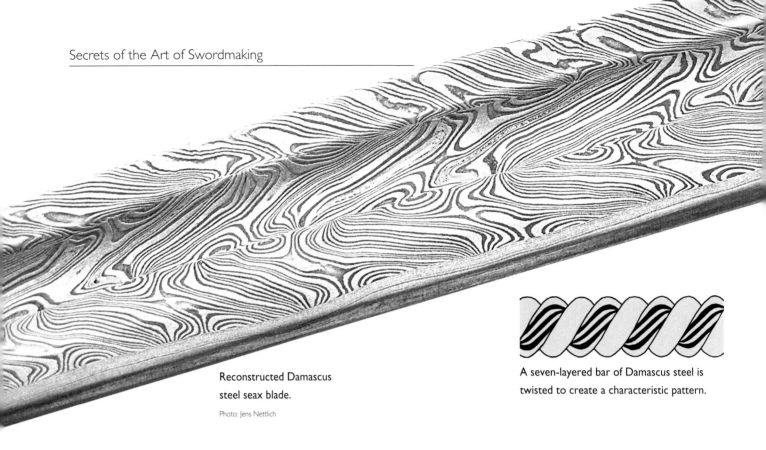

Reconstructed Damascus
steel seax blade.

Photo: Jens Nettlich

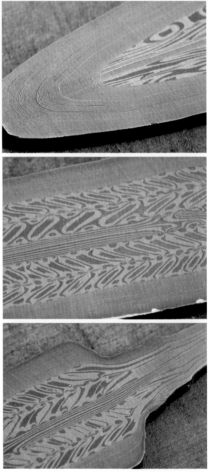

A seven-layered bar of Damascus steel is
twisted to create a characteristic pattern.

Alternately twisted and straight forged
Damascus steel rods were arranged to
form the blade.

Photo: Patrick Bärta

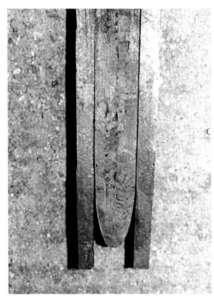

Pure steel cutting edge fillets are welded
onto the Damascus core.

Photo: Patrick Bärta

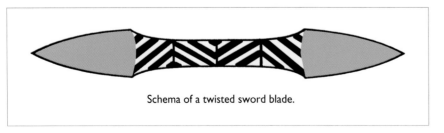

Schema of a twisted sword blade.

A "worm colored" sword blade of twisted
Damascus steel.

term *san-mai* is often also used in English. The following list shows the incredible number of layers that can be produced:

    1x = 14
    2x = 28
    3x = 56
    4x = 112
    5x = 224
    6x = 448
    7x = 896

The more or less erratic damascene pattern can "only" be affected by the direction in which the billet is divided and the number of layers, which is why it is called "wild," in contrast to the subsequent technique of forge-welding. To produce a controlled pattern, a billet of Damascus steel is notched at regular intervals with a file or a special hammer. Then, the swordsmith forges the billet flat again. The purpose of this forging is to re-distribute the structure of the steel, which is reflected in the resulting pattern.

Twisted Damascus steel was the one most important for medieval swords. To make twisted Damascus steel (called "Turkish damask" in German-speaking regions) the billet is not only folded over, but the drawn out, glowing hot rod is also twisted on its longitudinal axis. Twisting splinters the outer oxide layer, and reduces the level of impurities—improving the quality of the twisted rod of steel. Twisting allows you to see right away if the individual layers are welded firmly together. This technique allows the smith to create beautiful patterns, while ensuring at the same time an even stronger bond between the individual layers. Sword makers also attribute an additional effect of twisting the steel, which is that it makes the steel more shock-absorbent, something of course especially important for swords. Given the properties created by this forging technique, it is little wonder that the use of twisted Damascus steel soon became a mark of a high quality sword.

The twisted rods are then shaped into the body of the blade, and hard steel cutting edges forged onto its sides (on modern Damascus steel weapons only intended to "please the eye," these important "cutting strips" are usually omitted for aesthetic reasons).

The Sutton Hoo Sword (reconstruction by Patrick Barta).

Photo: Patrick Bárta/Tomás Baley

妙技精魂

Dramatic effect: the same
blade of mono-steel and with
Damascus steel veneer.

During the Early Middle Ages, it is likely that the patterns in twisted Damascus steel had not only decorative but also magical significance—but we no longer know what that magical symbolism was. To the human eye, the pattern often looks like a number of little worms. We also know from the Germanic heroic legends of the later Migration Period that the term "worm colored" was used to describe these blades; the earliest written record is probably in the *Theoderichbrief* (Theodoric letter, more on this below). In the Anglo-Saxon epic poem *Beowulf* (10th century), we find the corresponding designation, *wyrmfah*.

Worm-colored blades appear first in the Migration Period. At that time, such blades, as on a seax, were often composed of several lengthwise stripes of mono-steel and wild and twisted Damascus steel. Worm-colored swords were widespread and highly valued throughout the Early and High Middle Ages: So highly valued, that they were perfectly acceptable gifts for kings. Thus, in the 6th century, Theodoric the Great wrote a letter to the King of the Varner (*rex varnorum*; some historians identify him as Thrasamund, King of the Vandals, and Theodoric's brother-in-law), thanking him profusely for the Damascus steel blade that he had received as a gift:

> Swords which can even cut through armor, and by the nature of the iron (= steel) are more precious than the value of their gilding. Its highly polished surface gleams so that it clearly reflects the viewer's countenance, and its cutting edges taper so evenly, that one might think they were cast in a single piece and not composed of several rods. In its beautifully grooved center, one can believe one is seeing rippling worms, and the shading is so diverse, that the shining metal seems to be woven of different colors. Your whetstone has cleaned the same so carefully, your excellent sand has polished it so artfully, that it makes this shining iron virtually into a mirror for humanity. Nature has provided abundantly for your homeland, since it has thus made you famous: Swords, which by their beauty, could have come from Vulcan's workshop and which are designed with such elegant craftsmanship, that what is shaped by hand appears not to be a work of mortal men,

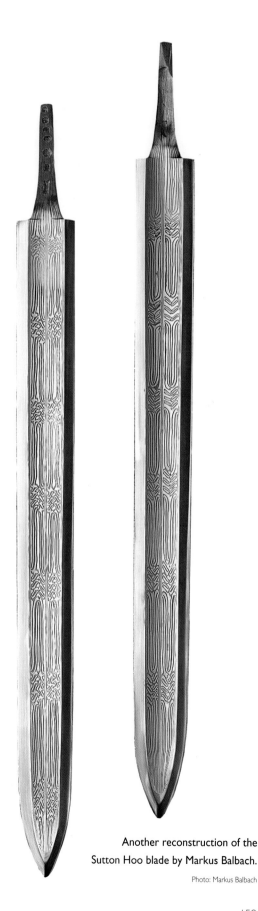

Another reconstruction of the Sutton Hoo blade by Markus Balbach.

Photo: Markus Balbach

but of divine origin. We therefore gladly accept the weapons which your ambassadors have presented to us as signs of fitting greetings, and as a good means for the preservation of peace, and we present you with an equally valuable gift in return, which we hope may be as gladly received, as yours was pleasing to us.

Unfortunately, the swords of which Theodoric speaks have not survived. However, a worm colored sword from around the same period was interred with an Anglo-Saxon king in the Sutton Hoo ship grave. The remnants were recovered, along with the other finds from the grave, and analyzed carefully. This is a beautifully decorated Vendel type long-sword. But what is really special is the worm colored blade, which has now been reconstructed several times by Damascus steel smiths—such as Manfred Sachse, Markus Balbach, and Patrick Barta. The Damascus steel core is composed of two sides of each four stripes of twisted Damascus steel. Two steel cutting edge strips are welded on the core. The bands are so constructed, that they were forged alternatively twisted and straight. Two bands each are twisted rightwards and leftwards. In addition, on the two sides of the blade, the twisted sections are each reflected by a straight one. A masterpiece of Damascus steel artistry: definitely worthy of a king.

Worm colored blades, strictly speaking, also include veneer or top-coated Damascus steel, which was already being made in the Early Middle Ages. To make these, a thin layer of Damascus steel was welded on each side of a "normal" blade, which is why this technique is also called "veneering." Usually different kinds of metal wire were used. The wires are braided and twisted, forged flat and then welded to the sword. This was one way to obtain the coveted damascene pattern, without having to use such complex and costly procedures to forge an entire blade. However, this process would not create the mechanical advantages of Damascus steel. It is, rather, purely cosmetic surgery.

During the High Middle Ages, Damascus steel disappeared for several centuries from the stage of (European) history. There are two possible explanations for this. One hypothesis is that only the secret of how to etch the Damascus patterns was lost, although overall, no Damascus steel was being forged. The blades were all *blank gefegt* ("swept" or finished bare). In this case, it is likely that only the flexibility of the steel was considered a criterion of quality. It is first necessary to test these bare-finished blades (tests for etching, X-rays), to determine which are made of Damascus steel and which are not.

The other theory is that it had been known since the Ulfberht blades were forged, that high quality all-steel weapons—which have been properly tempered—are superior to Damascus blades. Since then, thanks to the increasing use of water power, new sources of supply for forged steel developed, so that there was no more need to refine inferior steel by using Damascus steel forging methods.

By the 1960s, the art of forging Damascus steel was on the brink of extinction. Fortunately, this was prevented by the growing popularity of knife collecting. The legendary American blacksmith and knife maker Bill Moran brought collectors and makers back to appreciating Damascus steel. To make modern Damascus steel, usually the smith welds two or more different types of steel together, instead of steel and iron. The criterion for selection is often the visual contrast between the steels after they are etched (such as W1 carbon steel and pure nickel or nickel steel). Today, a collector has many possibilities for obtaining a Damascus steel sword.

A dagger with
controlled
Damascene pattern.

Photo: Harvey Dean

Modern Damascus
steel sword by
Kevin Cashen.

Photo: Kevin Cashen / Weyer

Sword Katachi style.

Photos and graphic design: Clemens Richardson and Volkmar Dietz

The Samurai Sword as an Object of Comparison

Again, there is the perception in this world, that you can limit swordsmanship exclusively to the technical handling of the sword; and thus it is hoped that, by mere practice of wielding a sword, through posture and skill alone, you can attain the proficiency to be victorious, but such as this is by no means sufficient for the way.

— (Myamoto Musashi, *The Book of Five Rings*)

Perhaps some readers are now wondering why I am even broaching the subject of samurai swords. Well, quite simply because in nearly all conversations and discussions about European swords, at some point, inevitably, the Japanese sword is brought up as an object of comparison. In my opinion, there are reasons for this circumstance besides all their obvious popularity due to movies, television, and computer games:

- The Japanese sword was still being used in the recent past.
- In contrast to European swords, most of which have only survived in badly damaged condition, samurai swords were well maintained. Centuries-old weapons look like new to the viewer. Even the original forging patterns can still be clearly recognized.
- The art of the Japanese swordsmith has been maintained in an unbroken tradition since the Middle Ages.
- With some modifications, swordsmanship has been handed down to the present time.

As a result, if you are interested in swords, you cannot get around the samurai sword. This discussion is anyway significantly facilitated by the abundance of the literature. Due to their high cultural value, Japanese swords are probably the best researched and documented edged weapons of all. Therefore, this chapter will be able (and willing) to give only a terribly brief overview. All readers interested in more detail are referred to the appropriate literature.

I must first add a disambiguation about the design of samurai swords. The vast majority of samurai swords, due to their curved single-edged blades, are by definition not actually swords, but sabers. However, the term sword has become so well established, that it would be rather pointless to dwell on it.

9.1 Development of the Japanese Sword

To be able to compare the samurai sword with European swords, we first require an introduction to the subject. Just as in Europe, in Japan, the sword was valued high above other weapons. However, this reverence has survived to this day in Japan. For centuries, Japan was dominated by wars between rival noble families, which made it possible for a very special form of warrior nobility to develop: the samurai. The samurai embodied absolute loyalty and contempt of death. There was only one choice: victory or death. For the samurai, their sword was more than a weapon, it was a symbol. Their motto was: "The sword is the soul of the samurai." Swords were (and still are) revered in Shinto shrines and sanctuaries, and play a major religious role. The weapons smith was the most highly respected craftsmen of all; this art was even worthy of emperors. Some swords are even considered national treasures. Because of this special feature of Japanese culture, many records on this subject have been passed down and very many old weapons have been preserved. Already in the Middle Ages, alongside the samurai themselves and the blacksmiths, actual blade experts developed, with blades including basically everything—from those of sword to spear. Therefore, we still have very old "specialized books" about blades which date from the 13th century.

Although the sword was the most revered weapon in medieval Europe, this devotion went a lot further in Japan. The best example is to compare the *Song of Roland* and a story from Japanese history. The 11th-century *Song of Roland* describes the adventures of the Frankish knight Roland in the service of Charlemagne. According to legend, Roland died at the battle of Roncesvalles in 778. To ensure that his sacred sword Durendal would not fall into the hands of the pagan Saracens—in reality, they were Basques—the besieged and mortally wounded Roland tried several times to break Durendal against a rock. When this failed, he threw Durendal into a river, where it disappeared.

In 1582, the Japanese prince Akechi found himself in a situation similar to Roland's—his castle was besieged and on fire. In this situation, Akechi sent a request to the enemy commander: "I have many excellent swords that I have treasured for a lifetime, and which should not perish with me [...] I would die happy, if you would halt for attack for a short time so that I can present these swords to you as gifts." The request was granted, and the swords were lowered from the burning castle and rescued. Thus, a samurai would rather give a valuable sword to his enemy rather than destroy it. "It was believed that a sword was the guardian of its own history, and that the spirits of its previous owners lived in it. The current holder of the sword was therefore only the guardian of the blade that had been given to him for safekeeping, so that he could pass it on to future generations," (Kapp and Yoshihara, p.18). If any such magnificent sword had an unworthy owner—such as a lousy swordsman—you would say: "The sword is weeping!"

History and Manufacture of Japanese Swords

The classification and assignment of Japanese blades is a science in itself. I am not just saying this: In Japan, this is really a scientific discipline. There are a great many categories among which the blades are divided. The following presentation of this science is therefore extremely brief and only a general overview.

It starts with the definition. The designation "sword" represents a generic term in Japan: Any edged weapon with a blade more than 5.9 inches (15 centimeters) long, a *hamon* ("blade pattern" or visual effect of hardening on the blade), and a tang with dowel hole, is considered a "sword." As result, this term comprises not only all "mature" swords, but also short swords and even daggers. The blade length (measured as for sabers) is therefore the first distinctive

category of a Japanese sword. The measure used here is the *shaku*, a unit of length (=11.8 inches [30.3 centimeters]). The Japanese concept of a "medium-length sword" is thus so different from the Western understanding, that in this country the terms short sword and dagger are usually interchanged.

Blade length	Japanese Name	Western Description
Up to 1	*shaku tan-to* (short sword)	dagger
1 to 2	*shaku shoh-to* (medium-length sword)	short sword
Over 2	*shaku dai-to* (long-sword)	sword

In addition to the length, there is a second comprehensive category used to differentiate the swords: their age. Here, the phases of sword history—which of course have their own titles—run parallel to the categorized periods of overall Japanese history. This sometimes leads to some confusion, since you have to distinguish between the sword period, and the "normal" period of history. It is similar in European history: here also, Gothic and Renaissance occur in the same time period. However, one is an art history term, while the other concerns the overall historical period.

The Ancient Sword Period (Koto): Up to 1596

Typical Japanese swords were not yet developed before the 10th century and the *chokuto* or *ken* types of weapons represented copies of or even imported Chinese and Korean swords. The officers considered Chinese swords to be superior weapons. These swords characteristically were straight, and sometimes had double-edged blades.

During the Heian period (794-1191), the administration of the empire disintegrated, there were countless wars, and the samurai caste developed. Battles were fought mainly on horseback. The straight swords were therefore gradually replaced by curved long-swords (with blades some 47.2 inches [120 centimeters] long). The quality of blade-forging improved significantly. Unfortunately, almost no

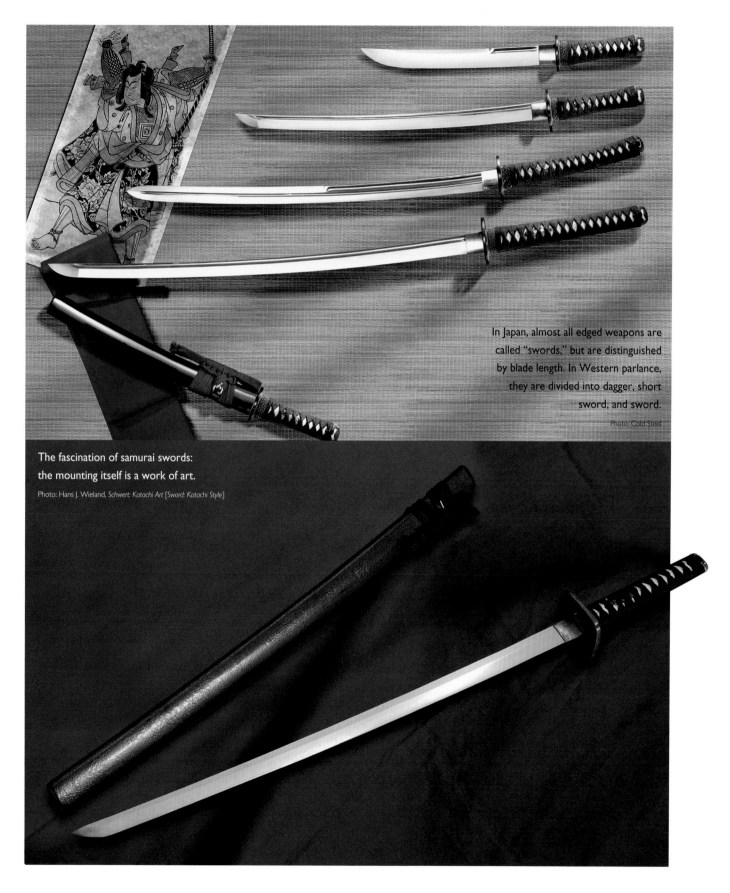

In Japan, almost all edged weapons are called "swords," but are distinguished by blade length. In Western parlance, they are divided into dagger, short sword, and sword.

Photo: Cold Steel

The fascination of samurai swords: the mounting itself is a work of art.

Photo: Hans J. Wieland, *Schwert: Katachi Art* [Sword: Katachi Style]

Chokuto, about 600 AD.

Before the "typical" Japanese sword developed, there were also several other blade shapes. The *kogarasu-zukuri* form comes of the transitional period.

Photo: Cold Steel

Different blade cross-sections: Right, the cutting edge is convex, so that it can be used to protect against heavy armor.

The characteristic samurai sword is slightly curved and single-edged.

Photo: Hans J. Wieland

Sword: Katachi Art

The *dai-sho* sword pair consists of the long-sword *katana* and short sword *wakizashi*.

Photo: Pieces of History

blades have survived from this transitional period. One of these rare specimens is *kogarasu-Maru* (= little crow)—the famous Taira clan sword—from the early Heian period. We find here an almost symmetrical, double-edged point, as is typical for many ken blades, on a curved, single-edged blade. The technical term for this form is *"kissaki-moroha-zuku-ri"* (with double-edged tip), but it is often called *"kogarasu-zukuri,"* after *"kogarasu-maru."* The swordsmith Yasatsuna, who was active around 900, is considered the forefather of "typical Japanese" swords: he made perfectly forged, single-edged blades with a slight curve.

Here, incidentally, is a significant difference to the European medieval sword: A characteristic, basic blade shape was developed in Japan, and there has been little deviation from this. The Japanese sword blade, due to the blade shape and manufacturing technique, can be used both for military (i.e., against an armored samurai) and civilian dueling (against an unarmored opponent).

In contrast, in Europe, the various types of blades were developed according to their purpose. In Japan, there are smaller differences, mainly concerning the blade wedge angle, depending upon the opponent's armor: "Thin and sharp edges were always used when the opponent had thick fabric or leather armor, while broader and somewhat duller cutting edges were designed for fighting against metal armor," *(Kapp and Yoshihara, p.42).*

The best swordsmith in Japanese history was active during the Koto period. The famous "five schools" of the art of sword making—Bizen, Yamashiro, Yamato, Soshu, and Mino—were developed. Soshu swords from the Kamakura period (1192-1336) are unequalled to this day.

The endless feuds among regional nobles began during the Muromachi period (1337-1573), and this led to a large demand for swords, so that the smiths started using mass production methods and no longer refined the steel themselves. Many swords have survived from this time, but only a few prime pieces.

The New Sword Period (Shinto): 1597 To 1876

A period of relative peace began in Japan: In the Azuchi-Momoyama period, Toyotomi Hideoshi ended the perpetual small wars. Tokugawa Ieyasu introduced the Edo period (1603-1867, the Shogunate). Japan was again ruled centrally with a firm hand by the shoguns, while the emperor was just a figurehead for the government.

Peace meant that swords lost much of their military significance, and they developed more into status symbols. This is reflected in specific effects:

- The *daito* were shorter; their average blade length was now mostly 2 *shaku*.
- As a status symbol, the weapon's appearance was important. Thus, sword-finishers put more and more emphasis on elaborate decorations. Not only the mounting, but also the blades were now often engraved.

Appearance became more important than the art of sword forging. This led to a significant decline in the quality of the swords. The tradition of the five schools came to an end, and swords were forged in all major cities. Edo (modern Tokyo) became the center of sword manufacturing.

Unfortunately, the lion's share of still-existing historical swords comes from the Shinto period. During this time, it became the fashion to wear a smaller long-sword (*katana*) along with an appropriate short sword (*wakizashi*, blade length about 17.7 inches [45 centimeters]), as a pair (*dai-sho*). The *dai-sho* mountings were designed as a set—like the European *Degen* and left hand dagger. While the *katana* was worn only outside the home, a man always kept his *wakizashi* at his side; at night, he laid it next to his bed.

Modern Sword Period (Gendaito): Since 1876

In 1868, the Emperor Meiji snatched power from the shogun government, and began to govern again himself. Within a short time, he introduced significant innovations based on Western culture. One of the most serious steps was to deprive the samurai caste of their privileges: In 1876, wearing a sword was prohibited. Many sword makers lost their jobs, and many swords were sold abroad.

At the beginning of the Showa period (1926-89), as the Japanese again began to focus on traditional values and the samurai culture, the art of sword making revived. In recent years, the craft of metal forging has been experiencing a revival. More and more Japanese-style swords are being forged in Europe and the USA. Contemporary swords are called *gendaito* (modern swords), and for swords made since 1955, the expression *shinsakuto* (newly manufactured swords) is also sometimes used.

Besides its age, a sword can also be defined by its mounting. Here, we distinguish six different sorts: The most common by far is the *buke-zukuri* mounting, from the Shinto period. The mounting of a *buke-zukuri* sword consists of the following:

- A ray-skin covered wooden grip is fastened to the flat tang with bamboo dowels (not with rivets!), and (for *tanto*, only sometimes) is wrapped around with bands (made of silk, leather, or cotton);
- A small pommel cap (*kashira*) and grip ferrule (*fuchi*);
- Grip ornaments (*menuki*)—small figures that were either wrapped in the grip or stuck into the grip without wrapping;
- A hand guard (*tsuba*);
- A scabbard (usually made of magnolia wood), which was painted and sometimes decorated with inlay.

The scabbard often had compartments for two of the following tools:

- Companion knife (*kogatana*); it was used as a multi-purpose or throwing knife (in Western literature, the term *kozuka* is often used for *kogatana*, although this is actually only the *kogatana* grip);

- Sword needle (*kogai*); a sword needle fulfilled various functions: It served as a hairpin and was also intended for stabbing the body of a slain enemy, to mark it as a "trophy," or to skewer the severed head.
- Metal chopsticks (*wari-bashi*); these are shaped like the sword needle split lengthwise.

When the sword is in the scabbard, the tool handles protrude through holes in the *tsuba*. Here is another parallel to late medieval swords, which were also often fitted with scabbards with compartments for tools. Japanese and European sets of tools look strikingly similar. While the function of the companion knife is the same, a sword needle serves a completely different purpose than an awl.

All the metal parts of the mounting, such as pommel cap, grip ferrule, grip inserts and *tsuba*, as well as the *kogai* and *kogatana*, were typically richly decorated. They were given the same finish and manufactured by the same craftsmen (except for the *kogatana* blade, which as a rule was forged by a swordsmith). Generally an alloy of copper and gold (*shakudo*), which was etched dark, was used for the decorations. In artistic terms, the *tsuba* is the most valuable part of the mounting. *Tsuba* were made both by simple arms makers and the most highly skilled weapons smiths, and now form a separate field for collectors.

The whole mounting could be removed with little effort, in contrast to European weaponry. This had the advantage that they could be easily interchanged, such as for repair or to decorate an inherited, traditional blade in a fashionable style. Ultimately, the blade was the most highly valued part (in terms of function, also the most important part). Thus, very old swords often will appear in relatively new mountings. If a sword was not worn for a long time, the mounting was removed and the blade given a special "safe-keeping" mounting to protect it. Here, we have the third significant difference from the European Middle Ages: The sword mountings were not intended to be interchangeable, and a warrior owned different swords for different occasions, while military or out-of-fashion models were simply "mothballed."

Dai-sho sword pair in their stand.

Photo: japanklingen.de

Grip of a *buke-zukuri* mounting.

Photo: Pieces of History

A *menuki* grip ornament wrapped over the ray-skin cover.

Photo: Pieces of History

Buke-zukuri is the most common mounting.

Photo: Oliver Lang, *Schwert: Katachi Art*

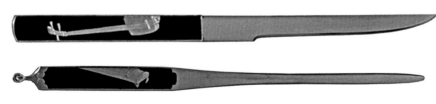

Companion knife (*kogatana*) and sword needle (*kogai*).

Photo: Pieces of History

Pommel cap (*kashira*) and grip ferrule (*kuchi*) are designed to match.

Photos: Oliver Lang, *Schwert: Katachi Art*

The *tsuba* itself is a collectible piece.

Photo: Pieces of History

The hand guard (*tsuba*).

Photo: Pieces of History

The mounting can be easily removed by pulling out the bamboo dowels.

Photo: japanklingen.de

The blade is the main distinguishing feature of a Japanese sword. We make the first distinction here by the shape of the blade. These include, in addition to the already known dimensions of blade length (*nagasa*) and curvature (*sori*):

- overall shape of the blade (*zukuri*), that is, its lateral form and cross section,
- shape and size of the point (*kissaki*)
- the center point of the curvature (*zori*)
- thickness of the blade ridge (*shinogi*)
- width of the blade upper surface (*shinogi-ji*)
- shape of the back cross section (*mune*), and
- details of the blade surface (*ji*), such as fullers and engravings.

You can make even more distinctions, which include terms composed of those for the lateral blade shape and cross section. There are two main categories for the blade shapes:

- *shinogi-zukuri* (with ridge) and
- *hira-zukuri* (without ridge).

Other distinguishing features, besides the blade shape, are created by the various forging processes (more on this below).

The hardness and sharpness of Japanese swords are legendary, as is the art of sword making itself. In principle, however, the technical process is not that much different for the way European blades are forged. In cultural terms, however, forging a Japanese sword is a spiritual, almost sacred, act. Before he begins, the swordsmith undergoes several prayer, fasting, and meditation ceremonies. Often he wears the white robes of a Shinto priest. In addition, the forge itself must be cleaned. This serves primarily to prevent contamination of the steel.

The first step in the forging process is refining the steel, this was, especially in earlier centuries, made especially by the swordsmith himself. The raw materials—iron-magnetite and iron-rich sand—were procured from the various provinces. These materials were processed into raw steel in a refining furnace (*tatara* oven). While a *tatara* furnace is slightly more sophisticated than a bloomery furnace, the principle

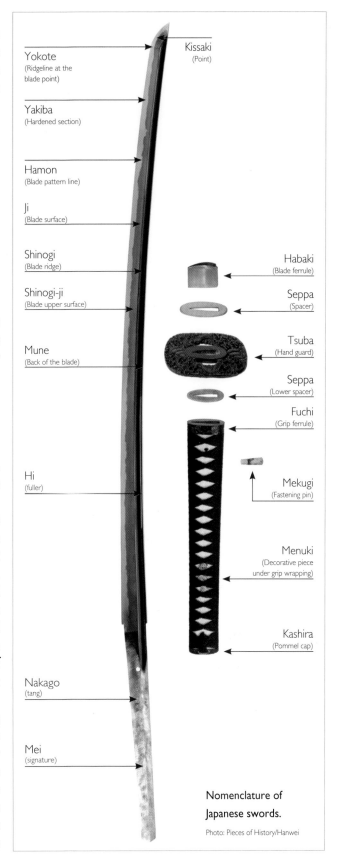

Yokote (Ridgeline at the blade point)

Yakiba (Hardened section)

Hamon (Blade pattern line)

Ji (Blade surface)

Shinogi (Blade ridge)

Shinogi-ji (Blade upper surface)

Mune (Back of the blade)

Hi (fuller)

Nakago (tang)

Mei (signature)

Kissaki (Point)

Habaki (Blade ferrule)

Seppa (Spacer)

Tsuba (Hand guard)

Seppa (Lower spacer)

Fuchi (Grip ferrule)

Mekugi (Fastening pin)

Menuki (Decorative piece under grip wrapping)

Kashira (Pommel cap)

Nomenclature of Japanese swords.

Photo: Pieces of History/Hanwei

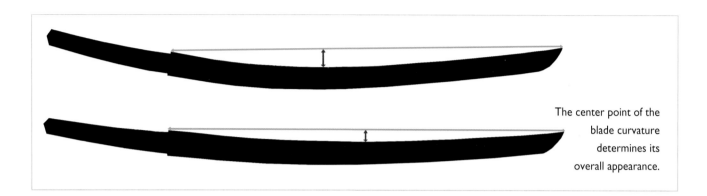

The center point of the
blade curvature
determines its
overall appearance.

Different blade forms: *Hira-zukuri* (without ridge, top)
and *shinogi-zukuri* (with ridge, below).

Photo: japanklingen.d

Tamahagane – raw steel used for a Japanese sword.

Photo: japanklingen.de

Shell and core are forged together.

Photo: Pieces of History

Forging a samurai
sword is a sacred act.

Photo: Kai Europe

is the same. Starting in the 16th century, iron and steel imported from abroad were frequently used, which of course saved the swordsmith a significant amount of labor. Today, there is still one single *tatara* furnace in operation, which only produces steel for sword making.

The most important aspect of forging a Japanese sword, is that the cutting edges are given a differentiated hardening than the rest of the blade body (more on this below). The blades are usually forged in two parts; the core and the shell. For the shell, the swordsmith takes an iron plate, and covers it with very hard pieces of steel. This billet is brought to glowing hot over a pine charcoal fire and then forge welded. The billet is folded in lengthwise and/or sideways and then welded together again. This later creates a characteristic pattern. This operation is repeated about six times. During this process, tools and billet are repeatedly cleaned, to produce an especially pure steel.

"The swordsmith now regulates the carbon content by the way he treats the steel in the forge. By heating the steel to 1,300° and by the constant hammering and folding it over again, the larger carbon crystals are broken up, and impurities reduced," (Kapp and Yoshihara, p.32).

In contrast to European Damascus steel, the folding process here does not consist of welding different steels together, but in homogenizing the layers of steel. However, a certain amount of inhomogeneous particles remain—these add extra strength and create the fascinating patterns in the steel. In any case, the Japanese folding process, like forging Damascus steel, is a refining process to qualitatively "spice up" the initial material. To make the shell of a Japanese sword, three or four such pieces are produced, which are again folded over each other several times. The different methods of folding produce different sorts of patterns on the finished blade. The result is a piece of steel made of thousands of welded-together layers (called "shadows" in Japan). The core is either made of pure iron or softer steel, and is folded over a few times.

The next step is welding the shell to the core. You can differentiate blades according to the different methods used for welding them together. A more complicated structure consists of a pure iron core,

Forging demonstration at the Kai Corporation Europe: Master smith Kanetusa demonstrates how to fold the steel.

Photo: Kai Europe

side surfaces and back of steel-iron layers, and a steel blade. The standard procedure is to insert the core into the V-shaped folded shell. The blade blank is then formed from this welded-together steel rod.

Now comes the complicated part: hardening. Here is where we find the actual difference from European swordmaking. The blank is wrapped in a mixture of loam or clay, sand, and charcoal—the exact recipe for this mixture was previously kept secret by the swordsmiths. The clay is applied only thinly on the future cutting edge, while the body of the blade and the back are wrapped in a layer about half a centimeter thick. At the point, a small piece of the back is left exposed, to also harden this. Also important are the thin, closely spaced transverse lines called *ashi*, which appear after the hardening process. The blade is now held in the fire with cutting edge downwards. So that the swordsmith can detect the correct temperature by the color of the blade, the forge is darkened. In some historical sources, this color is called the "February or August moon."

At this point, the blade is immersed in the water trough. The part in the thick covering layer cools more slowly, so it is therefore softer than the cutting edge. Depending on the method used, the blade is tempered immediately after quenching. For this, the blade is heated to about 160 degrees Celsius and then again briefly quenched. Tempering can be repeated several times as required.

The blade now consists of a soft core, a hard shell, and an even harder edge—so that, despite the hard edge, the body is flexible. The softer *ashi* lines lie within the cutting edge. They serve as a kind of "ship's hatch": If the cutting edge is damaged, the area affected usually runs no further than the next *ashi*—the damage is limited to the smallest possible area of the blade. The principle of differential hardening is now increasingly used by Western knife-makers, and several variations of the method described above have been developed.

Hardening significantly changes the steel's crystal structure: Due to the quenching, the exposed edge contracts much faster than the blade back in its clay coating. Thus, "the blade curvature can be altered by up to thirteen millimeters. To compensate for this effect, ideally, before the hardening process [...], the

swordsmith should give the blade a more limited curvature than the one he would like to have on the finished blade. Nevertheless, in most cases, re-working the blade is still necessary. [...] If the curvature is not strong enough, or not uniform, he can correct that by laying the blade on its back on a red-hot copper block, working it, and then again quench the sword in water," (Kapp and Yoshihara, p.94).

After hardening, the blade is examined minutely. Then it is ground and polished with extreme care (which takes about two weeks), while other craftsmen make the mounting. The terms grinding and polishing are a bit confusing here—in Japan both go together; neither process can be separated from the other.

This is due to the blade geometry of Japanese swords. While most European blades have two bevels, in which the actual cutting edge is formed only from the very narrow outer bevel, a Japanese sword has only one bevel. "Sharpening" means that the entire blade surface has to be treated; sharpening and polishing are a unified process, which is fundamentally different from the corresponding technique in Europe. This principle has the advantage of creating a blade geometry excellently suited for cutting, and a really sharp edge. But it also has a major drawback: A lot of steel is removed by each sharpening and the blades become thinner (such swords are said to be "tired"). On some old swords, the shell has over time been completely ground down, so that the core shows through at various points.

An average of twelve, but sometimes up to fifteen grinding stones of different granulation are used to polish a blade, until it reaches its famous sharpness. The entire blade is polished in each step in the process, and the work done in the previous stage is, so to speak, polished off. There are several methods for polishing, but in general, the polishing is done so that the fine touches resulting from the forging technique can be identified:

- *Hamon*, pattern line: After the last hardening process, the hardened cutting edge consists of a particularly light, crystalline steel with a boundary line scraped out by the smith from the clay covering.
- *Hada*, the grain pattern in the steel, and
- *Boshi*, the form of the hardened portion of the back (at the point).

Applying the clay covering for the process of hardening a samurai sword.

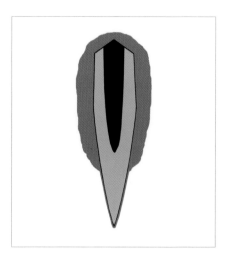

Blade with clay covering. It is applied only very thinly on the future cutting edge (below).

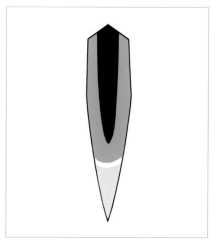

Cross section after hardening: core, shell, delimiting *hamon* and hardened cutting edge.

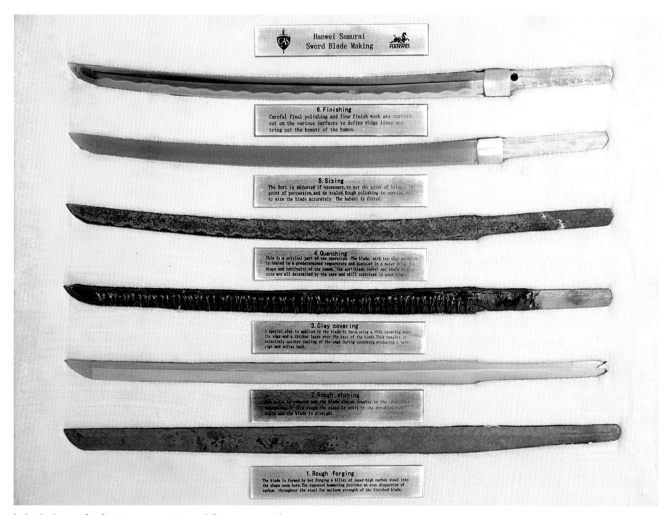

Individual steps for forging a samurai sword (bottom to top).

The upper part (*boshi*) of the point (*kissaki*) is likewise hardened.

Photo: japanklingen.de

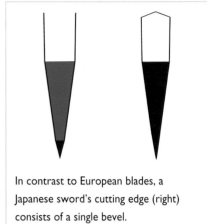

In contrast to European blades, a Japanese sword's cutting edge (right) consists of a single bevel.

Front and back of a *tsuba* are often different, but designed to correspond to each other.

Photo: Pieces of History

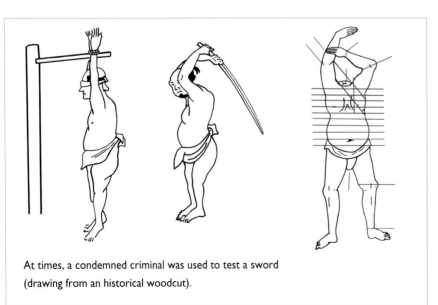

At times, a condemned criminal was used to test a sword (drawing from an historical woodcut).

A Japanese tang clearly displays the smith's signatures and typical filing traces.

Photo: japanklingen.de

A true connoisseur can distinguish the work of the individual swordsmith just on the basis of these patterns.

In addition to these forging technique features, the following features are also used for classification:

- details of the blade shape
- mounting
- the shape of the tang (in particular its end)
- file marks on the tang
- signature on the tang

All this information taken together, gives a complete picture. In historical Japan, it was often customary to test the finished polished sword and record the result on the tang. A successful test would considerably increase the selling price of such a weapon. There were specialized sword testers for this purpose, since an improperly executed stroke could destroy the delicate edge. The tests were mostly performed on wet, rolled straw mats (*tameshigiri*). Sometimes cutting tests were done on corpses, but the most-sought-after targets were criminals sentenced to death or prisoners of war—because you could test the sword on living tissue perfused with blood. Various strokes were used, with different degrees of difficulty. To carry out the test, the condemned was hanged from his tied hands, so that his body was hanging free (other methods were also used).

A very good sword could manage three bodies in one stroke, but there are also reports of five bodies, and one 16th-century tang inscription says the sword cut through seven bodies at one time.

The Ninja and Their Swords

At the end of this chapter, we come to ninja swords (*ninja-to*)—we need to treat them separately, because most of the misinformation circulating concerns these weapons. Originally, the ninja were mystics and anchorite families (*yamabushi*), who followed specific esoteric teachings; later, during the Middle Ages in Japan, they became feared assassins.

In the long-running guerrilla war against the "witch hunters" by the state religion, they developed the secret *Ninjutsu* system, the "art of stealth." The ninja were first used by the princes as scouts, then as spies, and finally as assassins. The families of mystics had evolved into clans of agents.

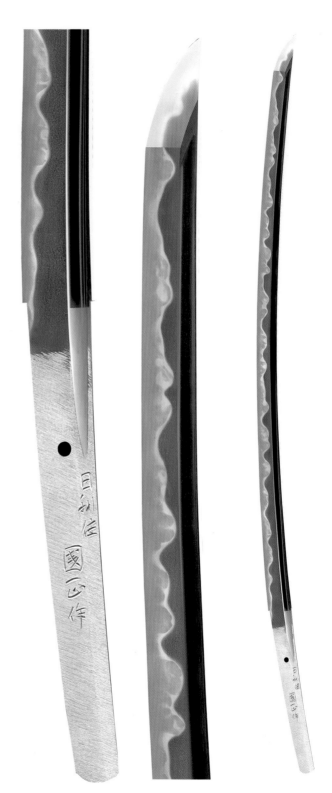

On a fully polished blade, the demarcation of the hardened cutting edge and the body of the blade is shown clearly by the blade pattern line (*hamon*).

Photo: japanklingen.de

The samurai and the ninja regarded each other with mutual total contempt: The ninja embodied everything the samurai despised. They had their own code of honor, and their actions were based on the Machiavellian motto: "The end justifies the means." As a result, they used a very different fighting style than that of the samurai; this was also reflected in the ninjas' relationship to their swords and how they used them.

Because Japanese sword makers were closely tied to the nobility, the ninja generally had no contact with them. Therefore, the ninja re-fashioned normal, captured samurai weapons for their own purposes. There were no constraints on this, since they did not follow the samurai ideology, which included devotion to their swords. The sword blades were shortened as required: Most ninja swords have a blade length of just two *shaku*, with many less than that. This short blade was particularly important for using special sword techniques. The ninja often used the "reverse grip": The sword was held one-handed, "upside down"—the blade jutting out from the wrist, with cutting edge down and forward.

Another difference between a samurai sword and ninja-to is the altered mounting: The lavish decorations were removed and simple, black *tsuba* attached. All parts except the blade were blackened for night use. The scabbard was often reworked, so that it could be used as a snorkel or blowpipe, and sometimes it was used to carry additional tools.

However, even these alterations were not "sacrilege" enough. The ninja were not afraid to poison their swords: The blades were immersed in a mixture of horse manure and blood. A wound from such a weapon could cause blood poisoning, muscle spasms, and eventually death. Some of the blades were hidden in walking sticks, called the *shikome-zue* mounting.

One characteristic of the *ninja-to* is its oversized, usually square hilt. If a ninja had to climb a wall, he leaned his sword against the wall, or rammed it in its scabbard into the ground, set his foot on the *tsuba*, and used the sword as an auxiliary ladder. Then the weapon was pulled up by the scabbard straps. An even more original use was as a "night vision device": If a ninja broke into a darkened room, he used the sword as a probe to feel out his opponents and kill them instantly.

They used an absolutely unique technique: The ninja would balance the scabbard by its mouthpiece on the point of the blade, holding the scabbard straps between his teeth. With this delicate arrangement, as soon as he encountered an opponent, he would feel the slightest contact—he let the strap slip from his mouth, the scabbard would slide off the blade point, and the ninja could thrust out in a single motion.

Just like the ninja themselves, various legends have developed about their swords, or rather, nonsensical rumors. For example, that they always carried their swords on their backs. Unless the back scabbard is specially designed, it is impractical to draw a sword from that position (and re-sheathing it even harder). No, the ninja, like the samurai, normally wore his sword sideways in his belt. Only in certain situations—such as when climbing—did he push the scabbard onto his back.

Another rumor is that, because they used special fighting techniques, the blades were basically kept dead straight. Since the ninja mostly used re-fashioned samurai swords, this is nonsense. In addition, a very slightly curved blade is rather an advantage for using the *ninjutsu kenpo* cutting techniques. Nevertheless, it can be seen that the ninja preferred only very slightly curved blades. There are some more recent Japanese swords with completely straight blades, but these are likely deliberately archaic, custom-made pieces that recall the Chokuto period. There are some very rare specimens, preserved from the transition period to Koto.

Finally, one more thing: So-called ninja swords with burnished blades and hollow grips containing survival utensils are nothing but toys, based on the manufacturer's fantasy. They have nothing in common with the real ninja.

Samurai Swords Today

Some fifty traditional bladesmiths are still at work today in Japan. They have to train for many years and have a state license to practice this craft. The demand is so great, that a customer must reckon with several years of waiting time to get a new sword. The prices for their blades are sometimes in the five figures. The best historical pieces are priceless. They are usually kept in temples, museums, or absolutely inaccessible private collections.

Probably due to the great interest generated by the movies, there are many samurai sword replicas. Most are purely decorative category D pieces. However, there are many high-quality swords being made. Even if these are not forged using original Japanese methods, the maker has to use the method of differential hardening to create a proper *hamon*. Beyond this, there are swords being forged in the Japanese way in the Western world. Many knife makers and swordsmiths have specialized in Japanese weapons, so that now there are a lot of samurai swords commercially available.

9.2 A Comparison Between the Katana and European Long-Sword

It immediately occurs to the uninitiated observer to compare a Japanese *katana* with a European long-sword and equate them, because:

- both weapons are intended primarily for two-handed use
- both weapon types are roughly equal in length, and
- fighting techniques and positions used are in some ways very similar.

Actually, there are more similarities than differences between long-sword and *katana*. However, the differences are significant and quite important for understanding these two types of weapons. Before we can compare a *katana* and long-sword, we have to deal with another problem. The Japanese sword—the *katana* in particular—is perhaps the most "hyped" weapon of all. No other weapon is the subject of so many tales and rumors, and, thanks to movies, videos, computer games, and manga comics, there are also a lot of self-proclaimed experts on this topic. As long as these fairy tales shape our image of the *katana*, any serious comparison between European and Japanese swords is a wasted effort.

Typical of the hype about samurai swords is that scene from the movie *Kill Bill*, in which swordsmith Hattori Hanzo describes his latest work: "If you should encounter god on your journey … then god will be cut!" Unfortunately, many people see this and other scenes not as (really) entertaining fiction, but take the whole thing at face value. And so one encounters statements such as: "samurai swords can cut European swords to pieces!" or "the blade was folded 1,000 times!"

This media hype is rather more supported than refuted by the European swords preserved in museums. While Japanese swords were perfectly maintained over the centuries and look like new, many swords from the European Middle Ages look much the worse for wear. Only a few pieces have survived the centuries in good condition as special relics. Considering this contrast, it is not surprising that you would not think that a European sword could ever equal the performance of a Japanese weapon under any circumstances.

Despite all the skills of Japanese swordsmiths, however, even the best Japanese *katana* is "only" steel—and any kind of steel can break. We should recall: Folding over Japanese blades and making European Damascus steel are two different methods to refine lower-grade raw materials. If you take a high quality modern steel as the raw material for making either a long-sword or a *katana*—steel which does not require further refining—this brings these two types of swords significantly closer to each other.

As for the differential hardening, this also was used, as we have seen, in medieval Europe—we just do not know anymore the exact method used. The last aspect remaining is that Japanese swords have a single bevel. But you can also obtain very good cutting properties from European sword edges with two bevels; it all depends on the sharpening angle of the cutting edge. Although we do not know exactly how a new sword was polished in the Middle Ages, we have no reason to assume that the blade had such a bad sharpening angle that it could not cut.

Therefore, it is not surprising that recent *tameshigiri* tests using reconstructions of medieval swords have shown that they can deliver as good a cutting performance as a Japanese weapon. Finally, both swords have one fundamental aspect in common: they are sharpened steel.

The preceding remarks are not to denigrate Japanese swords or belittle their achievements, but are intended to contradict some exaggerations and bring the Japanese sword back down to earth. Now, we can make a serious comparison between a *katana* and long-sword on this basis. There are many who

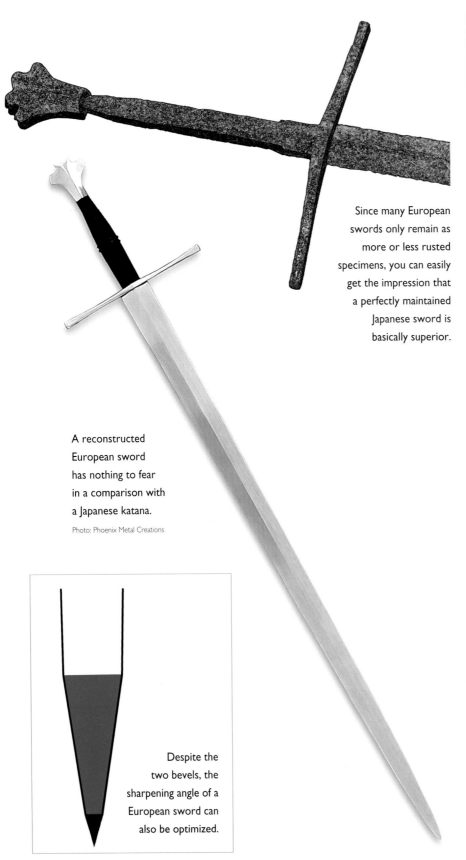

Since many European swords only remain as more or less rusted specimens, you can easily get the impression that a perfectly maintained Japanese sword is basically superior.

A reconstructed European sword has nothing to fear in a comparison with a Japanese katana.

Photo: Phoenix Metal Creations

Despite the two bevels, the sharpening angle of a European sword can also be optimized.

European swords also deliver an impressive cutting performance.

Photo: Museum Replicas, Herbert Schmidt

say that this is like comparing apples and pears—and that certainly has something to it. The determining factors for long-swords and *katana* are completely different, to say nothing of comparing medieval Europe and Japan. When the first Europeans arrived in Japan, the knights had long ago seen the last of their service, and the *katana* and long-sword never encountered each other. Nevertheless, a comparison is not far-fetched, and is an interesting mind game in any case.

It all starts with the objects we are comparing. For the *katana*, we are using an average model with a blade of just two and a half *shaku*. We will compare this *katana* to three European swords: A straight long-sword and two two-handed sabers. We are using a type XVIIIa long-sword; it is both very versatile, and was also very popular. In addition, it matches the *katana* in size very well. For the two-handed sabers, we will use a *Schnepfer* (Swiss saber) with a straight grip and a Hungarian saber with a curved grip.

Of course, different long-swords vary in size, but it is just the same with the *katana*. Although a long-sword is usually slightly larger and heavier, both weapons are comparable in terms of length. In terms of proportions, things look a bit different: the *katana* has a much longer grip in relation to blade length than the long-sword.

As we have seen, *katana* and long-sword correspond approximately in terms of size and two-handed use. Nevertheless, there are significant differences: The biggest, of course, in the shape of the blade. A curved, single-edged blade is completely different from a straight double-edged one. These create completely different propertiess, which are also reflected in how the sword is used.

Sword fighting expert John Clements points out here: "Medieval long-swords [were] in contrast to the powerful, cutting stroke of a curved, single-edged Japanese katana, made for hacking, shearing strokes, which were mainly done using elbow and shoulder. Despite the common elements of Japanese and European fighting stances and sword strokes, it is a mistake to assume that a straight, double-edged sword with a cross-shaped hand guard and pommel could be handled the way a samurai katana is, (Clements, 1998, p.80).

At this point, the European two-handed sabers come into play. The dimensions and proportions of these two weapons correspond more to those of the long-sword; the curved blade, on the other hand, to the *katana*. Sabers are used to make a pulling-cutting stroke, as the Japanese sword is. We can distinguish those types among two-handed sabers, which have a grip that curves along with the blade (as is the case with the *katana*), or is curved opposite to the blade curvature. Even this small difference affects how it is handled.

There is a bigger difference among the blade cross sections of *katana*, long-sword, and saber. This leads to completely different cutting properties. Another difference is in the distal taper: While the blade of a long-sword becomes much narrower from the base to the point, a Japanese blade –which is anyway much thicker—almost doesn't taper at all. There are *katana* which are almost nine millimeters (!) thick at the base and taper to only six millimeters thick at the *yokote*, while some long-swords are at least seven millimeters thick at the base and taper continuously to about two millimeters at the point.

Size Comparison

	Katana	Long-sword	*Schnepfer*	Hungarian saber
Total length (inches)	40.7	44.4	45.6	42.9
Blade length (inches)	29.3	34.6	37.0	34.2.
Weight (lbs.)	2.5	3.3	3.	2.8

This creates a totally different balance for the sword. The *katana* is therefore significantly stiffer than a long-sword. The way a saber or *katana* is sharpened, is completely unlike that of a long-sword. We should recall that many long-swords were only really sharpened along the top third of the blade, to make it possible to use half-sword techniques. *Katana* and most saber blades are, in contrast, consistently sharp, so that half-sword techniques cannot be used.

There are other technical differences between a *katana* and a European sword, due to the cross-guard and pommel design. The European "cross" represents an entirely different way to protect the hand than the Japanese *tsuba* does. The European cross-guard was developed to parry and block the opponent's blade. It is also used for binding, leveraging, choking, and wresting techniques. The Japanese hand guard is primarily intended to prevent the hand from slipping on to the blade.

The pommel is just as important. A Japanese sword does not get any counterweight from a pommel, which is why the grip is usually much longer relative to the blade than on a long-sword. This means also that certain techniques either cannot or only partially be used. One example is a technique known internationally as "slipping." This allows you, using a forward swing, to slide the grip through your hand and catch it again by the pommel—momentarily giving you an extra 5.9-7.8 inches (15 to 20 centimeters) of range, completely by surprise.

The comparison could go on forever like this. Nevertheless, we can say the following: As far as basic techniques, the similarities are greater than the differences—in particular as regards the two-handed saber. In terms of details, however, the different properties of the swords are really clear—and it is precisely these subtleties that a good swordsman takes into account.

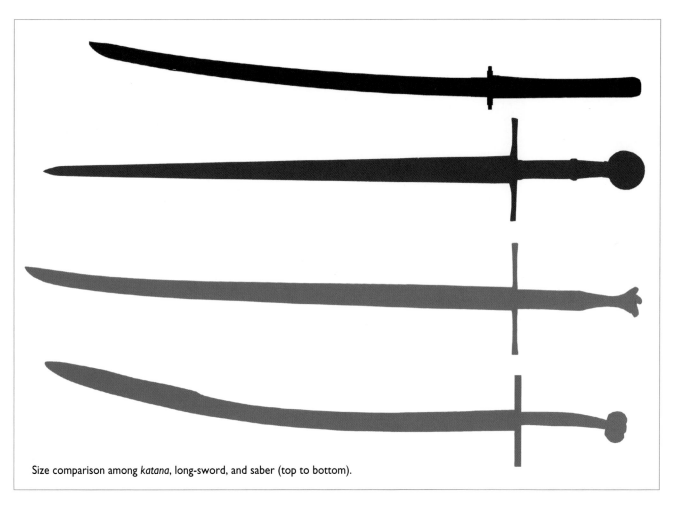

Size comparison among *katana*, long-sword, and saber (top to bottom).

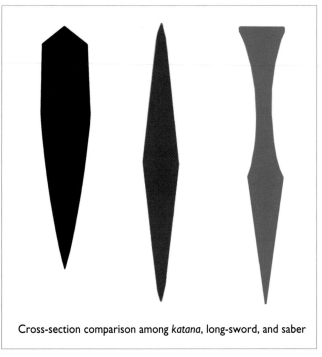

Cross-section comparison among *katana*, long-sword, and saber

Next to blade cross section, the crossguard and pommel make the biggest differences between long-sword and *katana*.

Photo: Pieces of History

Swords for Practice

This art is very serious and legitimate, and is on the very nearest and seeks what is briefest. (…) Because legitimate fencing doesn't want any pretty and out-of-hand parrying or broad fencing all around, which makes people careless and remiss.

— (Anonymous 14th-century sword master)

10.1 Stage Combat Swords

Stage combat swords are, as the name suggests, actually made for just one purpose: to make a staged sword fight look good as possible for the audience, while ensuring there is no danger for the actors. "Every performed fight on the stage is choreography, down to the smallest detail. All movements are set, and only the actors' stage skills will convey to the audience the rigor, refinement, and thus authenticity. [...] It remains important for us, that the steps, thrusts, stroke, and parries be done so as to be recognizable, without destroying the illusion of reality," (Ullmann, pp.11-12). Of course, this is something completely different than what the old masters taught: "[...] many of the techniques that can be practiced safely by a martial artist with modern protective clothing, are too dangerous and far too subtle for battle re-enactment or an staged fight," (Windsor, p.3). Thus, staged dueling is not practicing any historical martial art; instead, you strike and thrash at each other in a way that will have the most public appeal possible. Here we also find the infamous edge-on-edge parrying, which was never done this way. For this reason, stage combat swords are not only dull, but also have really broad "cutting edges": slightly rounded cutting edges three to five millimeters thick.

These dull blades mean that stage combat swords are very top-heavy and badly balanced. However, there are more and more manufacturers, who are focusing less on exhibition bouts and more on historical swordsmanship training, and also offer better balanced swords. The range of stage combat swords goes from roughly cobbled together "sluggers" from inexpensive backyard blacksmiths, to reasonably balanced models made by good craftsmen. Differences in price are correspondingly big. Before buying a stage combat sword, you should get as much information as possible on the Internet: request technical data (dimensions, weight, and so on) and ask about a breakage warranty and return policy. At medieval markets, for example, you can handle the swords and swing them around, making it possible to get a better impression. But even when you buy something at a market, you should insist on getting receipts and ask about return options.

10.2 Training Swords

Most modern training swords are made of wood. They are almost certainly very similar to those the knights used for training centuries ago. We find plenty of evidence in the historical literature that wooden swords (waster is the specific English term) were of fundamental importance for swordsmanship training. It is also clear—both from the literature and from the preserved remains of swords—that these were not just round poles, but actual carved wooden swords, with pommel, grip, cross-guard, and blade—along with a "cutting edge" and flat side. Sometimes, the wooden weapon's point was ball-shaped, to ensure extra protection.

At first, the term wooden sword might sound something like a children's toy, but a wooden sword can also cause serious injury. "When you train with it, be aware that this is basically a sword-shaped baseball bat: If you were to wield it with some speed against someone's unprotected head, the blow could be fatal," states re-enactor Christian Tobler.

Since it is not always easy to come by a high-quality wooden sword shaped like a medieval weapon, many training groups simply use practice weapons such as are used in Japanese swordsmanship. Wooden swords (*bokken*) and bamboo swords (*shinai*) are easily available from companies specializing in martial arts. In Japan, the *bokken* has a very special, traditional role. *Bokken*

Stage combat swords have rounded points and edges.

Photo: Pieces of History

are usually made of oak. In terms of length and dimensions, they are modeled as closely as possible on a real sword. However, a *bokken*—unlike a European wooden sword—does not have any guard. The removable plastic or leather *tsuba* on a modern *bokken* is added to meet with Western taste.

Although the *bokken* was originally developed purely as a training weapon, it later increasingly was used as a stand-alone weapon. A wooden sword could not cause the terrible slash wounds that a *katana* can, of course, but it was—if wielded by a master—absolutely deadly. Especially those warriors who could afford an expensive sword for some reason—such as the ronin (masterless samurai)—would seize on a *bokken*. "The better-off ronin proudly carried a bokken made especially for them, made of higher-quality wood, with their names carved or burned into them. They were made by carpenters who specialized in making the bokken," (Schultz-Gora, p.15).

It would seem incomprehensible to a layman, how anyone could compete against a samurai sword with a wooden *bokken*. The result of such a fight seems obvious. But this is not the case by any means. As always, everything here depends on the skill of the warrior. Myamoto Musashi (1584-1645), the greatest Japanese swordsman of all time, was known for the fact that he often used a *bokken*. The most famous of these battles took place in 1612, on an island off the coast. Musashi's opponent was an excellent swordsman who had a first-class daito. Musashi, in contrast, had carved himself a makeshift *bokken* out of an oar. He parried his opponent's blow, and at the same time struck him with a deadly blow to the head. After this duel, Musashi only used *bokken*—his swordsmanship was beyond compare. It was no longer necessary for him to fight with an actual sword.

In the Japanese martial art of *kendo*, the fighter uses a special training sword called a *shinai*. A *shinai* consists of four bamboo slats strapped together in a special way. A *shinai* blow can reach such speed and force, that the *kendoka* have to wear armor made of leather and bamboo to protect themselves from injury.

Swordsmith Stefan Roth has worked with the "Arts of Mars" school to develop a special *shinai* for medieval sword-fight training. The cross-section was adapted to conform to European swords; then the

Safe practice requires appropriate training swords.

Photo: Agilitas.tv

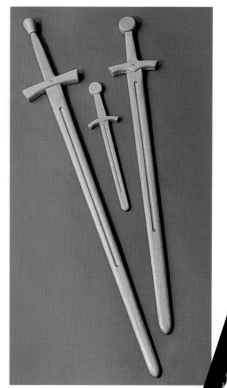

Modern wooden sword-fight training swords.

Photo: Museum Replicas

Modern aluminum alloy training sword.

Photo: Agilitas.tv

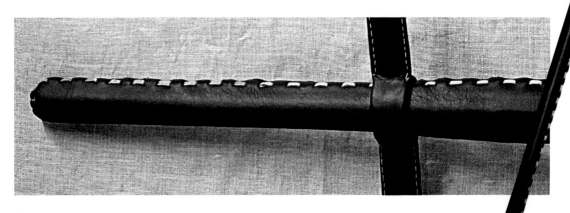

Special medieval swordsman's training sword: Bamboo *shinai* with leather sheath and cross-guard.

Photo: Seelenschmiede/Rot

shinai is sewn into a sheath made of heavy saddle leather. A cross-guard was added so that the *shinai* could be used to perform the special European swordsmanship techniques.

Since interest in historical martial arts is growing, there are ever-more specialized training swords available. They range from exact replicas of historical *Feder* (a name for medieval training swords) to blunt steel swords or aluminum alloy models, up to special models for sword fighting in armor. You should choose your weapon as required, as usually each school has its particular preferences or instructions.

10.3 Modern Cutting Swords

While you might assume that manufacturing sharp swords intended for combat is now outdated, just the opposite seems to be the case. More and more manufacturers and blacksmiths are specializing in making "real swords." There are two reasons for this. For one, for a collector, it is a very different feeling to own a sharp modern cutting sword rather than some more or less blunt decorative weapon. The frequently asked question, "What do you want it for?" is completely irrelevant for a collector. A collector's piece doesn't require having any practical purpose—otherwise all stamp collectors would have to be very diligent letter writers and beer coaster collectors all be alcoholics. For a collector, the awareness that this sword is "real" is enough.

Another reason is the growing number of people who practice historical sword fighting. For anyone who does sword fighting as a hobby, it is important to practice test strokes and cuts, and now and then use a really sharp sword for *tameshigiri* and other tests. "If you always practice strokes or techniques with a steel sword, wooden sword, or whatever, you generally won't be making any real cuts against a target. This affects how the body stays in balance during the movement and how you react to the impact on the target. There is a huge difference between trying to deliver real damage with a sword or give something a pat with it. […] The sad truth is that no sword will cut anything for you—that you have to do yourself," (Lindholm and Svärd, p.225).

"For those who have no experience in dealing with authentic swords, it is difficult to understand how different the steel in a cheap, weak, and heavy blade is from the steel in a lightweight, hard, and balanced blade. All the conceivable differences are immediately apparent when you practice cuts on various test materials, rather than thrashing around using blunt swords," (Clements, 1998, p.64).

As we have seen in preceding chapters, a sword is more than just a specifically formed piece of steel. For this reason, to perform a test, one needs not only a very well-made replica, but also a real weapon. And here we come to modern cutting swords.

The best are certainly swords handmade by a master swordsmith. These are in the top rank, both in terms of performance and price range. Of course, not every hand-forged sword is a masterpiece. Even Damascus steel swords, which are made of truly excellent quality steel, can sometimes be classified as flawed from a functional point of view—as far as sword physics is concerned. Whether an exact replica, modern re-interpretation, or pure fantasy sword—the same rules apply for forged swords as for industrial mass produced swords: harmonic balance is important!

Differentiated Hardening

An inexpensive alternative to the *tameshigiri* test is to use plastic beverage bottles. Water bottles, two liters or more, are best. Fill the bottles and put them on a platform. Then make a cut. Is the sword is bad or blunt, or the stroke poorly executed, the bottle will simply be swept off the platform. A good stroke will cut off the upper part of the bottle, leaving the lower part on the platform.

In terms of functionality and balance, Peter Johnsson's swords are among the best weapons on the market. This Swedish blacksmith, well known for his research on historical swords, makes both exact replicas and re-interpretations. The sword pictured on page 184 is a combination of different originals: An XVa blade combined with horizontal S-shaped cross-guard and *Fiederknauf* (pommel with pinnate center rib or feather design). With a blade length of 37.5 inches (95.5 centimeters), the sword is 123.5 inches long and weighs about 3.0 pounds (1.4 kilograms).

The "soul blacksmith" Stefan Roth and "dream blacksmith" Arno Eckhardt have made their names in Germany. Both forge accurate reconstructions and interpretations, and are also involved in historical sword-fighting. Arno Eckhardt is known primarily for his "fencing swords" for historical swordsmanship training. Stefan Roth focuses on Japanese swords in addition to European ones. One of his priorities is refining his own steel in a self-built bloomery oven.

Many small manufacturing enterprises in Europe, especially in Eastern European countries like the Czech Republic (such as Lutel), offer excellent swords at highly acceptable prices (however, there is also a lot of "junk" available). If you take the time to do extensive research on the Internet, you can find the appropriate offerings very quickly. The same rules apply for stage combat swords: be well-informed about warranties and return possibilities.

Most swords available on the Internet or by mail order today come from Asia. They are made in small enterprises (such as in India, Mongolia, or China) and then subsequently distributed under international brand names. Although they had a lot of defects at first, the quality of these swords has improved significantly in recent years, so that you can obtain a high-quality, functional sword in the price range of 250 to 400 Euros. One excellent example are the swords from Museum Replicas (made in India) and the Chinese manufacturer Hanwei, represented in Europe by Pieces of History, Ltd. and abroad as Cas Iberia.

Hanwei offers a wide range of swords (European, Chinese, Japanese …). The blades of the medieval swords are forged from 1065 steel, the mountings are of stainless steel. Until recently, Hanwei sword tangs

From time to time in historical sword-fighting, cutting tests have to be done.

Photo: Herbert Schmidt

A wide range of high-quality swords is available today.

Photo: Del Tin

21st Century Steel

There are three sorts of modern steel, based on carbon content:

0 to 0.2% C = steel with a low carbon content
0.2 to 0.5% C = steel with medium-level carbon content
Over 0.5% C = steel with high carbon content

Steels with high carbon content are important for sword making.

A wide variety of steel grades are used today for producing swords. Many smaller enterprises and forges in Eastern Europe only use the term "spring steel." Normally, that means that steel from discarded truck leaf springs is being used. Here, this term means flexible carbon steel, which is a good starting material. Larger companies generally use a specific type of steel supplied by a steel works. This way, they can decide exactly what properties they want the steel to have (such as machinability). Usually tool steels – non-stainless steels with high carbon content – are used to make swords. Larger manufacturers especially prefer 10xx series steels (such as 1050, 1065 or 1095; the last two digits indicate the carbon content) or 5160. Good craftsmen like to use highly alloyed tool steels, such as A-2 or L-6, which are difficult to work with and require special hardening processing.

STEEL TYPE

1095	5160	A-2	L-6	55Si7	CK-75	
0.90-1.00	0.55-0.65	0.95-1.05	0.65-0.75	0.55 to 0.60	0.70-0.80	% carbon
-	0.70-0.90	4.75-5.5	0.60-1.20	-	-	% chromium
0.30-0.50	0.75-1.00	1.00	0.25 to 0.80	0.60-1.00	0.60-0.80	% manganese
-	-	0.10	0.50	-	-	% molybdenum
-	-	0.30	1.25-2.00	-	-	% nickel
0.04	0.03	-	-	0.05	0.04	% phosphorus
-	0.15-0.3	0.50	0.50	1.50-2.00	0.15-0.35	% silicon
0.05	-	-	-	0.05	0.04	% sulfur
-	-	0.10-0.50	0.20-0.30	-	-	% vanadium
57-62	57-60	57-62	57-62	-	-	Hardness potential *

* = Attainable Rockwell hardness in HRC (Hardness Rockwell Cone). For swords, the target is a hardness of about 55 HRC.

PROPERTIES OF ALLOY ELEMENTS

	Ability to hold an edge	Hardness	Temper-ability	Rigidity	Tensile strength	Impact resistance	Abrasion resistance	Corrosion resistance
Carbon	X	X			X			
Chrome		X		X	X		X	X
Manganese			X		X		X	
Molybdenum		X	X	X	X			X
Nickel		X						X
Phosphorus		X			X			
Silicon					X			
Sulfur		X		X	X			
Vanadium		X			X	X		

Source: Columbia River Knife & Tool

Since we do not want to get too much into modern metallurgy, I am only providing a very simplified table of the properties of alloy elements. What is important here is to optimally balance the proportions. Phosphorus, for example, increases hardness and tensile strength and improves machinability – but in higher concentrations, it makes the steel brittle. We already discussed the properties of chrome and stainless steel at the beginning.

were still screwed in, but now they are—at the request of traditional re-enactment groups—riveted over the pommel. Hanwei also offers "practical" versions of many of its models. These include, in addition to sharp *katana* for cutting tests, basically blunt stage combat swords. New at Hanwei is a version with "antiqued finish": The swords are artificially aged so that they look like historical pieces.

Another example of swords made in Asia are the models offered by the American brand Cold Steel. Cold Steel's roots are in knives for tactical use: In the early 1980s, the company made the American version the *tanto* a popular item. Cold-Steel chef Lynn Thompson made big headlines with his spectacular knife tests shown widely in a video titled *Proof*. Thompson is a fan of bladed weapons of any kind, and soon began to include tomahawks, swords, and medieval pole arms (such as war hammers) in his product range.

Cold Steel swords are not replicas in the true sense. These are rather new interpretations of historical swords. However, some of the CS swords are so close to the historical originals that they can be considered category C replicas. The range includes medieval swords, Chinese and Japanese swords, oriental sabers, modern cavalry sabers, and Scottish basket-hilt swords.

The blades are forged from 1050 carbon steel and hardened. All swords come sharpened—they are not intended as decorations, but as weapons. Accordingly, Cold Steel's second DVD, *More Proof*, includes brutal sword tests. In addition to classical tests such as *tameshigiri*, the video shows cutting tests on halves of animals from the slaughterhouse. Sword points are thrust through discarded car hoods, and the pommels are used to crush stones. Very impressive!

"Shared Usage" Swords

For many people who are training in historical sword fighting, a sharp combat sword – in contrast to a wooden training sword – to be used for cutting tests is simply too expensive. For this reason "group swords" have become popular. Costs are shared by all.

Since Cold Steel deals not only in swords, but also knives and operates internationally, this brand's swords are, in contrast to the other modern cutting swords, available from many retailers of knives, martial arts articles, or Middle Ages-related products. The products are also readily available at Internet retailers. Although you may find what looks to be a good offer, you should definitely buy only from a dealer who gives the usual return guarantees, since test reports note that Cold Steel occasionally offers "lemons."

ASA Sword Works, based in Washington State, USA, has a completely different approach from Hanwei or Museum Replicas. CEO Angus Trim does not want to manufacture replicas, but purely functional practice swords, which are specially designed for cutting tests. The mountings are plain and unadorned: leather-covered bare wood and bare steel. Production is completely different from the Asian forging manufacturers: The 5160 tool steel blades are machined on the latest CNC machines and then tempered so that the blade body has a hardness of 52 HRC and the cutting edge of 56 HRC. Each blade is then tested for successful tempering. Finishing and mounting are done by hand. All this care comes at a price, and the swords are significantly more expensive than the models made by Hanwei, Museum Replicas, or Lutel.

Angus Trim takes another path also in the matter of mountings—upon customer request, he will also rivet the tang, although normally it is fastened to the pommel with an Allen screw. If the mounting becomes loose with frequent and hard use (cutting tests), the buyer can simply tighten the screw again himself—since, in these times, you just won't find a swordsmith who can make repairs on every street corner.

ASA Sword Works' product range includes medieval swords of various types, some Japanese swords, and various sabers in one-handed and two-handed sizes. All standard models are designed so that the customer can request modifications (such as to the pommel or cross-guard)—if these modifications do not affect the balance. The firm works closely with sword-finisher Christian Fletcher, who can further embellish the exteriors of simple battle swords. If anyone is interested in a modern *Lord of the Rings*-design cutting sword and has a well-filled wallet, he can certainly get what he wants from Fletcher.

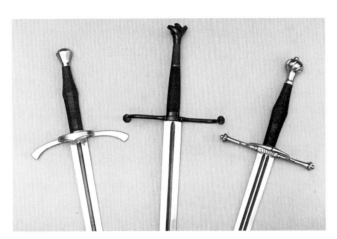

A lot of good, reasonably priced swords are
manufactured in the Czech Republic.

Photo: Lutel

Hanwei offers many models with
both "old" and "new" finishes.

Photo: Pieces of History

Cold Steel's swords aren't meant to be replicas, but rather new,
modern cutting interpretations of historical swords.

Photo: Cold Steel

Although the Wisconsin company Albion Armorers makes swords in a similar way as ASA Sword Works does—using CNC milling—their swords are designed with a more antique look. The mountings are cast in steel and conform to historical models; the tang is riveted over the pommel. Albion puts special emphasis on harmonic balance. In a very clever move, the company brought swordsmith Peter Johnsson on board as a designer.

Albion is now making his designs in series, producing absolutely high-quality swords in a price range of $700 to $1,500.

Perhaps the most exotic type of sword in this book is the group of "tactical swords." The term "tactical knives" is perhaps known to some readers: this means knives for (para) military use. These knives are generally kept perfectly plain and unadorned, and generally colored black and gray. They are usually made of modern high-tech materials, the best the industry has to offer. And tactical swords look just the same: classic blade shapes, no decoration, and the most advanced materials. For these swords, what matters is not how they look, but their performance. The tactical swords known to me so far, are all geared to the Japanese *katana*. From their simple, unadorned design and purely practical concept, they can be very well compared to the *ninja-to*. One example is the Katana-Tac by Canadian knifemaker Wally Hayes. Hayes—master smith in the American Bladesmith Society and a member of the Canadian Knifemakers Guild—makes both hand-crafted and ornate collector's knives and tactical knives for the Canadian Special Forces.

The Katana-Tac has a total length of 37.9 inches (96.5 centimeters) and blade length of 26.9 inches (68.5 centimeters). Although Hayes usually forges his blades and his own Damascus steel, the Katana-Tac model is not forged, but cut from flat bar steel. This comes from the idea that it should essentially be possible for a handyman—an "amateur"—to produce such a sword himself. Therefore, Hayes is also keen to have the production done using a minimum number of tools. Detailed instructions can be found in the video series *Katana* by Paladin Press. As the name suggests, the Katana-Tac is the tactical version of a samurai sword. It combines the traditional Japanese blade shape with the modern materials of a tactical

Cold Steel Combat Knives

In addition to popular swords – such as Viking or samurai swords – the Cold Steel company also dares to offer more exotic weapons. One example is its re-interpretation of a war knife, which Cold Steel calls its "Big Knife." The blade of this two-handed saber is 31.8 inches (81 centimeters) long and five millimeters thick. The entire weapon is 42.1 inches (107 centimeters) long and weighs about 3.9 pounds (1.8 kilograms). The tang goes the whole way through the hilt and is riveted to the wood grip panels. In contrast to historical war knives, there is no full hand guard on the Cold Steel hilt, only a finger ring. Pommel and crossguard are fully burnished. This war knife is a good example to show that Cold Steel doesn't make decorative pieces, but more or less plain weapons.

In addition to the usual cutting tests (such as *tameshigiri*), Cold Steel put its war knife through a particularly impressive cutting test on a thick phone book. You can easily test at home, using a knife (or a sword if you have it) just how much resistance the countless pages of a phone book offers. In just one stroke, Cold Steel's Big Knife cut the phone book in two clean halves – an impressive performance.

Photo: Cold Steel

There is no full hand guard, but only a simple finger ring.

knife. The first manufacturing step is to grind the blade from a piece of 1050 steel. This sounds simple, but it will be clear—at least when Wally Hayes reveals the master's tricks of the trade—that what you have to watch out for, is to make sure that the blade is given the right shape. The next step is hardening, using the traditional Japanese method. A special process using an insulating clay shell produces a blade with a very hard edge and softer back of the blade.

Hardening a Japanese sword is a complicated process, which Hayes describes exactly. He also explains the simplest way to build a charcoal-fired hardening oven in your back yard. Hayes does the mounting of the grip exactly as he does on his tactical knives. Of course, an ambitious handyman can also attach the mounting in the traditional Japanese style. The Katana-Tac mounting omits the typical ferrule on blade and grip, as well as the artistic design of the *tsuba*. The grip consists of a flat tang, with two plates of thermoplastic Kydex glued on. Then the grip is wrapped with parachute cord. The grip is then wound around in Japanese style, and soaked in resin. This creates a grip that is bombproof in the truest sense of the word, but, unlike the original Japanese grips, it cannot be taken apart.

The *hamon* on the blade is a distinguishing characteristic of traditional Japanese swords. It marks the boundary between the blade back and the hard cutting edge. While the method of correctly polishing a Japanese sword is a skilled trade in itself, in his video, Hayes shows us an easy way to make the *hamon* visible and to sharpen the blade. In the end, the result is a plain sword intended for practical use.

Angus Trim keeps his swords simple and intended for actual use.

Photo: ASA Sword Works

At ASA Swordworks, the mounting is fastened over the pommel with an Allen screw.

Photo: ASA Sword Works

The workshop of a "modern swordsmith." Here, he is just riveting the tang over the pommel.

Photo: Albion Armorers

Master smith Wally Hayes with his "Katana-Tac."

Photo: Wally Hayes

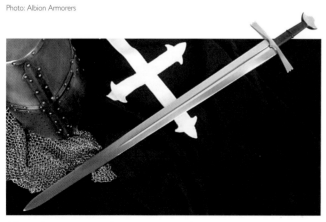

Albion Armorers manufactures very good swords at acceptable prices.

Photo: Albion Armorers

The Lord of the Rings and Other Movie Swords

From the ashes a fire shall be woken,
A light from the shadows shall spring;
Renewed shall be blade that was broken,
The crownless again shall be king.

— (*The Lord of the Rings*)

Many sword fans are inspired by movies. Big blockbusters like *The Lord of the Rings* brought new life to the interest in swords. Most movie swords are fantasy swords. The term "fantasy sword" basically means only one thing: this sword has no historical counterpart, no model. So a fantasy sword can be many things. This usually means a sword with a design based on fantasy media (whether comics, books, or computer games). The main difference to historical swords is the excessive ornamentation. We can divide fantasy swords into two categories:

- Swords, which in terms of ornamentation and the design of hilt and blade are so extremely "fantastic" (or rather, bizarre) that they could never, ever be used as battle-ready swords. Sword fans call such a weapon a "Sword-Like-Object" (SLO).
- Swords which, though their design is imaginary, are theoretically easily conceivable—that is, if fashioned appropriately, would be practical, battle-ready weapons.

Many of the fantasy swords commercially available are SLOs—such overdone pieces, that they could never be put to any real use. These are actually just metal sculptures that vaguely resemble the basic shape of a sword. SLOs are decorative items, not swords.

You should not start from the wrong assumption that fantasy swords are basically only—more or less cheap—wall hangers made of stainless steel. Many reputable manufacturers and blacksmiths include fantasy swords in their range of products. A good example of this are those by designer Jody Samson, which Albion Armorers makes into functional weapons. What is important here is to be aware of the criteria of quality and functionality, as well as the appearance of historical swords. Each buyer has to then decide, to what extent a design is fanciful or not.

As already noted, movie swords are basically also fantasy swords. The swords of film heroes and villains are generally given an especially complicated and fantastic design. They have to have an enormous recognition value, as well as fit the character of the figure who uses it. But many movie swords have a major shortcoming: To get the audience's attention, they are not only much-decorated or have an unusual design, but are also much larger than "real" swords. If these weapons were made of steel, they would be poorly balanced, and it would be impossible to wield them in the right way or quickly. Hence, films use a trick:

The blades are made of polished aluminum or even of plastic, making the sword "feather light," so that it can be wielded at a pace either impossible when using a steel version, or at most only after years of training.

One of the most popular swords in film history is the Atlantean sword from *Conan the Barbarian* (1981). In the movie, Conan (Arnold Schwarzenegger) enters the tomb of a warrior from ancient Atlantis and takes the sword for himself. This sword played a special role from the beginning, so it

Such a bizarre "sword-like-object" (SLO) has nothing to do with any real sword.

Photo: United Cutlery

197

The *Conan the Barbarian* sword is one of the best-known in movie history.

The proportions of Conan's sword are based on an historical executioner's sword.

had to be particularly striking. Very interesting, for example, are the engravings on the cross-guard and pommel. The cross-guard shows the downfall of the island of Atlantis: Volcano, waves and sea monster. The pommel also displays the volcano and the reed boats the survivors used to escape.

The overall proportions of the Atlantean sword are based on a historical German executioner's sword. The extremely broad blade and short cross-guard are essential characteristics of this type of sword. The only difference is that an executioner's sword has a "real" point. The Atlantean sword is clearly a "fantasy sword" in this respect, because never in history did warriors fight with swords of such proportions. With a total length of 39.3 inches (100 centimeters) and a 28.3-inch (72-centimeter) blade, the sword weighs about four kilograms, and is therefore extremely heavy for its size. It was designed to be so bulky because it is intended suit the muscle-bound Conan. In any case, the Atlantean sword, in contrast to many other movie swords, is still within the bounds of a genuine sword in terms of weight, so it is a "realistic movie sword." The Atlantean sword is currently available only as a pure decorative sword (category D); Albion Armorers no longer makes its fully functional model.

In terms of swords, the most important film ever is certainly *Highlander* (1985). The story of this immortal who fights on forever, very quickly became a cult object, thanks to the fast cuts used by director Russell Mulcahy, the mix of action, fantasy and romance, and, last but not least , thanks to the music of Queen. As the Internet expanded, *Highlander* fans from all over the world began to exchange their views, and interest in swords experienced a hitherto unprecedented boom.

A *Highlander* fan page generated an Internet discussion forum, where many of the posts are at a scientific level. *Highlander* was thus for many the "bone of contention"—the motivation—to start getting involved with swords at all.

The most striking weapon in the movie is the sword of villain Kurgan (Clancy Brown). Although the idea of having a collapsible sword in your briefcase is of course nonsense,

The famous Kurgan Sword from *Highlander*.

Photo: Stahlwarenhaus Hebsacker

The sword looks just as menacing as the film villain himself.

Photo: Davis/Panzer Productions

Of all films, perhaps *Highlander* has had
the biggest influence. Many *Highlander* fans
turned into sword fans.

Photo: Davis/Panzer Productions

Scene from
Kingdom of Heaven.

Photo: 20th Century Fox /
Museum Replicas

The Ibelin sword.

Photo: Museum Replicas

the design of the cross-guard and the protruding spikes alone give the sword that special something. The blade is only slightly tapered, so we are dealing with a hybrid of the Oakeshott system's types XIIa and XIIIa. Unfortunately, only a decorative version of Kurgan's sword ever came on the market.

Another striking movie sword is the weapon of the Headless Horseman in Tim Burton's *Sleepy Hollow*. The film production design was unanimously praised for its dark and creepy atmosphere, and the sword is no exception. This ghost rider's sword is basically a classical type XIIIa. The blade is broad (1.8 inches [4.8 centimeters]) and does not taper along the entire length. The sword is a total of 42.9 inches (109 centimeters); the blade 30.7 inches (78 centimeters) long. The two indentations just before the ricasso are the only fantasy element on the blade. The grip, however, is typical and distinctive, especially the snake head pommel with its red eyes. But despite these embellishments and somewhat too high weight of 5.7 pounds (2.6 kilograms), this sword is clearly a functional weapon. Both a decorative replica made by the company Factory X and a fully functional version by Albion Armorers are available on the market.

In the Crusader epic *Kingdom of Heaven*, the production design was not intended to be completely historical, but appropriate and consistent. Movie weapons specialist Simon Atherton was hired as the "weapons master." Atherton and his team have a lot of experience in bringing filmmaker's wishes into line with reality. "It's no use if something looks great, if you can't fight it," is Atherton's maxim—and therefore he designed weapons that are indeed striking, but as realistic and balanced as possible. He put special effort into *Kingdom of Heaven*: "First thing, I went to the British Museum and began to research. Then I bought every book there was. We have many books on swords ourselves, and looked through those first."

Atherton's efforts to be realistic sometimes led to clashes with director Ridley Scott—such as over the design of Saladin's sword. "In my research, I found out that the Saracens' swords of the time were straight. There was a small fight—Ridley said he wanted this beautiful, curved scimitar. And I spoke to historians in museums, who said 'no—they were straight,'" Atherton says.

Film weapons like the Ibelin sword have to have a high recognition effect.

Photo: 20th Century Fox

The Headless Horseman's sword from *Sleepy Hollow*.

Photo: Factory X

Detail of the functional *Sleepy Hollow* sword.

Photo: Albion Armorers

The "sword of the King of Jerusalem" is based on the historical sword of Edward III.

Photo: Museum Replicas

The production design for
Beowulf & Grendel tried to
create a realistic reflection
of the Early Middle Ages.

Photo: Universum Home Video

The Beowulf sword is a
new interpretation of a
Vendel type spatha.

Photo: Museum Replicas

Atherton asserted himself about the sabers, but he let himself be persuaded in other areas by the movie's script department: "We cheated a little, because we made a hand-and-a-half. Theoretically, these weren't that common at the time—they had one-handed swords." The actor portraying Godfrey, Liam Neeson, adds: *"My sword is quite large. To use it, you had to have some muscle in your arms."* The hand-and-a-half is more like the two-handed fighting style, which is simply what many moviegoers expect. But again, *Kingdom of Heaven* sought to present at least to a certain level of authenticity. In one scene, Godfrey demonstrated the *posta di falcone* to his son Balian with a two-handed sword. The "hawk guard" is actually historically accurate and is described in the fencing book *De Arte Gladiatora*. It isn't relevant that Master Vadi actually lived 200 years later, given a filmmaker's artistic license.

The most important weapon in *Kingdom of Heaven* is the Ibelin family sword: "It is a sword, that is almost like a co-star in the film. It is always there," says Liam Neeson, and Simon Atherton added: "Godfrey's sword, that Orlando inherits from his father, was the most fun. It really let me enjoy myself, and I spent a lot of time on it."

The Ibelin sword is a classic bastard sword, essentially representing a new mixture of historical styles: There were octagonal pommels, pommels with inscriptions, and engraved crosses. We know the animal heads on the ends of the cross-guards from Charlemagne's Sword. The 35.8-inch (91-centimeter) blade is a type XII, but this sword, with a total 44.8-inch (114-centimeter) length, is too large for that historical type (and the proportions are wrong for type XIIa: the grip is too short). Pommel and proportions aren't entirely correct historically, and the oddly curved grip with its partial leather cover is fictitious—otherwise, the Ibelin sword is a fairly successful recreation of an historical weapon.

The designer made things easier with the "sword of the king of Jerusalem." One of the books Atherton consulted was Ewart Oakeshott's standard work, *Records of the Medieval Sword,* where Oakeshott gave special treatment to the sword of Edward III. Since that sword looks really typical, it is not surprising that Atherton created an almost 1:1 copy for the King

The *Lord of the Rings* swords created a sensation among sword fans and gave the impetus for a new level of development.

of Jerusalem. The only practical difference is in the decoration of the pommel and blade, and the grip covering. On the original, Edward's coat of arms are on the pommel, instead of the Jerusalem Cross. The blade engraving of the Order of the Garter was eliminated for the film sword, and in the film, the grip is not covered with snake skin, but wrapped with raw leather cords.

The independent film *Beowulf & Grendel* was not a hit—it was mainly for fans of the genre—but was pleasing due to its accurate details. Weapons and armor very much correspond to the historical models. Thus, the sword of Beowulf (Gerard Butler) is based pretty much on early Vendel type medieval swords. The broad, scarcely tapering blade with an equally wide fuller is typical. It is also characteristic that pommel and cross-guard were made of metal bands and organic material—like bone—and riveted. Another nice detail is the characteristic Vendel-type ring-knob. Although the Beowulf sword is not an exact reproduction of an historical original, it nevertheless corresponds exactly to contemporary weapons—and is a truly realistic movie sword.

The swords from *Kingdom of Heaven* and *Beowulf & Grendel* are pleasing exceptions to the usual exaggerated and unrealistic movie swords. *The Lord of the Rings* swords are another exception. Some sword-friends claim that these were the best fantasy or movie swords ever made. These swords were indeed designed based on the knowledge of historical weapons experts. We can also see which creative details the production designer developed out of the often meager information, in this respect, in the novel. Unlike "normal" movie swords, here the details are so unobtrusive that you actually don't perceive them during the movie, but they still leave an overwhelming impression. *The Lord of the Rings* swords created a sensation among international sword fans and gave the impetus for the development of new designs. All this makes them so interesting, that I am dedicating more space to them here.

11.1 Swords In *The Lord Of The Rings*

The Bible is the bestselling book of all time. But the best-selling book of the 20th century is not the Bible, or even *Harry Potter*; it is J.R.R. Tolkien's *The Lord of the Rings*. Since it first appeared in the 1950s, the *Ring* trilogy has sold over 100 million copies—an absolute record! And not only that: This approximately 1,000-page story by Oxford Professor Tolkien founded the literary genre of "fantasy."

While dragons, sword fights, dwarves, wizards, and elves had earlier been something for fairy tales and children's books, *The Lord of the Rings* draws on the Arthurian epics of the Middle Ages or the violent pagan Viking sagas—and readers of all ages were thrilled! If we speak of 100 million copies sold, we can only imagine how high the number of "unreported cases" who have read *The Lord of the Rings* actually is. A classic tale of good and evil, honor, courage, loyalty and friendship—even after forty-five years, few other books can even approach it. For many years, the novel was considered impossible to film. The 1970s animated version was a failure, and only the first part completed. Tolkien's world of dwarves, elves, orcs, and hobbits was too fantastic; its description of a great adventure and a gigantic war too rich in detail.

What distinguishes *The Lord of the Rings* from other fantasy films, is the effort made to emulate Tolkien and create an entire world. "I only had one aim in mind: I wanted to transport the audience in a credible and convincing manner, to the fantastic world of Middle Earth," says director Peter Jackson. Thus, the hobbits' homeland, the Shire, was created on location in New Zealand. They dug hobbit holes in the landscape, planted vegetables, and laid down lanes—and then allowed it all to grow wild for over a year, so that it looked like a "mature" village. Other elements of the film were given just as meticulous and imaginative a treatment.

The actors were also given lessons in sword fighting.

Photo: New Line Cinema/ United Cutlery

Tolkien got his ideas from sources including the Anglo-Saxon heroic epics. Tolkien purists complain that therefore the movie swords should actually be based on the richly decorated spathae from the early Middle Ages.

Photo: Paul Mortimer

What of course interests us especially here, are the swords, in their respective "ethno-design" for hobbits, elves, and people. Perhaps some readers have seen the old cartoon *The Lord of the Rings.* That design was influenced by the "norms" of the 1980s fantasy movies: Muscle-bound barbarians in tight leather clothing. Jackson's film version, however, was intended to appear "realistic." The filmmakers' task was to harmonize between knowledge of medieval warfare and Tolkien's imagination. The first step was to consult experts in such fields as historical weapons and military equipment, as well as "practitioners," such as the popular Australian archer Jan Kozler.

Beyond archery lessons, the actors also had to take lessons in horseback riding, canoeing, mountain climbing, "Elvish," and of course sword fighting. What Viggo Mortensen, the actor who portrayed Aragorn, had to say about the first day of shooting is standard for this movie: "The first thing I had to do was a swordfight. Even before I spoke a single word of dialogue, I was forced to confront the physicality of my character." Famous stuntman Bob Anderson was hired to choreograph the sword fighting scenes. He had already worked with Errol Flynn and choreographed the swordfights in *Star Wars* and *Highlander*—the cult film for all sword fans. Anderson had developed a special training concept, because he wanted the film to have the most medieval, and most savage effect possible: "So I spent a lot of time on teaching the actors and stuntmen the right way to fence, and then I told them to forget it and be as bestial as they could."

The *Lord of the Rings* swords were developed by a design team at the Weta Workshop production company. In addition to the Weta team (Ben Wooton, David Falconer, Warren Mahy, and others), the weapons reflect in particular the influence of production designer John Howe—who with colleague Alan Lee was responsible for the overall design of the movie—and swordsmith Peter Lyon. Next to the Brothers Hildebrandt, Howe is perhaps the most famous Tolkien illustrator ever. In addition to his artistic talents, he had another quality important for designing the swords: Howe is a re-enactor, a *Söldner* (mercenary) in the Swiss *"Kompanie von St. Georg."* Therefore, he knows medieval warfare, weapons, and swords very well himself. He is co-author of several picture books on this subject (such as *Söldnerleben im Mittelalter* [*Mercenary Life in the Middle Ages*]).

In this respect, at least, one of the designers had a lot of practical experience in sword fighting. Blacksmith Peter Lyons—whom Howe characterized as a "mixture of librarian and ringer"—has a similar background. He came to reenactment and forging medieval weapons by way of fantasy role-playing games. No wonder that this team brought a reality-based influence into play from the very beginning.

Tolkien's ideas were, of course, the starting point for design. However, Tolkien himself said little on the appearance of the swords. He is more interested in the weapons' magical and symbolic properties, as well as their historical significance. If anything is mentioned about the weapons' appearance, it is mostly that they were splendid, sumptuously decorated swords. Gandalf's sword Glamdring is described in *The Hobbit* as having a "beautiful scabbard" and "jeweled hilt." Howe intervened already here to correct the design: "In any case, many fewer jewels on the hilts and scabbards."

Thus, although the weapons are still decorated, this is much more discreet than Tolkien had indicated. And this is just what some Tolkien purists criticize: In their opinion, the filmmakers should have used replicas of the richly decorated, often ostentatious Migration Period spathae for the movie rather than late medieval battle swords, since Tolkien got much of his inspiration from the heroic epics of that time. Apart from this criticism, however, most sword and Tolkien fans are quite happy with the relatively simple, battle-oriented designs of Howe and his colleagues. "Swords in films are almost always huge, ugly, and clumsy pieces that you could never lift if they were really made of metal. A sword should be balanced, elegant, and beautiful," Howe says.

Production design presented Howe and the others with a unique challenge—after all, none of these people had ever existed. They had the task of

Opposite to Tolkien's idea, the movie swords were spared "gold and jewels"; the weapons were decorated in Tolkien's "ethno-style," corresponding to the characters.

Photo: New Line Cinema/United Cutlery

The sword scabbards were made of the lightweight and extremely durable plastic material Kevlar and covered with leather.

Photo: New Line Cinema/United Cutlery

taking up Tolkien's ethnological descriptions, partly to expand upon them, and to transform them into images and designs. The newly invented ethno design played a special role for the swords, in addition to the fighting styles specially developed for the respective peoples. However, most swords in the movie are based on historical weapons, without being exact copies. Howe brought with him a large part of his own weapons collection as illustrative material for the Weta team: "It helped me a lot, that I could bring out a real sword and say: This is what it probably looked like back then."

To give the Weta team a real feeling for swords, they also tried them out practically. "It was especially great of John Howe, that he let us first make a few practice swords. He was a really good fencer and he finished off all the technicians from the workshop in the parking lot," says Weta boss Richard Taylor, and manager Tania Rodger added from her viewpoint: "I would really have to intervene here. How could I explain it to the authorities, if someone had been massacred on the parking lot?"

"Life-size" cardboard templates were made from the design team's first sketches. These templates went to Peter Lyons, who discussed them again with Howe and the rest of the team. After the draft design was completed, Lyon started production, transforming a two-dimensional sketch into a three-dimensional object. "My job was to make the weapons the best I could do—functional, apart from a blunt cutting edge. All the blades were made from tempered spring steel; if they had been sharpened, you could have trusted your life to these weapons," states Lyons. The mountings are made of steel or bronze, the grips of wood, covered with leather or wound around with wire. Finally, the weapons were artificially aged to make them look used.

Andril, the Flame of the West.

Photo:

United Cutlery

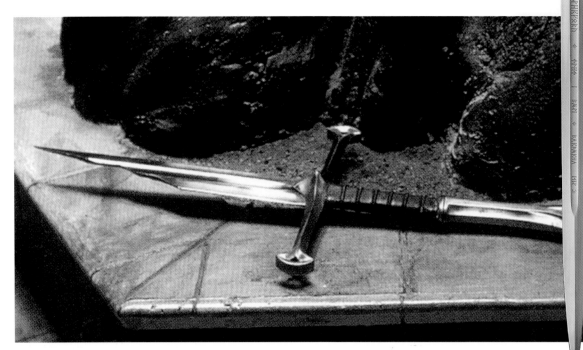

The sword Narsil was broken in the Battle of Mount Doom.

Photo: New Line Cinema/United Cutlery

The sword had to be newly
forged for *The Return of the King.*

Photo: New Line Cinema/United Cutlery

These swords are, as stated, designed to be modern cutting weapons: this also means that they are light enough to be carried by the actors on the set all day. The scabbards were made of Kevlar—a lightweight synthetic material, used to make bullet-proof vests—which was covered with leather and decorated.

Replicas of the most important swords in the movie, the "hero swords," are available from the company United Cutlery. These are invariably category D replicas—i.e., purely decorative swords with stainless steel blades. The grips are cast from solid metal and then hand engraved.

The sword Narsi-Andüril is probably the most famous weapon in the entire *Ring* trilogy. In the "Elder Days," Men and Elves joined together in a Last Alliance against the evil Sauron. King Elendil of Gondor was struck down by Sauron in the Battle of Mount Doom and his sword Narsil broke into pieces. Yet Isildur—Elendil's son—was able to cut the Master Ring from Sauron's hand with one of these pieces, breaking Sauron's power … and the actual story of the "One Ring" begins. During the War of the Ring, Narsil is repaired. The fragments of the blade are forged together, and the sword will be virtually reborn under the name Anduril (Flame of the West). Here we have an interesting parallel to the Germanic heroic legends of the Migration Period: in the *Sigurdlieder* (forerunner of the *Nibelungen Saga*), Sigurd inherits the fragments of his father's sword (which was broken by the divine power of Odin) and forges it together anew, with the aid of master smith Regin. The new sword was called Gram (in the Middle High German *Nibelungenlied*, the name is Balmung). We can clearly see where Tolkien got his inspiration.

Frodo's sword Sting.

Photo: United Cutlery

Celtic longsword with leaf-shaped blade, possible model for Glamdring.

Bilbo gives Sting to Frodo.

Photo: New Line Cinema/United Cutlery

The Elvish ethno-design
Sting has a leaf-shaped blade.

Photo: New Line Cinema/United Cutlery

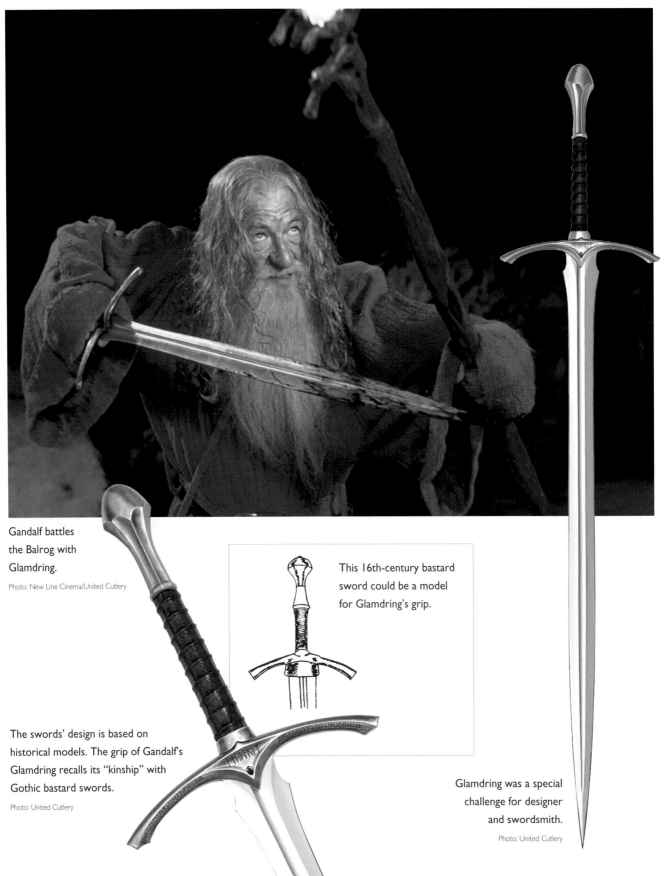

Gandalf battles
the Balrog with
Glamdring.

Photo: New Line Cinema/United Cutlery

This 16th-century bastard
sword could be a model
for Glamdring's grip.

The swords' design is based on
historical models. The grip of Gandalf's
Glamdring recalls its "kinship" with
Gothic bastard swords.

Photo: United Cutlery

Glamdring was a special
challenge for designer
and swordsmith.

Photo: United Cutlery

Tolkien himself describes Anduril as follows: "[…] on its blade was traced a device of seven stars set between the crescent Moon and the rayed Sun, and about them was written many runes." Elsewhere, Anduril (in comparison to Boromir's sword) is described as a long-sword. This is, of course, not very meaningful: the film version of Narsil (total length: 52.7 inches [134 centimeters]) basically corresponds to a battle sword. In profile, the sword recalls type XIIa with its long fuller, but the concave cutting edges rather belong to type XVIIIa (or XVIIIb). The lower part of the silver-plated mounting is covered with leather, and is intended to be reminiscent of leaves and stems. The broken pommel displays an inscription in the Elvish language Quenya, invented by Tolkien, as well as inlays of 24 carat gold.

The newly forged Anduril, apart of the engravings, is the exact likeness of Narsil. Here, they were able to carry out Tolkien's ideas somewhat more precisely: a sun is engraved at the base of the blade, and in the fuller runs an engraved runic inscription, interspersed with seven stars and finished with the symbol of the moon.

Glamdring and Sting, the swords of Gandalf (Ian McKellen) and Frodo (Elijah Wood), are of Elvish origin. *The Hobbit* describes how Gandalf and Bilbo find the swords, "For a troll, it would have been at most a tiny pocket knife. But for a hobbit, it was almost a short sword." During the War of the Ring, Frodo is given the sword by his uncle Bilbo. "[Bilbo] took from the box a small sword in an old shabby leather scabbard. Then he drew it, and its polished and well-tended blade glittered suddenly, cold and bright. 'This is Sting,' he said, and thrust it with little effort deep into a wooden beam." Elrond is able to make a more precise identification of the sword which Gandalf found in the troll treasure hoard, based on the engraved runes. "There are old Elven swords forged in Gondolin for Goblin Wars. […] This here, Gandalf, is Glamdring, the foe-Hammer, which the king of Gondolin wore ages ago." Apart from this description, and except for the jeweled decoration, we find no further indications about the swords' appearance.

The Elves are a nature-oriented people, despite their highly developed culture. Their designs are based on natural forms. Decorations typical of the Elves have a leaf and tendril pattern, which the production designer adapted from art nouveau style. The team selected two basic types for the Elves' swords: straight swords with leaf-shaped blades and curved sabers.

We know of short swords with leaf-shaped blades from ancient times; this type was widespread in the Bronze Age, around 1500-500 BC. They were not found at all, however, in the Middle Ages. This means we are seeing quite significant artistic freedom being taken here. Designer David Falconer created a very elegant weapon with harmonious proportions for the film version of Sting (total length: 56 centimeters). Cross-guard and blade are decorated with an inscription in Quenya.

For the film version of Glamdring, designer Ben Wooton significantly modified the sword as described by Tolkien: The lavish jeweled decoration of the hilt turned into two small, discreet semi-precious stones set at the base of the cross-guard. The runic inscriptions Tolkien described were added. At first glance, the sharply down curved cross-guard appears atypical for bastard swords, where a more or less straight cross usually prevailed. However, there is a small group of Gothic bastard swords, which have cross-guards shaped sharply downwards. They date from the mid 16th century and, although are certainly fully functional battle swords, served more for representative purposes. All these swords have a characteristic mounting with extensive engraving that is very reminiscent of Glamdring: "The pommel has a more or less stylized scent-stopper (pear) shape, there is a ring around the thicker part of the hilt, and the downturned crossguards have beveled ends," (Seitz I, pp.280ff). A particularly fine example of such a sword belonged to King Gustav Vasa, which was laid with him in his grave in 1560.

Glamdring (total length: 47.6 inches [121 centimeters]) is an interesting mix of Celtic long-sword and medieval bastard sword. Long-swords with leaf-shaped blades only appear in history during

The Elves' weapons and other military equipment are kept in a natural, organic design.

Photo: New Line Cinema/United Cutlery

The Elves' battle swords are designed for circular movements.

Photo: New Line Cinema/United Cutlery

An Elvish battle sword.

Photo: United Cutlery

the Hallstatt period. Around 650-500 BC, we find Celtic iron long-swords with a design still based on the Bronze models. These swords have a blade length of 37.3 inches (94.8 centimeters), which is very close to that of the Glamdring blade (35.8 inches [91 centimeters]). There are two differences, however: The Celtic swords' point is beveled, while Glamdring's is pointed, and the Celtic swords have basically no fuller (these first appear only in the Early Middle Ages). This special design turned out, as Peter Lyons acknowledges, to be one of the most difficult of all: "Glamdring was a partcular challenge, due to the long, leaf-shaped blade. It could very easily have become difficult to wield, I have honed a distinct distal taper in the widest part of the blade. The resulting sword was well balanced by the large pommel."

The second grouping of Elven swords are essentially sabers. The curved blades were chosen by the designers to make it clear that the Elves had a completely different, more elegant way of fighting than the men. Elven fighting style consists of using circular movements, for which curved blades are best. The battle swords designed by Warren Mahy are typical. The hilt makes up about half of these approximately 59.0 inches (1.5 meter) long weapons; it curves slightly opposite to the blade, giving the impression of a very elongated S. As the official companion book puts it: "The reason for such a long hilt was that it let you wield the sword with both hands, one at the base of the blade, the other on the pommel. This spread-apart grip was developed by the Elves to give them the greatest possibility for turning them around as they strike out with the sword, using this whirling stroke that characterizes their style of attack," (Smith, p.15).

For the Elven sabers, the designers combined two completely different design forms: Japanese swords with art nouveau—a stunning mix. The Elf saber Hadhafang (length of 38.1 inches [97 centimeters])

Arwen defending Frodo with naked blade.

Arwen's saber Hadhafang was a mixture of a Japanese sword and Oriental saber, with art nouveau decoration.

Boromir's weapon is an XIV sword with elements of type XVI.

Photo: New Line Cinema/United Cutlery

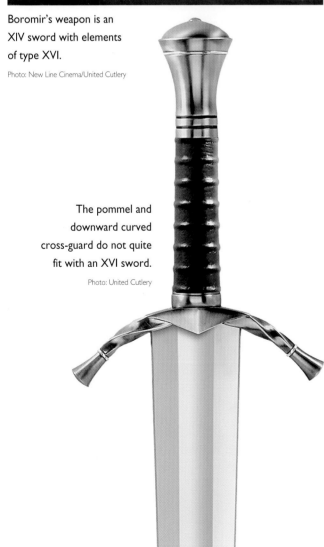

The pommel and downward curved cross-guard do not quite fit with an XVI sword.

Photo: United Cutlery

is an heirloom of Elrond's family. He fights with this saber in his hand against Sauron's orc hordes in the Battle of Mount Doom. Later Hadhafang is passed on to his daughter, Strider's beloved Arwen (Liv Tyler). In the movie, she uses the sword to protect Frodo's life from the Nazgul.

Hadhafang is a blend of a samurai sword and Oriental saber. On one hand, we find the typical Japanese blade shape with slightly beveled point, and on the other, the typical pistol-shaped saber grip, curved opposite to the blade. A peculiar detail of Hadhafang is that it has no cross-guard or hand guard. This is something only found on swords from Southeast Asia (such as Thailand). It is decorated with art nouveau-style tendrils, a design found on most of the Elves' possessions in the film.

Boromir's (Sean Bean) simple, purely practical sword poses a stark contrast to the sleek, ornate Elven weapons. If you saw this sword in a case in a museum, you could take if for an historical sword. The 30.3-inch (77-centimeter) blade is type XIV, with elements of type XVI: A broad blade with fuller, which runs down to a sharp point. The twisted cross-guard is also a style found in some historical swords, but those are not curved. The downward curvature of the cross-guard and flattened scent-stopper pommel are the only parts of this in total 38.9-inch (99-centimeter) long weapon that could make an expert suspicious and cast doubt on its historical authenticity.

The Rohirrim's swords are the only ones in the film which are based on early medieval weapons, and thus meet the demands of the Tolkien purists. Tolkien himself was reserved in describing them, speaking generally just of "long-swords." The external shape of the Rohirrim swords resembles the spatha. Thus far, this design is "historically accurate" for the weaponry of an equestrian people, since not only the Roman cavalry, but also the early medieval equestrian peoples (Scythians, Avars, Huns) carried straight,

The Rohirrim swords resemble
Early Middle Ages long-swords.

Photo: New Line Cinema/United Cutlery

King Theoden's
sword Herugrim.

Photo: United Cutlery

The hilts of antique Bronze and Iron Age swords serve as models for the Rohirrim's weapons.

Photo: Del Tin

Eowyn's sword is essentially a Viking sword with horse motifs.

Photo: United Cutlery

two-edged swords. The saber came later as a cavalry weapon, in the 8th and 9th centuries. The only basic differences between the Rohirrim swords and historical weapons are in blade width and grip design: The blade of the movie swords are much broader than those of historical cavalry swords—they resemble the Germanic spatha—and the mounting is borrowed from those of antique Bronze and Iron Age as well as Viking swords.

Eowyn's (Miranda Otto) weapon is a fine example of a sword of Rohan. The 31.1-inch (79-centimeter) blade is a classic example of type X, the "cross-guard" is based on ancient Bronze and Iron Age swords, and "enfolds" the entire base of the blade. The pommel of this 36.6-inch (93-centimeter) long sword resembles that of a type VII Viking sword: What is a cast piece in the replica, in the original is a typical Early Middle Ages composite pommel. As is characteristic for Rohirrim culture, both pommel and cross-guard are decorated with the predominant horse motif. Eowyn's sword is a particularly successful weapon.

Herugrim—the sword of King Theoden of Rohan (Bernard Hill)—is also a good example of Rohirrim weaponry. Tolkien himself describes Herugrim as "a long sword in a scabbard clasped with gold and was set with green gems." The movie version of the sword (total length: 36.6 inches [93 centimeters]) differs from this image primarily in the decoration. The 27.1-inch (69-centimeter) blade has two narrow fullers, which are typical for some spathae. The round hand guard and pommel are made of bronze and

Detail of Eowyn's sword.

Photo: United Cutlery

decorated with horse motifs. The scabbard is made of red leather and studded with bronze. There is—fortunately—no trace of gold or precious gemstones.

Every heroic saga of course has its villains. Their swords naturally look very different than those of the heroes. The swords of the Uruk-hai, for example, actually do not deserve to be called swords. Basically, these are long hacking knives with a spike protruding at a right angle at the point. This instrument matches the Uruk-hai's fighting style: Brute force with no technique.

The swords of Sauron's allies, the Easterlings, in contrast—simply described by Tolkien as "scimitars"—are based on the Chinese *da-dao* two-handed saber, which allows an elegant and effective technique, despite its ungainly appearance.

Beyond the common foot soldiers, there are also special villains. In *The Lord of the Rings*, these are the Nazgûl, the nine Ringwraiths. They were once mortal kings, until they were corrupted by the power of the magic rings. Now, under Sauron's command, the

The Black Riders on the hunt for the Ring.
Photo: New Line Cinema/United Cutlery

The Nazgûl swords reflect their own depraved character.
Photo: United Cutlery

The Witch King's sword.

Photo: United Cutlery

The Witch King of Angmar
is leader of the Ringwraiths.

Photo: New Line Cinema/United Cutlery

Nazgûl streak through Middle Earth as the Black Riders, forever in search of the Master Ring and its bearers. And these fearsome Ringwraiths of course require fearsome swords. In contrast to the heroes' elegant and beautiful weapons, the Nazgûl swords reflect their owners' depraved characters. The mounting—like all weapons from Mordor—is made of dark iron. The cross-guard is set with black thorns. One interesting detail is the asymmetric blade, for which there is no historical precedent. However, this design is not so "off" that it should be disqualified as an SLO.

The Nazgûl are led by the Witch King of Angmar, who is a powerful wizard. His sword is significantly different from those of the other Ringwraiths. In terms of proportions (total length, 54.7 inches [139 centimeters]; blade length, 39.7 inches [101 centimeters]) the Witch King's sword corresponds to the battle swords of the Late Middle Ages. Both the very long grip and blade with long ricasso are typical for this style of sword. The blade shape (type XVIIIb) is similar to that of the Sture Sword (p. 104).

Perhaps the most beautiful sword in the film trilogy is Strider's long-sword. In Tolkien's novel, Aragorn carries the fragments of Narsil with him everywhere in the sheath on his belt. Tolkien himself does not tell us how Aragorn survives duels with only a broken sword. This is a romantic motif from a fairy-tale, which of course is completely nonsensical in terms of military history and from any tactical viewpoint. Therefore, Jackson's screenplay differs on this point—absolutely correctly—from the original: In the film, the remnants of Narsil are kept in the house of Elrond in Rivendell. Until Aragorn is able to wield the renewed Narsil-Anduril in the battle against Sauron's hordes, he used his own long-sword.

Strider's long-sword (length: 47.2 inches [120 centimeters]) is an unadorned bastard sword—the typical purpose-built weapon of a simple mercenary leader. One characteristic detail is that he carries a companion knife attached to the scabbard, as we know from Late Medieval swords. The 35.8-inch (91-centimeter) blade is a slender version of type XIIa, but the mounting shows typical Late Middle Ages details, such as the iron reinforcement ring on the hilt and the scent-stopper shaped pommel. Of all

In the film, the remains
of Narsil are preserved
in Rivendell.

Photo: New Line Cinema/United Cutlery

Before Anduril
is re-forged,
Strider uses
another sword.

Photo: New Line Cinema/
United Cutlery

Strider's longsword is
an XIIA sword with Late
Middle Ages mounting.

Photo: United Cutlery

swords in *The Lord of the Rings*, this unadorned yet beautiful weapon most reflects historical models. The clear proportions and lines accurately capture the timeless elegance of medieval swords.

Following the motto "never change a winning team," the successful partnership of Weta and swordsmith Peter Lyon has continued since *The Lord of the Rings*. Another project is the movie version of *The Chronicles of Narnia*. These children's fairy tales about the magical land of Narnia, which are very popular in Anglo-Saxon countries, are the creation of Tolkien's friend and colleague Clive Staples Lewis. The first part of the film series—*The Lion, the Witch, and the Ward-*robe—was launched in theaters on Christmas 2005. The production design of the weapons and armor cannot deny the influence of *The Lord of the Rings*, and here also we find many interesting details—even if the Narnia films are more intended for children. In any case, the Narnia weapons are interesting enough to serve as a pattern for many reproductions.

A companion knife is attached to the scabbard of Strider's sword.

Photo: United Cutlery

Peter's sword for *The Lion, the Witch and the Wardrobe*.

Photo: Museum Replicas

The successful partnership of Weta and Peter Lyon continued their work together to make the swords for *The Chronicles of Narnia*.

Photo: Disney / Walden Media

12.1 Pommel and Cross-Guard Shapes
(Classification Based on E. Oakeshott)

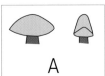

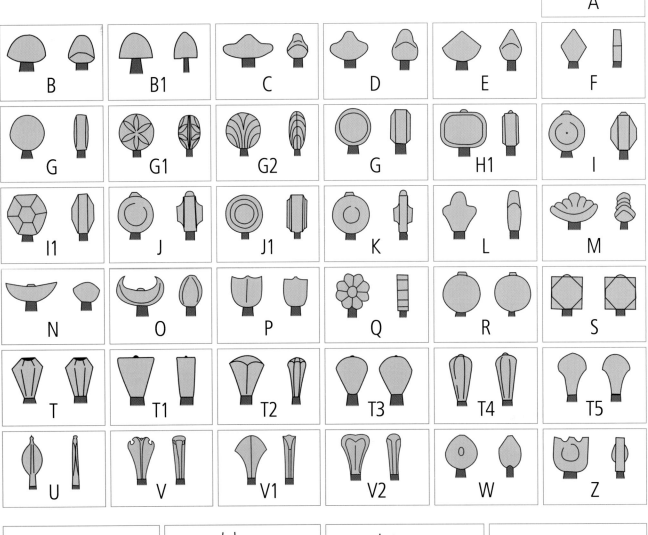

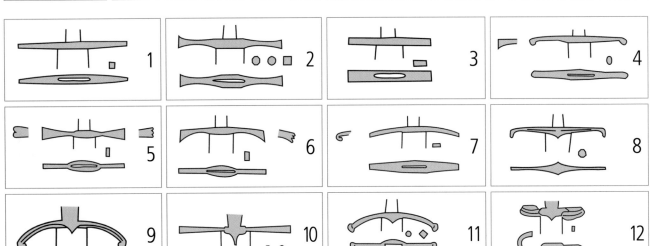

12.2 German Weapons Law on the Sword

Some readers may perhaps be wondering why a book on historical swords dedicates its own chapter to a 21st century weapons law. For a reason: If you want to collect swords, do sword fighting as a sport, or maybe "just" be a re-enactor, then you are affected by weapons laws.

Actually, the new weapons legislation that came into force in April 2003 is intended to disentangle and clarify the jungle of legal articles – regrettably, exactly the opposite is true, and everything has become more complicated. I have compiled below the sections relating to "swords."

Swords, sabers, and similar weapons are, under the law, so-called "cut and thrust weapons." The corresponding legal text can be found in §1 Abs 2.2a WaffG. [§1 Par.2.2a of the Weapons Act]. According to this, weapons in the legal sense include, "wearable items that are intended by their nature to eliminate or offset the offensive or defensive capability of persons, in particular cut and thrust weapons." Cut and thrust weapons are more exactly defined in German officialese in Appendix 1, Section 1, Sub-section 2, No.1.1, as, "objects which by their nature are intended, with the immediate use of muscle power, through cut, thrust, stab, stroke, or throw, to produce injuries." As we will see below, stage-combat and decorative swords are not weapons under this definition.

Having now clarified what a cut-and-thrust weapon is by law, we must also go into the regulations. Under §2 Par.2 of the Weapons Law, all weapons listed in Appendix 2 Sub-section 2 require a permit. Cut-and-thrust weapons are NOT on this list, so are therefore so-called "free weapons." So far, so good. But these free weapons are also subject to certain restrictions. According to §2 Par.1, their usage is, "only permitted to persons over 18 years of age." The legal term "usage" is defined precisely in §1 Par.3: "They have usage of a weapon [...], who acquires, owns, delivers, wields, spends time with, takes along [...] produces, processes, refurbishes or carries on business with them." To sum up, any legal adult may to purchase, own, and also use a sword – entirely without a weapons license or weapons possession card. Theoretically, I could go shopping at the supermarket, wearing my sword on my belt. In practice, however, you should never do anything of the kind – after all, there is still the risk of creating a "public nuisance." Wielding, or carrying a weapon, requires having your official identification, according to §38. This means you have to carry your personal identity card or passport with you; a driver's license is not specifically listed in the Act and is therefore not sufficient, in case of any doubt.

In addition, pursuant to §36 Par.1, weapons must be kept safe, "Who [...] possesses weapons, has to take the necessary precautions to prevent that these items are lost or are taken by a third party without authorization." This law is certainly intended primarily to apply to firearms, but also legally refers to cut-and-thrust weapons. Unfortunately, no regulations have been enacted on custody of cut-and-thrust weapons, so all sorts of "experts" are spreading the most abstruse theories. Their tenor ranges from "the law applies only to firearms," to "swords have to be chained to the wall." The fact is that the law clearly identifies "weapons" in general, not "firearms" explicitly, so it also applies to swords. As long as there are no pertinent regulations, you are not necessarily obliged to chain them to the wall by every means possible. Unfortunately, due to the still-lacking regulations, we are in uncertain legal territory here. Until there are new rules (which, based on experience, however, could drag on endlessly) a lockable cabinet should be sufficient to comply with the law. This also represents the understanding that storage in a self-contained apartment is sufficient, provided no minors have access to it.

Another point in the law on weapons applies to trade. According to §35 Par.3, the distribution and delivery of cut- and thrust weapons is prohibited in the travel industry, at set-time events (Middle Ages markets!), folk festivals, and collector gatherings. The responsible authority (usually the local police or regulatory office) can grant special permission, if this is, "not contrary to the public interest." After several occurrences, in which a person running amok has attacked and even killed people with a sword, however, the decision has been taken by many authorities to basically not allow any exceptions. However, according to §42 par.4, "commercial display […] at trade shows and exhibitions" is expressly allowed. Accordingly, you can not sell swords at a display without a permit, but can take orders for them.

§42 is also important for Middle Ages markets: According to Par. 1, no weapons should be wielded at, "public amusements, festivals, sporting events, trade shows, exhibitions, markets or similar public events." A general exemption to §42 par.1 applies, according to par.4.1, to, "the participants in theatrical performances and what are to be considered equivalent performances." Thus, there is, at least to some extent, a legal framework for stage fights and weapons demonstrations and Medieval markets. Beyond this, the organizers should however absolutely ensure that they obtain permission, based on §42 par.2 (which normally is granted).

Stage-combat Swords and Decorative Weapons

All of the above cited regulations and paragraphs in the Weapons Law do NOT apply to decorative weapons and stage-combat swords, because these by definition are not weapons in the sense of the law! This was clearly set out in the administrative regulations under the old weapons law, and since as yet no new regulations have been issued on this particular point, de facto, the old rules are still valid. The *Bundeskriminalamt* (BKA) [German Federal Criminal Police Authority] made this clear in a statement dated 11/242003: "After examination of the facts, the conclusion is that classification based on weapons' laws […] is not required, because the facts, with the help of the Waffenverwaltungsvorschrift [Weapons Administrative Regulations] (WaffVwV) and interpretation of the law make it clear that: Based on the factually still valid WaffVwV, the blunt Carnival sabers under discussion are not cut-and-thrust weapons." The Weapons Administrative Regulations state: "A device is not a cut-and-thrust weapon, which, although modeled on cut-and-thrust weapons […] but due to blunt points or blunt edges, is obviously only intended to be used for sports or as an ornament." Thus, decorative weapons are clearly classified as ornamental objects and stage-combat swords as sports equipment. The BKA has requested the Interior Ministry to include this passage in the new, yet-to-be-created, regulations.

These statements reflect the legal situation at the date of printing (December 2007) and again no liability is assumed.

12.3 Addresses

This list of course has no claim to being complete or timely. Internet addresses especially change frequently. Therefore, there is no guarantee of the specifics in all of the following addresses.

Organizations:

www.swordforum.com
Discussion forum all about swords.

www.myarmoury.com
Webpage about swords with discussion forum and valuable information for beginners.

www.kampfkunstverein-agilitas.de
Association for historical martial arts.

www.zornhau.de
Non-commercial school of historical swordsmanship, the site of a webring of German-language sites on historical martial arts.

www.freifechter.org
Non-commercial school of historical swordsmanship, webpage with lots of background information.

www.arsgladii.at
Non-commercial school of historical swordsmanship, webpage with lots of background information.

Retailers, smiths and manufacturers:

www.agilitas.tv
Training DVDs on medieval swordsmanship.

**www.albionarmorers.com +
www.albion-europe.com**
Manufacturer of detailed, practical swords (serially produced Johnsson swords and functional movie swords).

www.armart.antiquanova.com
Manufacturer of detailed, practical swords.

www.armor.com
(Arms & Armor) Manufacturer of detailed, practical swords.

www.atrimasa.com
(ASA Swordworks, Angus Trim) Manufacturer of functional new interpretations.

www.angele.de
Forging techniques, equipment and accessories, steel.

www.schmiede-balbach.de
(Markus Balbach) Damascus steel smith.

www.boker.de
(Böker Baumwerk) Retailer (decorative and samurai swords).
www.berbekuczviktor.hu
Weapons smith, stage-combat weapons, reproductions.

www.cashenblades.com
(Kevin Cashen); Damascus steel smith.

www.christianfletcher.com
Sword finisher.

www.coldsteel.com
Manufacturer of new modern cutting sword interpretations.

www.deltin.it
(Del Tin Armi Antiche) Manufacturer of modern cutting sword replicas.

www.arscives.com/vevans
(Vince Evans) Swordsmith.

www.filmswords.com
The film sword department of Albion Armorers.
www.hayesknives.com (Wally Hayes) Knife
maker, swordsmith.

www.herbertz-messerclub.de
(Herbertz Solingen) Retailer (Cold Steel swords
and decorative models).

Peter Johnsson
Swordsmith and designer: Grönstensvägen 12,
75241 Uppsala, Sweden,
Email: peter@albionarmorers.com

www.katachi-art.de
Retailer, Japanese and European swords
(Cas Iberia, Museum Replicas, Last Legend,
United Cutlery).

www.knifetom.net
Retailer of swords, knives, martial arts articles.

www.lutel.cz
Manufacturer of detail-accurate, practical replicas.

www.museumreplicas.com
Manufacturer of detail-accurate, practical replicas.

www.japanklingen.de
(Karl-Heinz Peuker) Collector and dealer of
original Japanese swords

www.phoenixmetalcreations.com
PhoenixMetalCreations@comcast.net

www.piecesofhistory.co.uk
www.cashanwei.com Wholesaler of detailed,
practical swords (Hanwei)

www.seelenschmiede.de
(Stephan Roth) Swordsmith, reconstructions and
modern interpretations.

www.schwertshop.de
Specialized dealer for swords, *bokken*, etc.

www.stahlwarenhaus-hebsacker.de
Dealer, decorative swords, film swords,
and stage-combat swords.

www.swords-and-more.com
Retailer (Hamburg), Japanese and European
swords, film swords (Hanwei, Museum
Replicas).

www.templ.net
(Templ Arms - Patrick Barta) swordsmith, exact
reconstructions of early medieval swords.

www.wkc-solingen.de
Manufacture and retail of swords and sabers.

www.dietraumschmiede.de
(Arno Eckhart) swordsmith, reconstructions and
modern interpretations.

12.4 Bibliography

No Editor, *Schwerter, Degen, Dolche - Kulturgeschichte der Blankwaffen*, Augsburg: 1994

Adams, Andrew, *Ninja - Geschichte, Philosophie und Kultur der Schattenkämpfer*, Niedernhausen im Taunus, Germany: 1991

Agilitas.tv (ed.), *Schwertkampf in der Rüstung für Anfänger* [Sword fighting in Armor for Beginners] (DVD), Krefeld: 2005

Agilitas.tv (ed.), *Langes Schwert nach Johannes Liechtenauer* [Long Sword by John Liechtenauer], Teil [Part] 1 (DVD), Krefeld, Germany: 2005

Agilitas.tv (ed.), *Kampf- und Kriegsringen* [Battle and War Wrestling] *Teil 1- mit dem Dolch* [part 1 with daggers] (DVD), Krefeld, Germany: 2006

Agilitas.tv (ed.), *Langes Messer Teil 1 - nach Johannes Lecküchner* [Long Knives part 1 - after John Lecküchner] (DVD), Krefeld: 2007

Arens, Peter, *Wege aus der Finsternis – Europa im Mittelalter*, Munich: 2004

Armart Antiquanova (ed.), *The Birth of a Sword* (DVD), Brno (Czech Republic): 2004

Bergland, Havard, *Messer schmieden – eine norwegische Kunst*, Hanover: 2002

Boeheim, Wendelin, *Handbuch der Waffenkunde – Das Waffenwesen in seiner historischen Entwicklung vom Beginn des Mittelalters bis zum Ende des achten Jahrhunderts*, Leipzig: 1890 Borst, Arno (ed.), Das Rittertum im Mittelalter, 3rd edition, Darmstadt: 1998

Clements, John, *Renaissance Swordsmanship - the Illustrated Use of Rapiers and Cut-and-Thrust Swords,* Boulder (Colorado): 1997

Clements, John, *Medieval Swordsmanship – Illustrated Methods and Techniques,* Boulder (Colorado): 1998

Davidson, Hilda Ellis, *The Sword in Anglo-Saxon England – its Archaeology and Literature*, Oxford: 1962, corrected reprint Woodbridge: 1994

Demmin, August, *Die Kriegswaffen in ihren geschichtlichen Entwicklungen – Von den ältesten Zeiten bis auf die Gegenwart – Eine Encyklopädie der Waffenkunde*, 3rd edition, Gera-Untermhaus, Germany: 1891

Dollinger, Hans, *Schwarzbuch der Weltgeschichte – 5.000 Jahre der Mensch des Menschen Feind*, Munich: 1973

Eliade, Mircea, *Schmiede und Alchemisten*, Stuttgart: n.d.

Embleton Gerry and Howe, John, *Söldnerleben im Mittelalter*, Stuttgart: 1996

Embleton, Gerry, *Ritter und Söldner im Mittelalter – Kleidung, Rüstung, Bewaffnung*, Herne, Germany: 2002

Evangelista, Nick, *The Encyclopedia of the Sword*, Westport, Connecticut: 1995

Fiedler, Siegfried, *Kriegswesen und Kriegführung im Zeitalter der Landsknechte*, Koblenz: 1985

Funcken, Liliane and Fred, *Historische Waffen und Rüstungen – Ritter und Landsknechte vom achten bis 16. Jahrhundert*, Niedernhausen im Taunus, Germany: 2001

Geibig, Alfred, *Beiträge zur morphologischen Entwicklung des Schwerts im Mittelalter*, Neumünster: 1991

Haedeke, Hanns-Ulrich, *Menschen und Klingen – Geschichte und Geschichten*, Solingen: 1994

Harding, David (ed.), *Waffen-Enzyklopädie, 7000 Jahre Waffengeschichte – Vom Faustkeil bis zum Cruise Missile*, Stuttgart: 1993

Harris, V. and Ogasawara, O., *Swords of the Samurai*, London: 1990

Hayes, Stephen, *Ninja, 4 vols*, Niedernhausen in Taunus: 1985-87

Hayes, Wally, *Katana – A Modern Craftsman's Guide to Making a Japanese Sword* (VHS video), Boulder, Colorado: n.d.

Herrmann, W. and Wagner, E.-L., *Alte Waffen*, (Battenberg Antiquitäten Kataloge [Antiquities Catalogue], Munich: 1979

Hils, Hans-Peter, *Meister Johann Liechtenauers Kunst des langen Schwerts*, Frankfurt: 1985

Höper, Herrman-Josef, *Damaszenerstahl – eine alte Schmiedetechnik*, 2nd edition, Münster: 1987

Hoff, Feliks, *Iai-Do – blitzschnell die Waffe ziehen und treffen*, 6th edition, Berlin: 1988

Hrisoulas, Jim, *TheComplete Bladesmith – Forging your Way to Perfection*, Boulder, Colorado: 1987

Icke-Schwalbe, Lydia, *Das Schwert des Samurai – Exponate aus den Sammlungen des Staatlichen Museums für Völkerkunde zu Dresden und des Museums für Völkerkunde zu Leipzig*, Berlin: 1977, 3rd edition 1990

Joly, Henri and Hagitaro, Inada, *The Sword and Samé*, reprint, London: 1962

Kapp, Hiroko and Leon, Yoshihara, Yoshindo, *Japanische Schwertschmiedekunst*, Eschershausen, Germany: 1996

Keegan, John: *A History of Warfare*, London: 1993, *Die Kultur des Krieges*, Berlin: 1995

Kluina, P. and Pevny, P., *Rüstungen*, Hanau: 1993

Koch, H. W., *Illustrierte Geschichte der Kriegszüge im Mittelalter*, Augsburg: 1998

Kölling, H. and Müller, H., *Europäische Hieb- und Stichwaffen – aus der Sammlung des Museums für Deutsche Geschichte*, Militärverlag der DDR, 4th edition, Berlin: 1986

Kohlmorgen, Jan, *Der mittelalterliche Reiterschild – Historische Entwicklung von 975 bis 1350*, Wald-Michelbach: 2002

Laible, Thomas, *Dolche und Kampfmesser*, Braunschweig: 2000

Landes, Roman, *Messerklingen und Stahl Technologische Betrachtungen von Messerschneiden*, 1st edition, Bruckmühl, Germany: 2002

Lanzardo, Dario (ed.), *Ritter-Rüstungen der eiserne Gast, ein mittelalterliches Phänomen*, Munich: 1990

Lindholm, D. and Svärd, P., *Sigmund Ringeck's Knightly Art of the Long-sword*, Boulder, Colorado: 2003

Marek Lech, *Early Medieval Swords from Central and Eastern Europe Dilemmas of an Archeologist and a student of Arms*, Wroclaw, Poland: 2005

Martin, Paul, *Waffen und Rüstungen von Karl dem Großen bis zu Ludwig XVI.*, Frankfurt am Main: n.d.

Menghin, Wilfried, *Das Schwert im frühen Mittelalter Chronologisch- typologische Untersuchungen zu Langschwertern aus germanischen Gräbern des 5. bis 7. Jahrhunderts nach Christus*, Stuttgart: 1983

Müller, Felix, *Götter, Gaben, Rituale Religion in der Frühgeschichte Europas*, Mainz: 2002

Müller, Heinrich, *Albrecht Dürer – Waffen und Rüstungen*, Mainz: 2002

Musashi, Myamoto, *Das Buch der fünf Ringe*, Düsseldorf: 1983, licensed edition, Knaur Verlags

Oakeshott, Ewart, *The Sword in the Age of Chivalry*, Woodbridge, U.K.: 1964, 6the edition: 2002

Oakeshott, Ewart, *Records of the Medieval Sword*, Woodbridge, U.K.: 1994

Ohler, Norbert, *Krieg und Frieden im Mittelalter*: 1997

Oshima, K. and Ando, K., Kendo *Lehrbuch des japanischen Schwertkampfes*, 10th edition, Berlin: 2003

Ozawa, Hiroshi, *Kendo – The Definite Guide*, Tokyo, New York, London: 1997

Peirce, Ian (ed.), *Swords of the Viking Age*, Woodbridge, U.K.: 2002

Perrin, Noel, *Keine Feuerwaffen mehr, Japans Rückkehr zum Schwert 1543 bis 1879*, Stuttgart: 1996

Phillips, G. and Keatman, M., *Artus – Die Wahrheit über den legendären König der Kelten*, Munich: 1995

Pinter, Zeno-Karl, *Spada si sabia medievala in Transilvania si Banat*: 1999

Pleiner, Radomir, *The Celtic Sword*, Oxford: 1993

Reid, William, *Buch der Waffen – Von der Steinzeit bis zur Gegenwart*, Düsseldorf: 1976

Reitzenstein, Alexander Freiherr von, *Der Waffenschmied – Vom Handwerk der Schwertschmiede, Plattner und Büchsenmacher*, Munich: 1964

Ritter, Heinz, *Der Schmied Weland – Forschungen zum historischen Kern der Sage von Wieland dem Schmied*, Hildesheim, germany, Zurich, New York: 1999

Sachse, Manfred, *Damaszener Stahl Mythos, Geschichte, Technik, Anwendung*, 2nd edition, Düsseldorf: 1993

Sachse, M., *Alles über Damaszener Stahl*, Bremerhaven: 1993

Sato, Kanzan, *The Japanese Sword* (Japanese Arts Library), Tokyo: 1966, Tokyo, New York, San Francisco: 1983

Schild, Wolfgang, *Die Geschichte der Gerichtsbarkeit – Vom Gottesurteil bis zum Beginn der modernen Rechtssprechung*, Hamburg: 1997

Schlunk, A. and Giersch, R., *Die Ritter – Geschichte, Kultur, Alltagsleben*, Stuttgart: 2003

Schubert, Ernst, *Fahrendes Volk im Mittelalter*, Bielefeld, Germany: 1995

Schultz-Gora, Axel, *Bokken das hölzerne Schwert der Samurai*, Berlin: 2000

Schulze-Dörlamm, Mechthild, *Das Reichssschwert – Ein Herrschaftszeichen des Saliers Heinrich IV. und des Welfen Otto IV.*, Sigmaringen, Germany: 1995

Seifert, Gerhard and Stefanski, Claus, *Der Blücher-Säbel Ergänzendes zu einem mehrfach behandelten Thema*, (Edition Visier) Singhofen im Taunus, Germany: 2001

Seitz, Heribert, *Blankwaffen*, Vols. I + II, Braunschweig: 1965, 1968

Sinclaire, Clive, *Samurai – Die Waffen und der Geist des japanischen Kriegers*, Stuttgart: 2004

Stenton, Frank (ed.), *Der Wandteppich von Bayeux – Ein Hauptwerk mittelalterlicher Kunst, Gesamtwiedergabe auf 71 Tafeln* [Comprehensive Reproduction on 71 Plates], Cologne: 1957

Talhoffer, Hans, *Talhoffers Fechtbuch – Gerichtliche und andere Zweikämpfe darstellend*, AD 1467, kommentiert von Gustav Hergsell, First edition, Prague: 1887, reprint: 1999

Time Life Books (ed.), *Minne und Schwert – Das Mittelalter, (Mythen der Menschheit)*, Amsterdam: 2000

Tobler, Christian, *Secrets of German Medieval Swordsmanship – Sigmund Ringeck's Commentaries on John Liechtenauer's Verses*, Union City, California: 2001

Turnbull, Stephen, *Samuraikrieger*, Eschershausen, Germany: n.d.

Turnbull, Stephen, *Ninja – Die wahre Geschichte der geheimnisvollen japanischen Schattenkrieger*, Zurich, Stuttgart: 2007

Ullmann, Volker, *Fechten für Theater, Film und Fernsehen – die Technik des Bühnenfechtens*, Wilhelmshaven: 2002

Vesey, Norman, *Waffen und Rüstungen*, Stuttgart: n.d.

Wagner, Eduard, Tracht, *Wehr und Waffen des späten Mittelalters*, Prague: 1960

Wagner, Eduard, *Hieb- und Stichwaffen*, Prague: 1975

Wagner, Eduard, *Tracht, Wehr und Waffen im Dreißigjährigen Krieg*, Prague: 1980

Warner, G. and Draeger, D., *Japanese Swordsmanship – Technique and Practice*, 6th edition, New York, Tokyo: 1987

Weland, Gerald, *Blankwaffen ein internationales Brevier*, Stuttgart: 1994

Wever, Franz, *Das Schwert in Mythos und Handwerk*, Cologne-Opladen: 1961

Wilkinson-Latham, Robert, *Degen und Schwerter in Farbe*, Munich: 1978

Windsor, Guy, *The Swordsman's Companion: A Modern Training Manual for Medieval Long-sword*, Highland Village, Texas: 2004

Yumoto, John, *Das Samurai-Schwert – ein Handbuch*, Freiburg im Breisgau, Germany: 1995

12.5 Categories

Attribution of illustrated sword replicas by category, as discussed in Chapter 6.

CATEGORY A
Page 53 right; 64 left above; 76 center and right; 81 above left, center and right; 95; 97 below; 100 center; 102; 104 center; 123 left; 127; 137; 148 left; 150; 151 above; 195 below left.

CATEGORY B
Page 8; 13 above; 18 below left; 22 above left; 29 left; 46 left and right; 53 left; 60 above; 64 above right; 64 below right; 66 below; 69 left; 71 above right; 76 left; 77 left; 85; 89; 100 right; 104 left; 105; 106; 112 above and below; 115 above; 123 above and right; 124 left; 126 left; 129 left and center; 131; 133 right.

CATEGORY C
Page 10; 25 center; 29 right; 56; 60 below; 69 right; 81 below; 82; 84; 87; 91 right; 94; 97 center; 100 left; 104 right; 107; 109; 119 above and below; 120; 121; 129 right; 180; 192 above right; 193.

CATEGORY D
Page 51.

12.6 Index